Information Technology and Organisational Change

For Judy

Information Technology and

Organisational Change

by

Ken Eason

HUSAT Research Centre
Department of Human Sciences
Loughborough University of Technology

Taylor & Francis
London · New York · Philadelphia
1988

USA	Taylor & Francis Inc., 1900 Frost Road, Suite 101, Bristol, PA 19007-1598
UK	Taylor & Francis Ltd, 1 Gunpowder Square, London EC4A 3DE

British Library Cataloguing in Publication Data

Eason, Ken.
   Information technology and organisational change.
   1. Information systems. Human factors
   1. Title
001.5

ISBN 0-85066- 391-1
ISBN 0-85066-388-1 (Pbk)

Library or Congress Cataloging in Publication Data
Eason, Ken.
   Information technology and organisational change/Ken Eason.
   p. cm.
   Bibliography: p
   Includes index.
   ISBN 0-85066-391
   ISBN 0-85066-388-1 (pbk.)
   1. Management-Data processing. 2. Information technology.
   3. Organizational change. 1. Title.
   HD30.2.E17 1988
   658.4'038-dc19

Cover design by Jordan & Jordan, 6 High St. Fareham Hants.
Typeset in 11/12pt Bembo by Chapterhouse, The Cloisters,
Formby, L37 3PX
Printed in Great Britain by T. J. International, Ltd. Padstow, Cornwall

Contents

Preface

It is widely acknowledged that information technology will revolutionise organisational life. And yet if you look at most organisations you will find that the pace of change is slow and there is not much sign of a revolution. In many organisations expensive equipment seems to be making very little contribution to the goals of the enterprise. It seems that researchers and suppliers are always in the midst of exciting new technological breakthroughs whilst potential user organisations are still trying to assimilate yesterday's technology. The pace of technological development poses the end user with the perpetual headache of trying to decide what is worth using and how to use it.

This book is dedicated to those non-specialists who are struggling to decide how best to use information technology. For nearly 20 years as one of the founder members of the HUSAT Research Centre, I have been working with my colleagues to understand the difficulties people encounter when trying to harness information technology and then to build tools and techniques which will help them in this process. As information technology has advanced the methodologies and tools for technical systems design have become progressively more sophisticated and efficient. By contrast the techniques by which users can specify their needs, evaluate alternatives, implement systems, make complementary organisational changes, etc. have hardly progressed at all. Most design methodologies pay scant attention to these issues. It is almost a truism to say that we need socio-technical systems design; the joint design of the technical and social sub-systems in the organisation. However, many forces keep the two processes apart. Technical design is the province of technologists who know little of social system design. Technical tools do not address the issue. Organisational change is the province of management but is seen as separate from technical change and there are few tools to help the fusion of the two kinds of change.

Through the medium of working with many organisations as they engage in technical innovation we have been slowly building up a set of methods and tools to manage this as a socio-technical design process. These methods are by no means finished but they have reached a state where we know they are helpful and usable by people who are not professional human scientists. They are offered in this book as a set of tools to set alongside technical design tools rather than to replace them. We believe that their use will speed the uptake of information technology in organisations by ensuring that its use is beneficial to the organisation as a whole and to the members of staff who become the individual end users.

The concepts, methods and tools described are a product of the work of many people. My debt to the present and past staff of the HUSAT Research Centre and the Department of Human Sciences is too immense to be listed; I hope that the many references to the work of my colleagues in the text will stand testament to their contributions. A companion volume to this text (Harker and Eason, 1989) provides a set of case studies from the work of the Centre. The development of these tools and techniques has, of necessity, been participative; we do not believe a tool is worthy of the name unless it has been tried and tested by those for whom it was designed. Many organisations, their managers, their technical staff and their end users have therefore indirectly contributed to this volume although the cloak of anonymity prevents an adequate expression of thanks for their pioneering efforts.

Fittingly, we have struggled just like everybody else to use the technology in the development of this book. I am forever in the debt of Eleanor Rowe and Lynne Sharp who dealt with three incompatible word processors in producing the text whilst Helen Symes, my wife Judy and I discovered the delights and limitations of drawing packages as we produced the diagrams.

Ken Eason
Loughborough
March 1988

Chapter 1
The Challenge of Information Technology

The Insidious Revolution

We are in the early throes of a revolution. Many commentators agree that the coming of the microchip brings cheap computing to the masses and signals the beginning of the 'information revolution'. In an influential book, Toffler (1980) calls it 'The Third Wave' following the agricultural and industrial revolutions as major forces shaping the way in which we live in the civilised world. This revolution is occurring because microelectronics offers us a way of storing, processing and communicating vast amounts of information quickly and cheaply. It also provides a way of integrating what have previously been separate ways of handling information; data processing on large mainframe computers, text on typewriters, photocopiers and printing machines, and communications via the telephone, radio and television. The integration of these separate technologies provides the opportunity for a single 'information' technology.

These may sound splendid and significant technical developments but do they really warrant the accolade of a 'revolution'? It is only when we start to list the applications that the technology makes possible that the significance can be appreciated. The key is the realisation that information is the basis for so many human endeavours. What you do not know you can do little about. But when you do know, all kinds of things become possible. A stockbroker in London has previously paid little atention to detailed stock movements in Tokyo but now, via satellite and computer, worldwide, 24-hour dealing becomes a reality. Integrate shopping and banking and your account can be debited directly from the shop and old-fashioned money need never change hands. Get in your car and ask the on-board computer to plan your route, taking account of all the information it can obtain about current road works and traffic flows. If the car breaks down, get the expert system to provide the expertise of the best mechanics to diagnose the problem. Get to your hotel, plug in your computer, check the day's developments at the office and leave instructions for the next day. Back in your factory robots connected to computers assemble products with the minimum of human intervention. The list of potential applications grows longer every day and is limited only by our ability to think of them. Nearly every activity that involves the human processing of information can, in theory, be changed by this technology.

But it is only when we start to examine the ramifications of these disparate applications that we begin to see why there is talk of an information revolution. Figure 1.1 lists some of the predictions, many of them using the terminology of Toffler, that have been made about the broader effects of information technology.

1

Figure 1.1
Some predictions about the impact of information technology

The Paperless Office

The Unmanned Factory

The Electronic Cottage

The Collapse of the City

The Global Village

The Demise of the Expert

The Leisure Society

A popular view is that the gradual spread of electronic information handling will replace paper as the medium of communication so that, in time, newspapers, books and postal communications will disappear. The familiar sight of an office piled high with paper will be replaced by the quietly humming visual display terminal. As the office changes, so the factory will gradually become uninhabited as assembly robots, remote controlled vehicles and computer controlled machines do all that is necessary to produce the goods that we need.

If it is possible to obtain a rich information exchange from home, why bother going to work? By working over computer networks from the 'electronic cottage' people can communicate with colleagues, write programs, act as secretary to someone who is miles away and could, in theory, even control a process in a factory remotely. If the work can be done in this way, why bother with the tedious and time-consuming journey to the city office block every day? Office blocks could empty, city centres could become deserted and rush hours could become a thing of the past. Access to an information-rich environment could also mean that we are no longer limited in our daily contacts to the people and issues in our locality. If we can communicate just as easily with a person on the other side of the world, maybe we will choose only to communicate with those with whom we share specialist interests and the world will become a collection of specialist networks. We could then choose where we want to live rather than where we have to live in order to be near our work.

If it is not only information but knowledge that becomes widely available we could all, with the tutorage of an expert system at the appropriate time, engage successfully in many of the activities which currently require professionals, whether it is mending a car, decorating a home, buying a house or diagnosing an illness. But if they are not needed to do this work what becomes of the experts? This is but one example of a general prediction that the technology will progressively take over greater proportions of the activities that have so far been the responsibility of human workers. The negative view is that the technology will lead to mass unemployment; the positive view that we will live in a leisured society in which the work ethic will no longer be relevant.

The purpose in listing these predictions is not to suggest they will come true. Most of them are probably wrong and they are almost certainly over simple. The main purpose is to make clear that what begins as a change in technical capability has, through the applications it makes possible, the power to change the way in which we live our lives.

In all probability the reader of this list will experience mixed emotions. Some of these changes sound desirable and beneficial; others the loss of some of life's most worthwhile features. Every application of a technology is likely to be a mixed blessing. The technology itself may be neutral but what we do with it may bring benefits and losses to each of us. Of greater significance for the balance of society, it may bring benefits to some at a cost to others. This is particularly true of an information technology because it can accentuate the difference between the 'haves' and the 'have nots'; those who have the money and power to obtain vital information and those who do not.

One of the earliest and most hopeful conclusions from research on the impact of information technology is that it is not a deterministic technology, i.e. it is not inevitable that it will have certain types of impact, for example, lead to unemployment in every application. It is a very flexible technology which can be used to support many different objectives; it can be used to support democracy or dictatorship, the creation of job losses or the development of more interesting jobs, etc. Whilst we are undoubtedly undergoing a revolution it is, therefore, a revolution we should be able to shape; we should be able to exploit its flexibility to give benefits for the vast majority of our citizens.

If there are decisions being made which are shaping the society of tomorrow, where are the decision-makers with this heavy responsibility and how are they exercising their powers? The strange feature of this technology is that it is pervasive and insidious. It is not like the nuclear industry or space technology which requires massive investment in specialist centres. In these industries there are groups of decision-makers who shape the fates of whole industries. In information technology, products are cheap and widely available and across each Western nation there are thousands of applications which in sum are starting to shape first the world of work and subsequently the world of leisure.

This book is about the human and organisational consequences of these applications and is therefore concerned with the manner in which these issues are treated during the design process. The findings of many research studies of the information technology design process are that it is a technology-driven process in which there is very little consideration of the broader ramifications of the technology, for example, Eason *et al.* (1974). We therefore have the paradox that we are reshaping our society through a multitude of technology-driven applications but that very little thought is being given to the world that is being created. At best, the result may be that we do not exploit the technology as well as we might; at worst, we may create more conflicts and dysfunctions in society with calamitous results. An examination of the design process shows that it is dominated by technical and cost issues; what size memory, how much data has to be transmitted, how many terminals, etc. There are numerous textbooks that spell out the stages of technical systems design and very few of them even mention that the systems that result could have fundamental organisational consequences. Many people involved in applications development, both technical specialists and potential users, are now aware that information technology is a great force for organisational change. Unfortunately the tools they have for systems design do not allow them to control this force. The purpose of this book is to try to rectify this imbalance; to begin the process of establishing tools and techniques deliberately to shape the human and organisational changes that accompany technical change. The aim is not to produce an entirely different design process but to create a set of tools that can be used alongside technical system design techniques. By this means we may have user-driven rather than technology-driven applications and the technology will then be truly in the service of its users.

Since the emphasis will be upon human and organisational issues there are several areas that will not be covered in this book. There is, for example, no presentation of information technology itself because other texts present excellent, non-technical, descriptions — see, for example, Eaton and Smithers (1982). In keeping with the application theme, Chapter 2 discusses not the technology itself but the benefits that might be derived from different uses of it. There is no systematic treatment of the technical methodologies for developing information technology systems because many texts exist for this purpose — see, for example, Parkin (1980), Lee (1982). Specific aspects of these technical methodologies are discussed when they abutt the user-centred techniques being presented.

The Origins of the User-centred Techniques

The techniques for user-centred design described in this book have been developed over a period of 18 years by the staff of the HUSAT (Human Sciences and Advanced Technology) Research Centre which is part of the Department of Human Sciences at Loughborough University of Technology. HUSAT was founded in 1970 by Professor Brian Shackel to correct the tendency of technical design processes to pay inadequate attention to human and organisational issues. The Centre has deliberately sought a mixture of research and action research commissions. In its research role it has undertaken many studies of the human implications of emerging forms of information technology and of new applications of the technology. An example is the multi-national study of the impact of computer-based information systems upon management reported in Bjørn-Andersen, Eason and Robey (1986). In its action research role it has worked with teams of system developers in many organisations to help design and implement new systems. The aim of this involvement is to ensure the design process is more user-centred; to help users and technologists work together to create a system which users can and will want to use. The term action research conveys the philosophy behind this work; the aim is to develop techniques which can be used in the design process and to study how effective they are in use so that they can be refined and developed.

The many studies that have contributed to the development of the techniques described in this book cover a wide range of application settings. The studies can broadly be classified under two headings:

1. Supplier studies, and
2. User organisation studies

In the former case the work has been to help the companies that create information technology products to understand their user populations and to design their hardware and software accordingly. In the latter case it has been to help user organisations apply the products of the suppliers to the benefit of their business objectives. This book is restricted to the application of the technology in user organisations. Many of the techniques are also applicable to the supplier design process, but, because user issues often have to be considered without direct user contact, the problem of being user-centred deserves separate treatment.

The majority of the user organisation studies which provide the basis for this book might be described as office applications but a broad definition of this term might be necessary to encompass not only banks, insurance, local government and government departments but also services such as the major utilities (electricity, gas, etc.), hospitals and education. Manufacturing has not been as well represented in these studies in terms of shop floor organisation but the office or 'white collar' side of manufacturing is included. The bulk of these studies is based on applications in Great Britain but in recent years more of the work has been undertaken in other European countries. Another way of expressing the origins of the work is in terms of the types of users who have been the targets for these systems. In addition to managers, clerks and secretaries we have studied the needs of doctors, economists, accountants, engineers, architects, teachers and the public. The systems being introduced have varied from the very small to the very large and from standard office applications of word processing and electronic mail to highly specialised systems developed for a particular industry.

In presenting the user-centred techniques reference will be made to many of these studies but no attempt will be made to give comprehensive descriptions because a companion volume has been prepared (Harker and Eason, 1989) which presents a series of case study accounts of these studies. Specific illustrations of most of the techniques to be described are to be found in these case studies.

The Content and Form of User-centred Techniques

Out of this varied and rich background has gradually emerged a range of techniques to assist different parts of the systems design process. They are organised in this book under the following heading:

1. *Techniques for Organising Project Teams.* A central theme in user-centred design is that an appropriate mix of users and technologists is needed for the different kinds of design decisions that have to be taken. Therefore, before we attempt design we need techniques to establish who is doing the designing.
2. *Techniques for System Specification.* One of the most difficult issues is to establish user requirements for a system. Users must be involved in establishing what they want but they do not know what can be provided or what effects it might have. The processes that are necessary to cope with these problems include organisational and task analysis, broad conceptual design and the early evaluation of consequences.
3. *Organisational Design.* If the technical system is to be of major significance to the business it is likely to require organisational change. The common pattern is to make technical change and follow it with enforced organisational change. In a user-centred approach this is reversed so that desirable organisational changes are first identified and the technical system designed to serve this structure.
4. *Technical Design for Human Use.* Many techniques are available for the design of the technical system but they do not pay sufficient attention to the needs and characteristics of the people who must use them. We need techniques, therefore, that enable technical designers to cope with issues of usability and acceptability.
5. *Implementation and Support.* To the many technical issues involved in implementing a system must be added the many user and organisational issues associated with implementing change. In particular, the needs for training and continuing support are vital if the potential of the technical system is not to be wasted because people do not know how to use it. The implementation phase is also the time when many of the ergonomic issues of workstation and environment have to be addressed if users are not to be asked to work in conditions of discomfort and stress.
6. *Evaluation.* It is tempting to think of design as a neat, linear process but if every step is not checked, and repeated if found wanting, an expensive disaster may be the only result of implementation. Technical evaluations at all stages are now common but evaluation against the human and organisational criteria of success are also necessary and cannot be left until implementation.
7. *Information Technology Strategies.* Most user-centred techniques are for use within a specific project context. However, their use can best be facilitated within a broad information technology strategy which identifies appropriate roles for technologists, user management and end users within the development and operation of information technology systems.

The process of being user-centred can be seen from this list to be diverse, to operate at many levels and to be necessary at all stages of the design process. A chapter is devoted to each of the topics in this list.

A number of principles have underpinned the presentation of the user-centred techniques. It may be expected that a book on techniques would take the form of a manual with detailed, step-by-step accounts of the procedures to be followed. This is not the strategy followed for two reasons. The first is that we have found in practice that the detailed procedures we need for one situation are different from those needed in another. Specifying user requirements for standard office technology in a small organisation is, for example, not the same as specifying the specialist requirements of doctors in a large teaching hospital. The second reason is that people who use these techniques need to relate them to their existing design philosophies and techniques. It is therefore better that they work out the detailed way of using these techniques for themselves. The process of customising these techniques for local use also ensures that they are digested and understood so that the people using them understand why they are engaging in these activities. The danger of large, comprehensive and detailed procedures is that people may slavishly follow them without understanding and may use them inappropriately. The presentation of each technique is therefore a rationale for the technique (why it is needed and what it does) and the general procedures to be followed with examples where appropriate. The term 'tool' or 'technique' is not therefore being used in the highly formalised and detailed way that may be expected. Rather it is a statement of the issues and a general procedure for tackling them so that people can tailor it to their own situation.

Another general principle is that this is not an attempt to provide a comprehensive, integrated design methodology to compete with existing methodologies. Rather it is an attempt to create a set of techniques for those human issues in design that are not well represented in most technically orientated methodologies. The techniques are therefore envisaged as a kind of toolbox from which they can be taken and used in many different ways in association with many diferent technical design methods. In practice, we have found that this is possible for most techniques in most circumstances. It may be, however, that following the technical design methodology prevents the use of a user-centred technique. It is, for example, quite common to find that the technical timetable does not allow for early user evaluation and redesign if necessary. If this is the case then user management and project leadership may have to vary the technical methodology to accommodate the user-centred procedures. It is a good test of the flexibility and adequacy of an existing design methodology to examine what problems would result from the employment of techniques designed to support user and organisational issues.

Although the techniques address different issues at different levels they are based on a common approach to identifying design solutions and this approach will therefore recur through this book. It is depicted in Figure 1.2.

To be user-centred a technique must be undertaken by people with two kinds of contribution to make. Firstly, we need experts who understand the specialist issues and, secondly, we need 'stakeholders', the people who have something to gain or lose from the solution adopted. These people have to establish a framework for design which includes two major elements, the design options (what could be done) and the design criteria (what we are trying to achieve). The design options may come from analysis of the users and their tasks together with evidence about technical and organisational options that have been developed and tried elsewhere. The establishment of the options may be the area where specialist skills are most necessary.

Figure 1.2
General form of a user-centred design technique

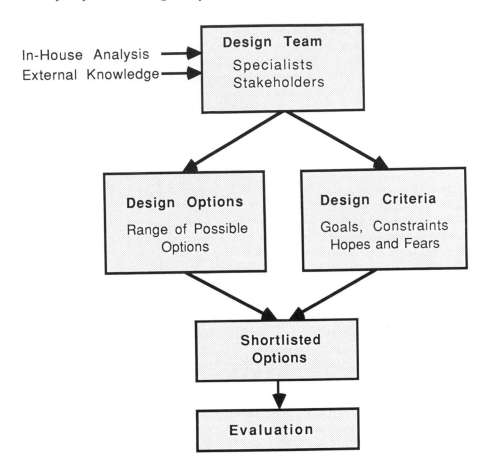

The design criteria must come from the explicit aims of the organisation in implementing information technology and the range of goals, constraints and outcomes to avoid that the 'stakeholders' in the organisation may consider important. The potential users are therefore likely to play a major role in establishing the criteria. Judging the options against the criteria is likely to lead to a short list of possibilities which can be detailed and evaluated more thoroughly before being fully developed and implemented. This general procedure can be applied to a wide range of design issues including the selection of the overall technical system, the design of jobs, the organisation of workstations in the work environment, and the selection of implementation and support strategies. This procedure embodies the two key features of exploiting information technology; the availability of *options* shows there is flexibility at all levels and the identification of *evaluation criteria* ensures that user values and goals play a part in the selection between them.

The final principle relates to the potential user of these techniques, for any technique must be constructed so that it is usable by the people to whom it is relevant. It is actually very difficult to define the user of these techniques. They are directed at anyone who is associated with the development of information technology systems in organisations and who is particularly concerned with the fit between the technical system and its organisational context. Obviously the techniques will be of relevance to any person with a technical responsibility within a project design team. They may, however, be seen as of even more relevance to those user management teams who are increasingly aware of the need to pay close attention to information technology development because it is shaping the nature of the processes they manage. At present there are few methods by which user management can exercise this responsibility and these techniques may help fill this vacuum. Unions and other staff representatives are also increasingly recognising the impact of information technology upon the jobs and conditions of work of their members. They, too, lack the techniques to identify the issues to which they should give their attention and these user-centred techniques can help them pursue their objectives.

There is, however, a group of people who should find these techniques of special relevance. Within user organisations there are many new roles emerging to cope with the activities necessary to implement and operate information technology systems; these roles are emerging according to need and there are no agreed titles, terms of reference or statements of the qualifications and experience necessary to fill the roles. These staff may be called user representatives, liasion staff, user support staff, trainers, co-ordinators, implementation teams, and so on. They may be seconded to these roles for the duration of system development but increasingly the roles are becoming permanent features of the new forms of orgnaisation. Many roles are filled by users, some from technical staff who play a more user-centred role and some from outside as organisations seek people who do not have specialist technical skills but have the ability to smooth the path to effective implementation. The normal methods of systems development are of marginal value to people in these roles and it is to this growing army that these techniques are really dedicated. These people occupy a hinterland between the user departments and the technical specialists; they bear the brunt of the conflicts between user needs and system provisions and they have very little formalised methodology to help them. These techniques have in many situations been developed because we have found ourselves playing such roles or we have needed to find ways of supporting people inside the user organisation who are playing these roles.

What should be the characteristic of techniques to help such people? Since the people come from very varied backgrounds no assumptions can be made about their knowledge and experience. The techniques are therefore presented, as far as is possible, without recourse to jargon or specialist knowledge. The techniques have been developed out of the theory and practice of human and social science as it has been generally applied in organisations. The concepts of participation and the planning of change, for example, owe much to the practices of organisational development. The methods of organisational analysis and of job design are developments from socio-technical systems theory and the general job design literature (see, for example, Davis and Taylor, 1972). Many of the issues in the design of the technical system arise from the growing literature on human–computer interaction (see, for example, Shneiderman, 1986), and the procedures for workstation analysis, environmental design, etc. belong to the tradition of applied ergonomic practice (Galer, 1987). Although the techniques have antecedents and in many cases a rich theoretical basis, little of the background is given beyond references to enable the context to be developed by those with a specialised interest. This is done to assist the varied population who may wish to make direct use of these techniques and only want to assess the justification for the technique in the information technology context.

Conclusions

The book is structured so that Chapters 5 to 11 contain the descriptions of the user-centred techniques. Chapters 2, 3 and 4 provide the context within which they are to be used. Chapter 2 is an appraisal of what could be achieved with information technology and an assessment of the state of the art which identifies the degree to which we are falling short of achieving these objectives. Most of the reasons for the shortfall are human and organisational rather than technical. Chapter 3 examines the design methodologies that have been and are being used to introduce these systems, which sheds more light on the reasons for the shortfall in the achivement of objectives. It also indicates the range of design methodologies to which these user-centred techniques have to relate. Chapter 5 provides a summary of the techniques presented in the context of a set of principles a user-centred approach attempts to follow. Although no attempt is made to provide a new, integrated and comprehensive design methodology, the techniques are united by a perspective on design that emphasises certain objectives and values. This chapter seeks to make these explicit so that those who use the techniques can judge the degree to which they are compatible with the objectives and values of other design methods and tools.

The challenge of information technology is that it is a flexible technology which will transform society. Because it is flexible we have the opportunity to transform society in ways that reflect human values that are shared by the majority of the population. The danger is that this will not occur because each design process will continue to be dominated by technical considerations. Society may then be shaped not by the malice of powerful, self-seeking decision-makers but by the accidental effects of decisions taken for technical reasons. To avoid this danger and to ensure we use the technology to create the world we want, we need design techniques that cross the boundary between human affairs and technology and which complement and balance the power of increasingly sophisticated technical design techniques. This book is a small contribution towards the development of a more user-centred approach to information technology design methods.

Chapter 2
The Achievement of Benefits from Information Technology

Success or failure?

Information technology may represent a fundamental way of transforming society but each application will be undertaken in order to achieve specific benefits. The technology can be employed to achieve a wide variety of benefits and in this chapter we will examine the main types of benefits and their organisational ramifications.

Because any kind of technical innovation represents a risk, we will also examine the problems of implementing information technology. We will begin by looking at some of the evidence about the success or failure rates of information technology projects. These data are difficult to attain but frequently there are disasters; even more often there is disappointment and frustration. The commonly-voiced complaint is that the technology is being oversold; the hype is such that it cannot achieve what it purports to achieve. It is difficult to put figures to the shortfall. Suppliers are not likely to advertise application difficulties and user organisations are not overkeen on their problems being made public. Nevertheless, there are some studies that give an indication of the scale of the problem and the nature of the outcomes. Figure 2.1 summarises the position. It shows the embedding of an information technology system in the organisation such that the organisation is ultimately more effective in achieving its objectives. In some ways an apt analogy is the transplanting of an organ in the human body (although fortunately, information technology systems are rarely the equivalent of vital organs which can cause the demise of the host if they fail). The range of outcomes is otherwise rather similar. If the application is successful (and the transplant takes), success will enhance the effectiveness of the organisation. If it does not take one outcome may be rejection — the organisation may simply reject the information technology system as 'foreign material' and revert to its normal way of working. Another common cause of failure is that the system is implemented but causes major complications elsewhere in the organisation. As a result there may have to be the equivalent of massive doses of drugs to deal with the secondary problem, for example dealing with staff resistance, coping with problems of health and safety, training, repairing damaged relations with customers, etc.

The frequency of these different outcomes presented in Figure 2.1 are the estimates made by Mowshowitz (1976) of the impact of information technology systems

11

Figure 2.1
Success rates in information technology applications

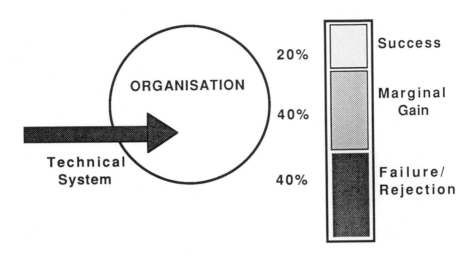

in North America. He suggests that 20% of systems implemented achieve something like their intended benefits, 40% fail and the remaining 40% make only a marginal impact on the organisation. Whilst no comprehensive survey exists for Great Britain, a number of limited studies point in a similar direction. Of the 20 Office Automation projects sponsored by the Department of Trade and Industry, only 15 were continued when the trial period was over (DTI, 1986), and some that continued had not achieved the planned objectives. Wroe (1986) examined ten systems implemented by small builders of which four were rated as successes, four were discontinued before implementation and in two cases the firms were still struggling after a long implementation period. McCosh (1984) reports 15 small-scale, decision support systems which he was personally involved in designing. He estimated that five were a success. In a notoriously difficult application area this is a good rate to achieve. One might anticipate that word processor applications would be more straightforward. In a survey of 92 systems (Pomfrett *et al.* 1985) the general rate of benefit achievement was 77% which implies a significant failure rate. In general we find that the implementation of information technology systems is a high risk process. Complete failure is not uncommon and marginal impact with unwanted and negative consequences is commonplace.

In order to understand the difficulties that are encountered the following section examines the different benefits one might hope to achieve and the specific issues involved in attaining them. This is a useful way of formulating a list of the issues that systems development must handle and which the strategies proposed later in the book are designed to serve.

Types of benefit

An organisation can be viewed as a collection of resources deployed to handle a specified workload. In these terms we can employ information technology to increase the work undertaken (or improve its quality) or we can use it to replace or reduce the resources we need to deploy.

Figure 2.2 presents a classification of information technology benefits based upon a continuum from resource reduction to work enhancement. It groups the benefits into four types. The first is cost savings. The major cost in offices is staff costs and the reduction of the number of people employed (or their more effective deployment) is often a major target. Other costs may be reduced; if everything is stored electronically, we may save the costs of paper and the space needed to store bulky paper.

Rather than reduce the cost of resources we may choose to seek higher productivity from existing resources. Thus, a group of secretaries may be expected to process many more words or a telephonist may be expected to control the transmission of many more messages.

The third major group of benefits arises as a result of an expansion of the quantity or the quality of the work done directly in pursuit of the organisation's objectives. The technology may be used to improve the information available to executives or to improve the support for their decision-making. Expert systems may be used to provide specialist knowledge that might otherwise not be available and computer aided design (CAD) systems might be used to improve the quality of design.

Finally, and most importantly if any dramatic revolution in user organisations is to occur, there is the use of information technology to seek new and valued objectives

Figure 2.2
Information technology benefits in the office

that could not otherwise be contemplated. This may involve internal objectives such as new forms of integration and communication or it may involve external objectives in new areas of business.

Organisations using information technology systems may be seeking any or all of these benefits. But it would be unrealistic to assume that all organisations are clear about the benefits they seek. There are many applications which are stimulated by concern for the way other companies, especially competitors, are applying the technology. There may be a fear that competitors may be successful, that the advertisements for information technology products may be right, and that they may be left behind. They may also want to give the impression of being an up-to-date, efficient, high technology organisation.

We will now examine each of these forms of benefit in some detail and look at some of the evidence about what happens when organisations try to achieve them.

The Reduction of Resources

There are a variety of ways by which information technology can enable an organisation to accomplish the same amount of work with less resources. If the medium of information processing is electronic there may be no need to use paper and the 'paperless office' may become a reality. Not only would that save paper but also all the equipment that goes with it, from stationery cupboards and photocopiers to filing cabinets, and all the space they require.

Unfortunately, until all the parts of a task are handled electronically, including communications to and from the outside world, there is a need to translate from the electronic to the paper medium and the 'electronic office' remains a dream. Also the workstation required for computer-based work which may include a visual display unit (VDU), desk, chair, printer, modem, document holder, disc drive, etc. often takes up more space than it saves. A study by the Central Computer and Telecommunications Agency (CCTA, 1980) found that up to 40% more space was required in some applications when computer systems were introduced.

The resource that most organisations try to reduce by employing information technology is the human resource which is often quoted, for example, as more than 70% of the costs of running an office. This reduction can be accomplished by direct replacement: the computer, for example, can automatically prepare an invoice, search and retrieve a document, add up columns of figures, etc. It can do so much faster and more accurately than a human being and, on many counts, seems a desirable proposition. But resources may be reduced by means other than direct replacement. If a person is given a tool which enables them to perform a task twice as quickly, they should over time be able to do the work of two people and hence, if the amount of work is fixed, one person less is needed on the payroll.

It is this kind of thinking which has provided the rationale for most early computer systems. The cost–benefit justification of the majority of data processing systems has relied upon staff savings; they are the tangible savings which can be set against the development and operational costings of the computer systems. On a wider scale it is the staff savings which have been the major focus for predictions of the long-term effects of information technology. In 1978 and 1979, when there was a sudden awareness of the major impact that microelectronics could make on business, a series of reports was issued forecasting the effects on job numbers. Forecasts were made, for example, about the impact of office automation. The Siemens Report (1978) forecast a 40% reduction in office jobs by 1990 and the influential Nora Report (Nora and Minc, 1980) produced a French forecast of a reduction of 30% in office jobs by 1990. In Britain, Barron and Curnow (1979) suggested there would be a 10-20% loss in typing, clerical, secretarial and managerial jobs in 15 years, and several unions, for example APEX (1979) and ASTMS (Jenkins and Sherman, 1979), made forecasts suggesting a similar loss of jobs.

These reports were forecasts based upon assumptions about the degree to which information technology could replace human labour and on an analysis of the number of such jobs in the economy available for replacement. We have now had a number of years of experience of implementing the technology and we can review these forecasts in the light of data about actual impact on job numbers. A recent report by the Institute for Employment Research at Warwick University (1984) concludes that whilst there may be some gains and some losses in the implementation of office automation, there is unlikely to be an overall change in job numbers. A report by the Japanese Ministry of Labour (1984) on office automation reaches a similar conclusion. An Office of Technology Assessment report to the US Congress (1985) concludes that by the year 2000 there may be some slow-down in the growth of office jobs but no actual decline.

These reports seem to stand in stark contrast to the earlier predictions of wide-spread change. Why the difference? Our own studies, for example, a survey of 92 word processing installations (Pomfrett *et al*, 1985), a survey of the designers of 45 systems across a range of applications (Eason and Harker, 1986) and intensive studies of five cases of advanced office automation (Olphert and Eason, 1985) lead us to conclude that there are wide discrepancies between theory and practice:

1. *The Overestimation of Routine.* Information technology can directly replace routine prescribed activities but spontaneous adaptation to novel circumstances must remain a human activity. It is very easy to assume clerical and secretarial work is routine when in fact it may require many subtle variations on a theme to cope with emerging circumstances. Plans to replace large numbers of clerical staff tend, as a result, to become more modest when the extent of the non-routine is appreciated. The word processing survey also revealed that the average secretary spent less than 40% of her time typing, the rest being occupied by a wide variety of tasks in support of her superiors. Many organisations seemed to believe they would save many secretarial posts by introducing word processing but found it was making a contribution to only a part of the secretarial role. Again the potential for reduction was much reduced.

2. *Organisational Change.* Most attempts to reduce job numbers as a result of implementing information technology involve some degree of organisational change. Usually this takes the form of centralisation. If, for example, there are

small groups of secretarial staff scattered across an organisation, the only way to cut numbers substantially is to create a smaller central group and offer a centralised service. When attempts are made to introduce such a change there may be serious objections from powerful people about to lose a personal service and there may not be the organisational will to push through the changes.

3. *New Jobs for Old.* Jobs may be lost but others may be created to operate the technology. In the survey of systems designers (Eason and Harker, 1986) 15 of the 45 systems led to job losses but 15 led to new job creation. Overall the job losses outweighed the job gains but in many organisations there was marginal change. The new jobs ranged from relatively routine data input to development and support staff, training and helping users to make use of the system. The process of introducing the change almost invariably requires extra staff on a temporary basis in order to implement change whilst 'keeping the shop open'. Sometimes it seems appropriate to keep the extra staff that are acquired.

4. *Job Reductions as a Convenient Fiction.* It is remarkable how many organisations go ahead with information technology developments on the basis of savings from staff reductions and yet never check whether they achieved the objectives. In the survey of 45 systems, the respondents in 16 cases could not even estimate job changes due to the introduction of the system. It is hard to avoid the conclusion that, in many instances, the figures for staff reductions are provided as the cost–benefit justification for the system but are unrealistic and are not vigorously pursued. It is a way of getting a development approved because it shows tangible benefits whereas the staff directly concerned might be hoping for less tangible benefits more difficult to present as a convincing case for expenditure.

5. *Resource Reductions are Job Losses.* Reducing staff numbers may be a benefit to the organisation but it is job loss to the staff concerned. Such savings are likely to be fiercely resisted by the staff and their representatives. The implementation of the system is therefore likely to involve lengthy negotiations. Many unions in the United Kingdom have negotiated New Technology Agreements with employees which, for example, insist that job reductions are achieved not by making existing employees redundant but by natural wastage, early retirement and redeployment. The overall effect is to reduce opportunities on the labour market. It may be a long time before the savings for the organisation are realised.

6. *The Impact of Enhancement Objectives.* In many organisations we hear that 'we may not have achieved resource reductions but we have achieved many indirect benefits'. These may vary from being able to provide high quality presentation of documents (with consequent positive effects on clients) to being able to offer new and valued services. There is more on these enhancement objectives below. The discovery of these benefits tends to take the pressure off the drive for resource reduction; indeed, as we shall see later, the goals of enhancement and of resource reduction may be incompatible.

Collectively these findings suggest that the potential for benefits from staff reduction may have been overestimated (at least with the technology available today), that it takes considerable organisational effort to achieve what benefits may be possible and that other kinds of benefit, covertly or overtly pursued during systems development, may become more important. This is not to say that significant benefits from staff reductions have not been achieved. They tend to be made in large, routine clerical operations where the potential for savings is correspondingly large. In the majority of applications this is not the case and other benefits may be more significant.

The Optimisation of Resources

It is a short step from reducing resources to optimising the resources that exist already. It is often easier to implement a system if the ground rule is not to reduce resources but to get more work from existing resources. We may thus introduce a banking system so that the existing bank clerks can service more customer accounts, a new telephone system so that existing telephonists can cope with more calls, or a word processing system so that the existing secretaries can produce more 'key strokes'.

Many systems are introduced on this basis perhaps because greater productivity will be beneficial or because the reduction of resources would be vigorously opposed. These are perhaps the easiest types of benefit to achieve but there are a number of issues to overcome and problems to face before they can be achieved.

1. *Is Greater Productivity Beneficial?* The ability to service the requirements of more customers is obviously beneficial but can the same be said for other forms of productivity gain? Is the generation of more internal messages on an electronic mail system necessarily a benefit? In the surveys we have conducted, many recipients have complained of the need to search through more 'junk mail' to locate significant messages. Information technology makes it easy to generate greater volumes of information and to distribute it widely but these 'benefits' can simply add to the information overload of those on the receiving end. 'Keystroke' measures of the productivity of clerical or word processing operators have become popular but survey results raise questions about how often more keystrokes is actually beneficial. Many secretaries believe, for example, that the existence of word processing encourages authors to write more, demand more re-drafting and to start from a poorer first draft. The secretaries faced with this growing volume of work doubt whether it is effective, to which many authors counter that it is helping them to prepare better documents. What the extra work may not be doing is producing more documents going to the outside world. Whether the extra productivity is beneficial is much more open to debate than at first appears. It follows that it is important to trace the link between extra productivity at the keyboard and the effective achievement of organisational goals before seeking this kind of benefit from information technology. High terminal usage figures are, of themselves, no evidence that an organisation is getting benefit from information technology. How many terminal hours have actually been devoted to 'landing on Mars'!

2. *Productivity may mean Greater Control.* If the aim of introducing the technology is to obtain greater productivity there is a tendency to use it as a means of enforcing the new rate of working. This can be done in a variety of ways. The computer can pace the operator by, for example, automatically channelling a customer enquiry to a clerk as soon as the previous one is completed or by 'timing out' an operator if an

action is not complete within a specified time. Secondly, the computer can be used as a monitoring agent, maintaining a continuous check on progress and notifying a supervisor when it drops below a threshold or producing performance tables at the end of the day. Thirdly, the computer can control the way a task is undertaken by only permitting certain activities in specified sequences, not allowing an operator to proceed until earlier parts of the task are complete, etc.

The power of the computer as a mechanism of control, as shown by these examples, is very considerable. It can operate continuously and be completely impartial and therefore has advantages over the human supervisor. However, the person engaging in a task under these conditions will feel stressed, paced and rigidly controlled. These are all the parameters of jobs on assembly lines which studies have repeatedly shown, for example, Walker and Guest (1952), lead to low morale, limited job interest and a tendency towards a 'negotiate for everything you can get' mentality. Downing (1980) calls office automation 'the white collar assembly line' for these reasons and Bjørn-Andersen (1985) points out that many of these features, especially undisclosed monitoring of human performance, would not be acceptable in the Scandinavian countries. Using the technology as an impersonal agent of control may seem attractive but it often produces a strong negative response from employees and (as we shall see in Chapter 6) is at variance with good job-design practice. It may be much better to set overall targets with employees and allow them to use the system to monitor their own performances so they can set their own immediate targets and find their own ways of improving their performance.

3. *Full-time Computer Use and Health Hazards.* There have been many complaints that using visual display units leads to health problems, for example eye strain, backaches, facial rashes, repetitive strain injury and even pregnancy complications (for further details see Pearce 1985). Typically these complaints are associated with the applications described here which aim to maximise the productive use of information technology equipment. In these applications employees are often full-time VDU operators engaged in repetitive work. This produces the constrained postures and fixed visual conditions that can lead to muscular strain. Part-time use of VDUs or variable use of the kinds described later in this chapter rarely lead to these problems. Where there is intensive use attention to the classical ergonomic issues of seating, workstation design, the visual environment (see Cakir *et al.* 1980) is vital. Even then there may well be demands for the implementation of specific work/rest pause regimes to give regular breaks from the VDU work and other measures to ensure employee health such as the transfer of pregnant women to non-VDU work.

4. *Organisational Change and Human Learning.* Introducing systems of this kind normally involves organisational changes in reporting structures, monitoring systems, job content, etc. It will also involve employees learning different ways of engaging in their tasks. Obviously they will have to learn computer skills but they may also have to learn different working practices. Implementation procedures will be needed to cope with these changes if the benefits of the information technology are to be obtained.

Once again these factors show that the achievement of better utilisation of resources not only involves technical decisions but a variety of managerial, human and organisational decisions; what will actually yield benefit to the organisation, what will be the consequences for employees, what will be their reactions, what training and other kinds of changes will ensue? An important point to note is that information technology is not simply a technology you purchase, plug in and start to reap the benefit. It is raw material that can be used to shape a way of working that will be beneficial.

The Enhancement of Work

The applications described so far do not change what the organisation offers the outside world; they make the organisation more effective in its use of resources. Companies that have been employing computer systems for some years now feel that they have largely exhausted the possibilities in this direction. They accept that it is not a direction which will lead to radical change in their organisations or to the utilisation of the full potential of information technology. They are reaching for ways of using the technology to enhance the work they do. It is convenient to divide this type of application into the 'hand tool' approach to the use of information technology (using it to increase the power of individuals) and the organisational approach, where the technology is used to enable the organisation to seek new ways of achieving its objectives or to seek new objectives. First we will examine the 'hand tool' approach.

The possibilities for using information technology as a tool to aid or support a specific human activity are numerous. They range from general purposes tools, for example, the ability to calculate, store and retrieve data, store and manipulate text, etc. to tools specific to tasks, for example, computer-aided design. In each case the aim is to give the person some advantage in pursuing the task — to enhance the task performance. Word processing enables the unskilled typist to produce good quality outputs because there are no messy errors corrected on the paper. An integrated workstation gives the full power of a publishing house to a single operator; to present type in many fonts, integrate it with tables and diagrams, vary the size of characters, etc. Planning with network control software means it is possible to vary an element in the plan and examine its impact on the whole plan. Similarly a spreadsheet enables the financial planner to change a single estimate and quickly see its implications for overall costings. Not only does computer-aided design enable the designer to build a three-dimensional model that can be examined from any angle but it makes it possible to test the effects of changing an element of the structure. These are all examples of the power of simulating the task and manipulating the simulation before making final decisions. A further example is the way a decision support system (DSS) can be used by managers to ask 'what happens if?' questions of a model of their company affairs.

This list could be extended indefinitely. Almost any task which involves a significant amount of information processing could be beneficially supported by information technology. Human beings are slow and inaccurate when processing information and, unaided, tend to cut corners by guessing, approximating and not looking at all the options. A device which will do the work at their behest could make a tremendous difference to the performance of many types of task.

The falling costs of information technology have made it possible for many organisations to contemplate applications of this kind. Providing computers for these applications is to serve the discretionary, intermittent user, i.e. someone who will use it truly as a tool, when and where it is relevant to the task in hand. It is the manager who needs a DSS, the designer who needs CAD and the accountant who needs a spreadsheet. They will not use them all the time and they will only use them if they are useful. Many organisations are now making widespread developments of this kind but, as before, there are problems and issues to face before the benefits are achieved:

1. *Is it Beneficial?* It is not easy to put a value on the service provided by a tool which might help someone perform a task better. Is the design that results from using CAD better? Are the project costings produced using a spreadsheet actually better? What value can be placed on being able to produce letters free from errors every time? These kinds of benefits may be valuable but in indirect, intangible ways not comparable with the resource reduction savings of other types of application.

   An additional problem is that it is often not clear whether staff will find information technology applications beneficial. It is often necessary to give people a chance to experience applications before they can judge whether they will be able to use them to advantage. All these factors mean that applications that seek enhancement benefits seem more like 'steps in the dark' than those that optimise resources. In the word processing and office automation surveys we found many systems developers who were now very cautious about cost justifying the next generation of systems. Having used tangible resource saving arguments for earlier systems, they were now moving into enhancement applications convinced there would be benefits but without being able to give convincing demonstrations. One solution is to start small, for example with a limited number of Personal Computers, to gather experience to demonstrate benefits and to expand on this fruitful base. Maskery (1986) gives several examples of this exploratory, evolutionary form of system development for managerial and professional users.

2. *Easy to Use Systems.* The users of these systems are often unskilled in computer use. It is rarely possible to train busy professional people in skills they may only use occasionally. This puts a premium on the use of easy to use, easy to learn systems (or 'user friendly' in the popular parlance). Systems for this kind of application must not, for example, assume well-developed keyboard skills from their users and should not use elaborate, obscure computer command structures. If systems do have these properties, the effort required will be too great for busy people and, whatever the potential benefits, they will exercise their discretion and not use the services that have been provided. For an analysis of the properties required in a system to serve users of this kind see Eason (1984a).

3. *Functionality, Usability and Acceptability.* The ease of use problem relates to three system and application characteristics which are particularly important to discretionary users. Our investigations of computer users suggest they operate on an implicit cost–benefit evaluation basis when it comes to establishing whether and

how they will use a system (Eason, 1981). In this implicit evaluation the benefit is the value they will get in completing their task and the cost is a mixture of the effort, time, risk and financial penalties involved. If benefits do not exceed the costs in the long run use will not be maintained. The cost side of the evaluation is dependent upon two features of the system, its usability and its acceptability. Usability reflects the degree to which users are able to use the system with the skills, knowledge, stereotypes and experience they can bring to bear, i.e. they do not have to develop new skills or internal 'models' in order to appreciate how to use the system. Acceptability reflects not whether they *can* but whether they *will* use the system. There is an array of potential 'costs' which relate to the organisation context of use; fear of failure, fear of losing status, power or influence, fear of providing more explicit evidence by which others may judge performance, etc. These 'costs' relate more to the culture of the organisation than they do the system itself. The benefits should arise from the functionality of the system but, as discussed above, there may be no obvious benefit for a user in relation to his particular tasks. This is often the case for the new user who has very little idea how to assess the benefits of the functionality of a system to the work he does. For these reasons, the initial cost–benefit evaluation can seem all cost and no immediate benefit. It usually needs a low key, exploratory introduction to clear these initial obstacles so that users can begin to find benefits for themselves. In practice many systems have been stillborn because these problems were not appreciated and too much was expected too soon.

4. *The Assumption of Organisational Equilibrium.* Since the individual work enhancement approach is simply adding another tool to the armoury of the user, it is often assumed that this kind of application will not lead to organisational change. Indeed it is often an explicit reason for adopting this approach; 'we want to keep our organisation as it is so we are introducing information technology as a tool to help people do their existing jobs'. This seems a straightforward objective but neglects the fact that, if people really find the tool beneficial, they start behaving in different ways, for example, enlarging the job they are doing. This affects the formal or informal demarcation lines between jobs and may lead to unanticipated stresses in the organisation. It is well known, for example, that journalists producing copy electronically threaten the role of the typesetter. The manager who starts handling some of his own text production, changes the work going to a secretary or a word processing centre. The planner who really begins to plan an extensive work programme in detail is actually planning the work of a lot of people and can easily erode their autonomy. This creeping kind of organisational change can easily lead to counteraction. It can look as though some people are 'stealing a march' on others. Benefits from the technology can be blocked by the suspicions of others. McCosh (1984), for example, in reviewing the implementation of Decision Support Systems identifies, as one of the main reasons for failure, the resistance of managers senior to those using the system. McCosh does not expand on why this occurs but it is easy to imagine the reaction of senior managers when their juniors start to produce and justify clever ideas by use of systems they do not understand and did not initiate. An organisation is a collection of interrelated work roles and a change in one will

destabilise others. This kind of application needs to be just as much concerned with the implications for organisational change as do other applications.

The problems of individual work enhancement are then of a different character to the other applications we have considered but they remain about the same broad themes; the human and organisational learning and change that is necessary before the benefits of information technology can be obtained.

Organisational Enhancement

If information technology is to have the dramatic effects on organisational functioning that many commentators suggest, it needs to be harnessed directly to the achievement of important organisational objectives. It may do this by making it easier to achieve existing objectives or by making it realistic to establish new ones. Taking this route should enhance the work not just of individuals but of the entire organisation.

Examples of this kind of approach are numerous as are examples of their failure. Most common are examples of systems to make it easier for organisations to achieve existing objectives. A company may wish to get its products to its clients whilst limiting its stocks. Real-time systems giving up-to-date data on stocks which are accessible by staff in many locations make it possible to minimise stocks and to use the data base for reordering and for planning production. This approach is relevant whether the 'product' is consumer goods, airline seats or hospital beds. The aim is often to achieve a better degree of integration between the parts of the organisation. Indeed some writers, for example, Wright and Rhodes (1985), consider that the principal aim of implementing information technology is to achieve integration. They examine the current aim in production industries of CIM (Computer Integrated Manufacture) which uses information technology to bring together the design, machining, assembly and other functions so that fast, flexible and effective production can be achieved. The integration may be across many different functions. Bjørn-Andersen *et al.* (1986), for example, describe a case in which integrated data bases enabled a company to relate the marketing and production functions much more clearly so that the production facilities only made what was profitable to sell.

Beneficial integration can also be achieved across organisations. The current interest in EFTPOS (Electronic Fund Transfer at Point of Sale) involves collaboration between retailers and banks to enable funds to be debited directly from customers' accounts at the time a purchase is made.

Almost any organisational objective can be supported directly by information technology; marketing, sales, production, research, monitoring the outside world, maintaining security, storage and distribution, etc. Applications can be identified in each of these areas. In many there is a gradual shift from existing objectives to new ones; from existing services or products to new ones. Most service organisations are offering a wider range of services, confusing the traditional boundaries between organisations. Banks, building societies and other financial institutions are now in direct competition and information technology is an underlying reason why this is happening.

Many of the changes may be organisational in character making it possible to achieve other objectives. Pomfrett and Damodaran (1989) give an example of an organisation taking out a tier of its regional marketing structure by using information technology to enable salesmen to communicate with the regional headquarters from their homes. The concept of Telework, i.e. using information technology to allow staff to work from home is now becoming a practical reality; see, for example, the Rank Xerox Experiment (Judkins *et al.*, 1985). An alternative is the Local Work Centre (Hedberg and Mehlmann, 1984) in which a number of organisations share offices wired for all forms of information technology local to the homes of their staff.

This list of possible organisational enhancement objectives could be much longer, as long as the myriad goals of organisations. Many applications, however, lead to failure. All of the problems discussed so far can appear in these applications; there can be resources to reduce, jobs can be created that are stressful for staff, systems may prove unusable by professional or managerial grades of staff, etc. There are, in addition, some other problems.

1. *Defining the Organisational Need.* These applications should start from the identification of objectives the organisation can beneficially pursue. They should not start from a new technical opportunity because this may not mirror a real organisational need. Frequently this is how they do start and the result can be a system that does little for the fundamental problems and opportunities of the organisation.

2. *Developing Specialist Systems.* Whilst the systems implemented may belong to the families of applications described above, each will have to be uniquely developed to meet the organisational need and to match the organisational structure. Attempts to provide standardised solutions at this level have often led to disasters. An excellent example is the development of Management Information Systems (MISs) in the 1970s. In many organisations grandiose plans were drawn up to provide rather rigid information services to all managers. The result was what Ackoff (1967) called 'management mis-information systems'; services that provided piles of irrelevant, out-of-date data but little usable information because the services were inadequately matched to the needs of managers. Many systems fell into disuse. The need is to specify the technical service required to meet the unique organisational need and this requires a combination of technical knowledge, business requirements and inside knowledge of the organisation in question.

3. *Organisational Change.* Above all other considerations, the pursuit of organisational enhancement using information technology demands organisational change. Computer integrated manufacture needs dramatic changes in the work roles of people in production units. Inviting a substantial proportion of employees to work from home needs completely new ways of running the business. It has often been failure to think through and implement these changes that has led to lack of success. The result can be a new form of technical systems harnessed to an old form of social system, the incompatibility of the two preventing the achievement of the original objective.

The Problems of Achieving Benefits

We are now in a position to summarise the issues which confront the organisation seeking benefits from information technology. At the beginning of the chapter the question posed was whether the problems of achieving success were the result of the technology being oversold; was it that it could not live up to the extravagant claims? This review suggests that the claims for information technology are real — especially in its ability to enhance the work of staff individually and collectively. The overselling seems to have occurred not in the statement of potential benefits but in the problems of achieving the benefits. The worst offenders are those who claim that it is easy; 'you buy it, switch it on and the fruits of the new age are yours'. Nothing could be further from the truth. Success depends upon confronting and resolving issues of the following kinds:

1. *Tangible vs. Intangible Benefits.* Some of the benefits, i.e. those relating to cost reductions, are of a tangible nature against which specific costs can be allocated. Others are of a much more intangible nature because they involve indirect effects on the work of other people. A Decision Support System, for example, is only beneficial if the managerial decision performance improves as a result. If the organisation engages in a tight and explicit cost–benefit analysis, before launching its information technology project, it is likely that tangible benefits will be sought as a much more concrete expression of the benefits that can be achieved. It is only by doing so that a project can be shown to be cost beneficial. An organisation that seeks intangible benefits is, to some extent, engaged in an act of faith and will be unlikely to be able to show clear-cut benefits being achieved over the costs the project is going to incur. This problem is having a braking effect on the introduction of really radical organisational changes because they involve many intangibles. Indeed the pace of implementation of information technology and the type of application may be determined by the degree to which management adopt a very tight definition of tangible benefits. If this is the approach adopted, the applications are likely to be of the resource reduction or optimisation form and the broader, enhancement objectives are less likely to be pursued. Methods of identifying and costing enhancement applications are one of the major requirements if the full potential of information technology is to be realised.

2. *Identifying Worthwhile Benefits.* There are a profusion of benefits that could be pursued in any organisation. But great choice makes choosing difficult. Every organisation has a unique set of objectives, culture and problems and the appropriate way of using information technology in one organisation is not necessarily the same as in another, even if it is in the same business. Every organisation needs to be able to assess the way of using the technology which is best suited to its requirements.

3. *Benefits Come from Human Learning.* With the exception of the cost reduction types of benefits, all the benefits accrue as a result of human learning. It is not possible for the organisation to improve its productivity or for the nature of its work to be enhanced unless and until the staff concerned are able to master the information technology and use it to improve the work they undertake. This in turn means that

the benefits can take some time to come to fruition and depend heavily on the kind of learning programmes implemented with the information technology systems. If insufficient attention is paid to this aspect of implementation the result is expensive high technology that the staff of the organisation are unable to exploit, a scenario that will be recognised in many workplaces.

4. *Benefits to Some and Losses to Others.* Whilst this chapter is devoted to the benefits of information technology, it is obvious that the benefits for some people are in fact losses to others. Nowhere is this clearer than in the example of staff savings, which are also lost jobs, and lost opportunities for people looking for jobs. Quite clearly the achievements of benefits of this kind is going to involve the resolution of conflicts of interest within organisations. It is not so evident that the achievement of work-enhancing benefits will lead to conflicts of this kind, but in any organisational environment an improvement in performance by one group can have an effect, perhaps beneficial, perhaps detrimental, on other groups so we have yet to see whether the same kinds of organisational conflict result from the achievement of the less tangible benefits.

5. *Conflicts Between Types of Benefit.* It might be argued that a project could achieve all the different kinds of benefits, for example, both those that come from resource redeployment and from work enhancing. However, these different types of benefits are often in conflict with one another. We may take the example of the manager being given an executive workstation. The assumption may be that with this workstation he will be able to enhance his decision-making performance and his managerial performance as a result of the new forms of information he can obtain, the easier communications he has with other people and so forth. It could be, how- ever, that the organisation will take the opportunity of saving money by removing his secretarial support on the premise that he can now fulfil his information processing for himself. It is likely that a manager in this position will find that he spends his time performing basic routine information processing tasks and is there- fore unable to use the service from the system to improve his managerial perfor- mance. In some organisations this has become known as the 'hidden costs' of office automation. The result of trying to achieve too many types of benefit can be that none of them are achieved.

6. *Benefits Lead to Secondary Effects.* The kinds of benefits that are being discussed can have quite far reaching effects in an organisation. It is not possible to reallocate staff to reduce costs, to improve productivity, or to improve organisational performance more generally as a result of the introduction of the system, without changing other facets of the organisation. It may be, for example, that jobs are changed, career patterns are disturbed, payment and evaluation systems have to be revised, industrial relations agreements have to be revised and organisational structures have to be rethought. Unless these issues are effectively managed, the system may lead to unwanted organisational problems or may be rejected or inadequately exploited because it does not match organisation practice and custom.

When the people on the receiving end of information technology applications, be they managers, staff or their representatives, first contemplate the problems they have to confront their first thought is usually that they will need to develop their technical knowledge. Most guides to help the would-be user concentrate on the technical aspects of the technology. Whilst not denying the importance of technical issues, the analysis presented in this chapter suggests that in choosing and developing a system, there is a major role for the users which has more to do with knowing their information requirements, establishing the purposes for which information technology could be used and working out how to handle the human and organisational issues associated with the change. It is to these matters that this book is devoted. In the next chapter we will examine how these matters are addressed in typical application design processes.

Chapter 3
Systems Design Methods and Organisational Change

Introduction

To obtain the benefits of information technology there are many human and organisational change issues to be confronted in the system development process. How are these issues considered in the design methods available for the creation of systems to be implemented within organisations? The purpose of this chapter is to review the methods that are currently in use with this specific question in mind.

Design Methods

There are many variants in system design methods and many ways of classifying them. As a result of changes in the technology and the recognition of the need to consider organisational issues, the methods have been changing quite dramatically in recent years. Figure 3.1 is a classification which emphasises the way methods relate to the organisation in which they are used and which indicates the shifts in focus that have

Figure 3.1
A classification of application design processes

Location	Dominant Participants		
	Technical Specialists	Specialists with Users	Users
Centralised	**1.** eg. Traditional Data Processing Design	**2.** eg. Structured Design Methods	**3.** eg. Participative Design Methods
Decentralised	———	**4.** eg. Local Technician Developed Systems	**5.** eg. End User Developed Systems

occurred in recent years. It is adapted from the classification used by Wainwright and Francis (1984) to characterise design processes in use in their sample of office automation systems.

It is based on two major dimensions. One distinction is between those design methods which are primarily undertaken by technical specialists and those which include, in some significant way, the users for whom the system is intended. The second dimension refers to the location of the design effort. It may be a centralised design process conducted at corporate level or a decentralised effort undertaken within a user department. This produces five major forms of design:

1. *Traditional Data Processing Design*. Inasmuch as a young industry such as computing can have a tradition, it has been the development of bespoke (purpose-built) data processing systems within the client organisation. This has been a centralised approach where design is dominated by computer specialists located at head office and developing systems to run on large mainframe computers.

2. *Structured Design Methods*. Recognition that the potential users of a system should have a voice in its construction has led to many methods which embody the concept of computer specialists working with users. Where large-scale centralised systems are being developed, Structured Design Methods for example, LSDM (Burchett, 1985) and SSADM (Cutts, 1987) are becoming very popular because they provide a disciplined way of working through the stages of design to ensure consistency, documentation, change control, etc. These methods also formalise the relationship between the end users and the designers into an explicit customer–contractor contract.

3. *Participative Design Methods*. Many authors, especially Mumford *et al.* (1978), Kling (1977), Hirschheim (1985) and Dray (1987), consider that it is not sufficient to provide users with a formal role within a technically dominated design process. Hirschheim, for example, considers that successful system design is primarily an exercise in organisational change and as such user-dominated socio-technical design methods should be employed such as Mumford and Weir's (1979) ETHICS method or the socio-technical method of Pava (1983). In these methods participating users analyse organisational requirements and plan appropriate social and technical structures which will meet human and organisational needs. These methods constitute a major change from the design methods currently in use which emphasise technical goals.

4. *Local Technician Developed Systems*. Many end-user departments are now taking computing into their own hands and developing systems for themselves. The availability of cheap microcomputers and 'off-the-shelf' software applications makes this a practical proposition which would have seemed impossible a few years ago when all computing depended upon a large, centrally located, mainframe computer. One way of accomplishing this form of decentralised computing is to employ a local technical expert who can help identify requirements, select systems, set up systems and support the users. This may be done by a Department employing their own systems manager or programmer, using an external consultant or by the organisation establishing a local Information Centre (Bird and Firnberg 1984). This concept has become very popular in recent years; it usually entails some part of the DP Department being decentralised

to the user location and providing advice on both the organisation's mainframe services and the wide array of services that can be obtained on micros. In effect the Centre operates as a kind of 'Information Shop' with a significant after-sales maintenance and user-support role.

5. *End-user Developed Systems.* The availability of cheap microcomputers also makes it possible for end users to do without any kind of specialist design help in their organisation. They can, for example, visit a local retailer, purchase a system and either make use of the standard software or attempt to program a system to meet their own requirements. It is increasingly common to find examples of such do-it-yourself 'end user developed systems' scattered around organisations.

We thus have a complete range of applications from the centralised, 'bespoke' large-scale system in which the specialist staff create unique suites of programs for the organisation through to the localised, off-the-shelf purchase of standard micros and their packages for use by a person with no technical specialist support. It will be apparent that these different methods will evoke different kinds of organisational consequences and will contain within them different ways of managing these organisational consequences. In the following sections we will look more closely at each of these five possibilities.

The Traditional Data Processing Approach

In general the procedures whereby a data processing application is created for a mainframe computer within an organisation have traditionally followed the phases described in Figure 3.2.

The methods are essentially linear. The process starts with a project selection phase which leads to a statement of the project to be pursued with a set of terms of reference for a design team to undertake its work. This then proceeds to a full-scale feasibility study which produces a report to the sponsors (the potential customers of the system) which specifies the costs of the development, the benefits that would accrue, and the

Figure 3.2
Systems analysis and design

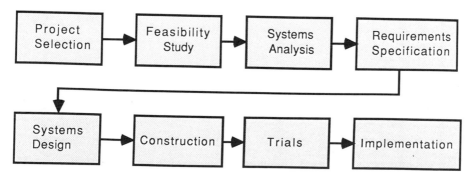

systems development plan that would be necessary to develop the system. If approval is given for undertaking the project, there would then follow a systems analysis stage in which the systems designers would analyse the requirements for the system in terms such as the information flows and the volumes of data to be stored and transmitted in order to fulfil the system's objectives. This process would lead to a requirements report which specifies the size and nature of the system that will be necessary to perform the task. Following this phase, systems design proper can begin as the systems designers attempt to fabricate a way of meeting the requirements. Commonly this involves the detailed specification of the programs, the definition of the data bases, and, if hardware is not already available within the organisation, the specification and procurement of an appropriate configuration of equipment upon which the system can run. The system can then be constructed usually with an extensive period of part- and whole-systems trials as system testing is undertaken. Finally the system can be implemented and procedures for operation, maintenance and support put in place.

Taking a broad view of the introduction of a system as an exercise in the creation of a new technical system and a change in the organisational framework, we can note the following about this kind of design process:

1. *Technical System Design.* Clearly this design process is intended to create a computer-based technical system. There is very little formal recognition that the system will be operated by a number of human beings who will themselves be operating in an organisational environment. It has to be said that in the earlier generations of computer systems it was a difficult feat to develop a complex technical system and get it to function as anticipated, and it could well be that this lack of explicit formal concern for the organisation environment in which the system was to work was largely a matter of having to solve the technical problems before you could worry about the organisational problems.

2. *Design Team Composition.* The process of creating a technical system is dominated by the concept that it will be created by technical specialists. There are occasional references to the customer, i.e. reports are made to the sponsor about costs, benefits and requirements, etc. and the design process proceeds inasmuch as the customer is prepared to pay. However, there is no mention of incorporating users within the design process.

3. *Establishing a Specification.* This design process divides neatly into two parts: the first is a series of analyses leading to a specification; the second is a design process attempting to meet the specification. The process of arriving at a firm and agreed specification which will thereafter be adhered to is therefore a central feature of this approach. A basic problem is that it allows for very few second thoughts.

4. *One-shot Implementation.* This design procedure is also characterised by the philosophy of defining, designing and implementing the system in one series of steps. The concept is that once the system has been implemented, the design team can disband or move to other work and it will thereafter be a question of operation and maintenance of the system. This may be contrasted with the concept of a steadily evolving and changing system, which is never complete.

There is little pretence that this traditional approach is engaging with the organisational issues which must be faced before there can be successful implementation. One way of characterising the way technical design and organisational change are handled in this process is depicted in Figure 3.3.

Figure 3.3
Technical design before organisational learning

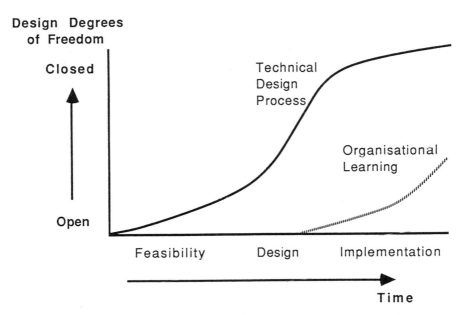

The technical design process is the subject of formal procedures and moves from the feasibility study stage where there are many degrees of freedom in the design to the stage of implementation where the technical options have been frozen to provide a specific solution. Towards the end of the design phase potential users become aware of the planned technical change and gradually become aware of the organisational implications. This is not part of the formal procedure and is usually an uncoordinated and unplanned phase of organisational learning.

It is this kind of sequential design process which has been the subject of most of the computer impact research. There is now a considerable literature documenting the effects of large-scale data processing systems running on mainframe computers — see, for example, Eason *et al.* (1974), Gotlieb and Borodin (1973), Mowshowitz (1976), Buchanan and Boddy (1983) and Bjørn-Andersen *et al.* (1986). If the system is implemented the result is often a variety of unexpected and, for many of the users, unwanted results. It is convenient to summarise them under the following five headings:

1. *Task Support Problems.* The failure to look in detail at the work of each type of user often means that the system delivers an inappropriate service to the users, i.e. does

not provide what is needed to undertake the task, or makes unreasonable demands for inputs from the user. It may also demand more time and effort than the user can provide given the constraints of the working conditions. It has been known, for example, for a computer system to expect a detailed account of a patient's symptoms and the planned treatment regime at a time when the doctor is struggling to keep the patient alive.

2. *Job Content Issues*. The implementation of the system may assume or require changes in the content of the jobs of users. Under some conditions, for example, jobs may become more repetitive, more tightly controlled, subject to continuous monitoring, paced by the system and requiring less skill from the operator. This is by no means the only set of outcomes that is possible but, when it does occur, it is not welcomed by the people on the receiving end.

3. *Formalisation*. Computer programs demand explicit and disciplined procedures. It is hardly surprising, therefore, that the introduction of computer systems requires users to behave in more formal and disciplined ways. Systems that co-ordinate the work of many users perhaps across a number of departments tend to require more standardised and formalised procedures between users. Whether these effects are welcome depends upon the degree to which the order imposed fits the task requirements. If it does not the users will experience unwanted bureaucracy and the organisation may find it difficult to adjust to changing business circumstances (Bjørn-Andersen and Eason, 1981).

4. *Power and Influence*. To have access to information is a necessary precursor to the exercise of power and influence and computer systems may redistribute access to information. They may thus have unexpected and perhaps unwanted effects upon the power structure of the organisation. The change most often predicted is towards centralisation with senior staff having more ready access to information and therefore better able to exert power over their subordinates (Whisler, 1970). However, later research (Bjørn-Andersen *et al.*, 1986) suggests the direction of change can also be in other directions towards decentralisation, when subordinates in possession of more information can influence their seniors, or laterally, where one department can influence another because it is better informed.

5. *Personnel Policies*. The changes wrought in the organisation inevitably bring needs to amend personnel policies. They may affect recruitment, training, payment systems, career development and progression, manpower planning, etc. Changes on these fronts and others may mean there are major industrial relations matters to resolve.

These are the issues which can be seen when a system has been implemented. But, of course, if the organisational learning that begins as a system nears implementation brings these issues to the attention of the users, the result is often a long-drawn-out implementation process — sometimes leading to a failure to implement the system. This reaction of users is often classified as resistance to change, which suggests a blanket, unthinking opposition. This does little justice to the thoughtful and ingenious way many users may respond. Keen (1981) captures the active nature of users' reactions in what he has called 'counter implementation strategies'. These are measures designed to impede the development of the system or its implementation and engaged in by people unofficially because of anxieties and frustrations about the system. Counter-implementation strategies include the following:

1. 'Lay low' – if you do not want it to succeed then the more you keep out of the way and do not give help and encouragement, the more likelihood there is of failure.
2. 'Rely on inertia' – any change process is up against organisational inertia and if you can be too busy when asked the implementation process may come to a halt.
3. 'Keep the project complex, hard to co-ordinate and vaguely defined' – if the goals are ambiguous or too ambitious there is every chance of failure as energy is dissipated in many different directions.
4. 'Minimise the implementers' legitimacy and influence' – if the designers are kept as outsiders, other users will probably not allow them to work effectively.
5. 'Exploit their lack of inside knowledge' – the design team probably know very little about the detailed nature of the work and if they are denied this knowledge, the system will probably prove to be inadequate when it is implemented.

The description of the design process as a political process with implementation and counter-implementation forces at work will accord with the experience of many people engaged in the process, if not with the textbooks on system design, which rarely mention these realities of organisational life. It is clearly dysfunctional for the organisation to proceed in this way.

    Along with many other professionals in the human and social sciences, we have often been asked to assist organisations with implementation procedures when a system is ready for installation. Unfortunately at this stage it may already be too late to resolve implementation problems. If the process depicted in Figure 3.3 is being followed the technical design will have been fixed by this stage. If analysis shows that the system is not well matched to the needs of the organisation or to its individual users, the choice is either to abort the system or to try to ameliorate the undesirable effects. Given the financial and psychological investment of the developers in the system it is small wonder the choice is usually to press on with implementation and suffer the consequences of a sub-optimal socio-technical system. We must conclude therefore that if we are to deal adequately with the organisational change issues they must be addressed much earlier in the design process so that the technical and organisational work can proceed in parallel rather than in sequence.

Structured Design Methods

The design of large-scale systems is changing dramatically for a number of reasons, e.g. fourth-generation languages and tools, different kinds of applications, etc. One major cause of change is the introduction of structured design methods which provide a well documented and consistent set of procedures by which technical systems can be created. These formal methods include a number of important innovations, for example, an emphasis upon describing the entities the system deals with as well as the processes in the application. By formally requiring documentation in specific forms at all stages, these methods also inject discipline into change control, i.e. when one part of the system is changed the consequences for interdependent parts are thoroughly examined and the outcome is recorded in a form readily understood by other designers. These and other changes mean that these methods now provide a means by which large-scale, complex software developments may be managed with some confidence. Some of the best known examples of these methodologies are the Jackson Methodology (Jackson, 1975), LSDM (Learmouth Structured Development Methodology) (Burchett, 1985) and SSADM (Structured Systems Analysis and Design Methodology) (Cutts, 1987).

One of the concepts embedded in these methodologies is the customer–contractor relationship, i.e. the customer is perceived as commissioning the design team to develop a system to meet specified requirements. At various stages in the process, the designers are obliged to provide the customer with evidence of progress and customers are empowered to assess the progress; design cannot proceed until they are satisfied that the resulting system will be in accord with their requirements. On the face of it, this provides the users with the involvement and the right to ensure systems meet their needs from the beginning of the design process. An example of the kind of stages to be found at the top level of a structured systems design is given in Figure 3.4.

The stages in these methods are not unlike those in traditional DP methods and the linear sequence remains. As far as the customer is concerned the general principle is that, at each stage, users review progress and the next stage does not advance until they have accepted the output. Thus the initial analysis has to be vetted as acceptable to the users, and the specification for the new system has to be accepted as the kind of system the users want. At stage 3 the designers present users with alternative ways of meeting the specification and the users are, at this stage, required to select the way they wish to proceed. Further forms of reviewing and accepting occur at the detailed levels of developing the system.

These techniques have been in use for a relatively short time and it is a little early to offer systematic evidence about the effects of this arrangement upon users and therefore upon the success of systems designed by these methods. However, there have been widespread efforts to involve users in the phases of traditional data processing design procedures and the circumstances seem very similar to those users will find in structured systems design. From the results of studies of users under these conditions we can identify a range of problems they might experience:

1. *Technical Knowledge*. Users asked to review proposals by specialist staff are often at a disadvantage in that they cannot readily understand the technical proposals being put to them because they do not have the background knowledge to appreciate what is being said. A complex flow chart, for example, full of files, terminals, etc., with notes about rates of transmission from one point to another, and the amount of storage available in one place rather than another, is not something that the average user, taken from his normal job to advise on this development, can actually pass sensible comments about. It is a long way from this kind of technical specification to the experience of using a system to improve one's work performance.

2. *Communicating with Specialists*. A related problem is that there may be considerable

Figure 3.4
User involvement in structured design methods

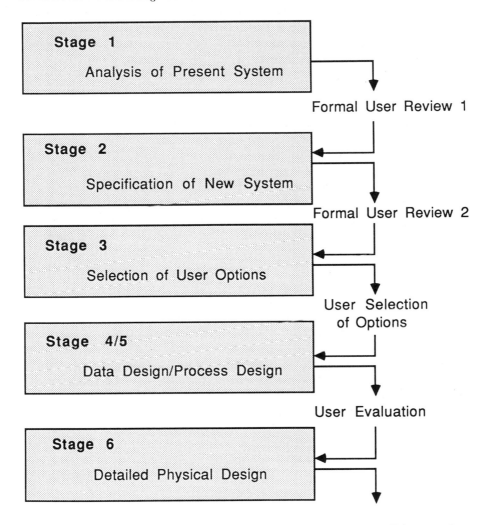

difficulties in communication between users and specialists. Even if the specialists are part of the same organisation, they may speak a quite different technical language to that used by the user departments and neither side may adequately appreciate the difficulty the other side has in understanding the significance of what they are saying. It may also not become apparent to the people concerned that there are these difficulties because users feel inhibited about revealing their ignorance in settings which may contain many important people within the organisation.

3. *Defining Needs.* One of the duties systems specialists may expect to see performed by user representatives is that of detailed definition of user requirements. It is not easy, however, for anybody to step out of the work role and accurately report how

that work is undertaken. It is, for example, well known that managers asked to report how much of their time they spend in meetings, on the telephone, or travelling, etc. are usually inaccurate in their judgements. The designer does not of course merely wish to know how a person undertakes his work, but needs to know what kinds of requirements arise from this work which is a stage further removed. In practice users find it very difficult to arrive at judgements of this kind.

4. *Seeing Opportunities.* A related issue to that of defining needs is that ideally the users in the systems design process will not be reporting what they need in order to support the job as they now do it, but will be examining information technology possibilities in order to see what new opportunities they provide. The intention must be to make a significantly different approach to engaging in the work of the enterprise if the full potential of the technology is to be harnessed. Users who find it difficult to report their existing work and who find it difficult to understand technological descriptions, which may be couched in an unfamiliar language, are not in a good position to see these opportunities and to judge opportunities that technologists might offer them.

5. *Which Users?* A system may have many potential users so which of them will review system progress? Too often it is a user manager when an end user is necessary because detailed job knowledge is required or it is a junior user when a major, strategic issue requiring managerial desision is on the table.

6. *Resolving Conflicts.* Introduction of users into the design team adds a new dimension to the conduct of systems design. It means that the technical specialists are, to some degree, under the control of the users, but the nature and degree of this control by the users and which of the users is exerting this control can often be ambiguous and can often cause conflicts within the design process. Furthermore, a large system may well require representation from a number of different user departments. It is most unlikely that all of these users will define the requirements of the system in the same way and there may be fundamental differences in their aspirations. The technical staff require an agreed specification before they can proceed to detailed design and in some way it will be necessary to resolve the differences between users.

7. *Technical not Organisational Design.* It had been hoped that the involvement of users in systems design would mean that the problems and issues of organisational change would be identified early and suitable procedures initiated for the implementation of necessary and appropriate changes. Experience has shown that users working within design teams find themselves concentrating, as the technical systems staff do, on the technical issues. The primary concern is to judge whether the specification for the technical system is appropriate and whether the technical solutions being proposed are going to be adequate for their job. Once again there is a tendency to leave the broader, organisational consequences until such time as the technical system is more or less complete and these consequences are more evident. It is salutory to note that the extensive documentation of these methodologies does not include methods of engaging in job design and organisational change. It is a method of arriving at a technical not a socio-technical solution.

8. *Acting Quickly.* The above list of problems is quite extensive and to be managed effectively will take time and concentrated effort. Unfortunately time is not usually

on the users' side during systems development as can be seen from Figure 3.5 below, which is a repeat of the earlier figure, displaying the way in which the technical design proceeds from feasibility through design to implementation in a one-shot implementation process. With users involved in the design process, we can hope that the organisational learning process, i.e. the awareness of users about the organisational issues accompanying implementation, can begin very early as the technical design process begins. However, if the principle design philosophy is to arrive at a specification and then rapidly to design a solution to meet the specification, then users have to make their views known about the specification and about the early principles of the design solution very early in the design process. The principles of setting deadlines and freezing the specification before design underpin structured design methods as they do traditional DP design.

As Figure 3.5 indicates, the requirement to follow a design process of the one-shot implementation form means that the users have a limited window for their contributions to design. The fact that they are ill-prepared for this role and experience many difficulties in fulfilling it, means that they are frequently not able to make good use of the limited opportunities that offer themselves. Quite often they find themselves presented with complex documents at the beginning of the week and have to attend a meeting at the end of the week to ratify the proposals that are contained therein.

It is common for users faced with the problems of responding sensibly to the needs of designers to conclude cynically that the customer–contractor relationship is simply a way of ensuring it is the customer's fault if the technical system is not successful when implemented. If the customer has approved each stage of the development, the designer can always say you approved the specification or you approved this

Figure 3.5
Technical design with user involvement

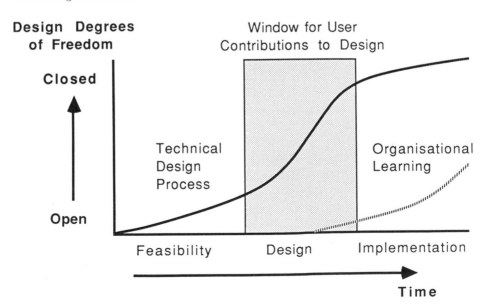

particular design. In defence of the system designer, it should be said that no design can be completed if the customer keeps changing the specification. Finding ways of helping users to specify requirements and evaluate ways of meeting them whilst giving systems specialists a clear brief and time to design solutions is one of the main needs in systems design.

Whilst we should not make hasty judgements about recent innovations, it seems unlikely that structured design methods as presently constituted are going to offer much improvement as a way of handling the organisational change aspects of systems design. There are two main reasons for this conclusion. Firstly, these methodologies are designed for technical systems design and give little procedural help in the many topics to be addressed under the heading of organisational change. Secondly, although they provide the user with an opportunity to influence technical design, they provide little time or procedural support to help the user make adequate use of this opportunity.

Participative Design Methods

If, as Hirschheim (1985) proposes, systems design is seen primarily as an exercise in organisational change, an approach to systems development very different from traditional DP design is needed. Many methodologies have been proposed which take this as their rationale and most of them emphasise the participation of users throughout the development process.

As an example of a participative design methodology a summary of the Effective Technical and Human Implementation of Computer Systems (ETHICS) Method developed by Mumford and Weir is presented in Figure 3.6. It is a procedure users can employ to plan their future system. Mumford (1983a) has elaborated the procedure to 25 steps. The general procedure is that a systems analysis procedure which explores goals, values and sources of job satisfaction in addition to information flows, key tasks, etc. leads to the ranking of efficiency and job satisfaction needs. The next stage is the design of socio-technical systems solutions. This requires the identification of technical and business constraints and the technical resources available in order to specify the technical objectives. In parallel a similar process is conducted to identify social constraints and resources in order to specify social objectives. After checking whether the technical and social objectives are compatible, a search can be made for technical solutions and social solutions (forms of work organisation) which again can be checked for compatibility and ranked according to their ability to meet the social and technical objectives. Once an outline solution has been selected work can begin on the detailed work design necessary to implement the system.

This programme performs the difficult feat of keeping social system design (organisation change) integrated with technical design through the analysis and design stages. Mumford has reported several case studies (1983a, 1983b) using this methodology which is gradually evolving as experience of its use grows. However, as yet, the process has not spread widely and neither have any other methods that are based on participative socio-technical design. There appear to be at least two major problems. It

Figure 3.6
The ETHICS Method

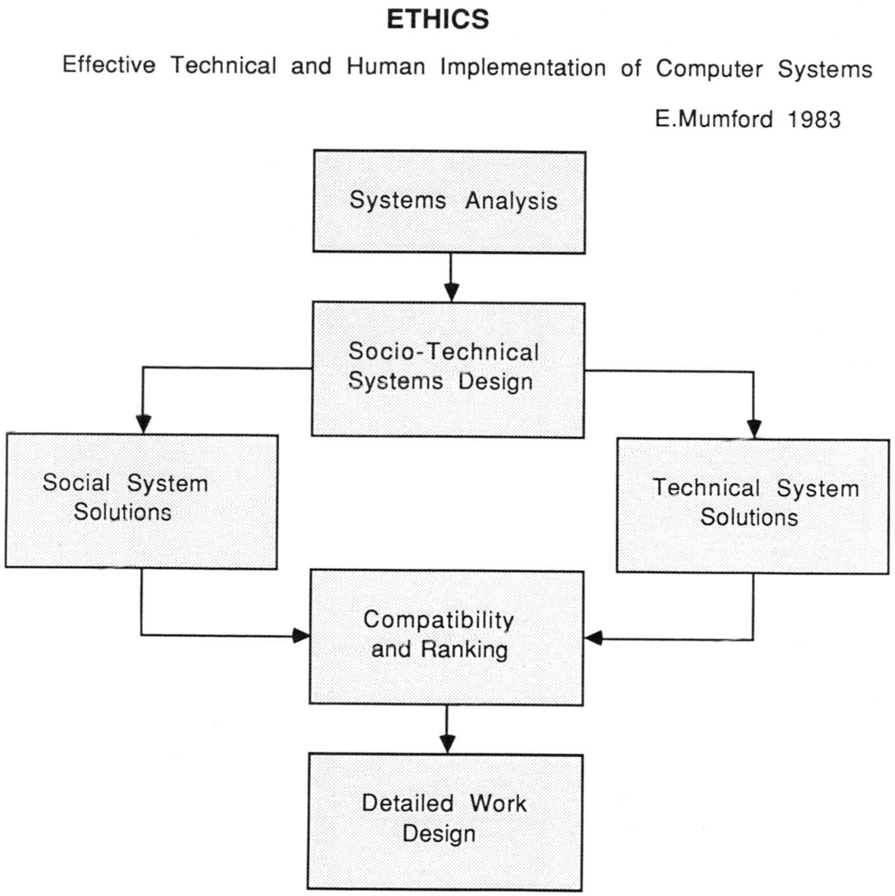

ETHICS

Effective Technical and Human Implementation of Computer Systems

E.Mumford 1983

needs an expert, such as Enid Mumford, to support the users through the steps in the process. It is a complex process for people who are unfamilar with design, never mind socio-technical design, although, with help, they can most certainly use it successfully. The second problem is the degree to which it can be integrated with traditional data processing systems design. There are few points of contact and it is difficult to see how both processes can be undertaken in the same development. Many of these concepts underpin the methods presented in Chapter 7 which have been developed for use in conjunction with traditional technical systems design procedures.

End-User Developed Systems

If centralised methods of systems design, whether or not they provide for user representation, do not provide local users with systems they find useful or acceptable, it is likely they will seek alternatives. Their motives may be many. It may be that they consider they have unique requirements, not met by design processes that seek similar solutions across many departments. It may be that they recognise that centralised systems are often implemented as control mechanisms and if they develop their own local solutions, they may, in effect, be asserting their own autonomy rather than accepting centralised control by impersonal computer systems. They may simply be impatient waiting for a central team to get round to their needs. Whatever the reason they may look for their own solutions and the way the technology has developed in recent years has made it ever more realistic and cost effective for them to do so. The development first of mini-based systems and then of microcomputers has made it possible for department heads and section heads to purchase computer systems from within their own budgets. There is, as a result, a massive movement in progress in which small-scale systems are being purchased and developed in many different places within an organisation and this movement has been christened 'end-user developed systems'.

Figure 3.7 combines the two different ways in which end-user developed systems are created and some of the issues that surround this method of developing systems are presented.

The two different techniques for developing these systems are to get technical support to realise a user's specification for a system and for the users to do it themselves, without technical support. The 'do-it-yourself' approach has been made in-

Figure 3.7
End-user developed systems

	Users 'Do-it-yourself'	Users with Technical Support
Description	- Use of Packages - End-User Programming	-External Consultants - Programming Techniques -Information Centres
Issues	- Poor task match, - Reliability, Support and Expansion problems - Effort required	-Unrealistic Demands
Consequences	-'Computer Anarchy'; non-integration of information flows	

creasingly possible by the array of useful business packages that are available for micros, especially for accounting (for example, spreadsheet packages), for communications and for word processing. These computer systems also have programming capabilities and in many instances end users have made use of these facilities to try and create systems unique to their own circumstances.

Although these developments have been relatively recent there is already evidence of the results that business users obtain by this method. It would appear that where the application is of a general nature, e.g. in word processing, the purchase of packages and running them within an organisational setting can be very effective. However, where the users' requirements are in some way unique it is quite frequently the case that the package is soon found wanting and users find that it takes considerable dedication, time and effort to tailor applications to their own requirements. They are either faced with using a system which is poorly fitted to their requirements, changing their requirements, or discontinuing the use of the system they have purchased.

In many circumstances they rapidly outgrow the capability of the system they have purchased. They discover that they wish to use more storage than they have available, that performance degrades quite quickly as they begin to load the system, or that they cannot add to or expand the system as they would wish to. They may also experience difficulties with the reliability of the system and when they have problems with it they lack the local technical support to help them with these problems. They are, in many ways, in the position of people who have used public transport for many years, have become frustrated by having to travel as the times of the public service to the destination provided by the service rather than at their own time and to their own destination, and have therefore moved to private transport so they may have complete control over their travelling arrangements. Unfortunately it also brings responsibility for operating, maintaining, and understanding the private system which was not necessary when it was a public system. In a recent survey by Wroe (1986) a number of small building firms tried to develop their own systems, often without very much external support, and found that the effort required was often well beyond that which they envisaged when they purchased the system, and that the end products often fell far short of their aspirations. Similarly Hemming (1986) found that computer systems in general medical practice succeeded to the extent that doctors were willing and able to provide the considerable amount of personal effort needed to develop an appropriate system. This kind of development therefore requires a level of dedication from the user which most would not anticipate — given the type of advertising which suggests there are instant 'user friendly' solutions in every purchase that one makes.

The alternative to do-it-yourself is to purchase a small-scale system with the advice of a technical specialist and to use technical specialists to develop systems which are specific to one's requirements. This may be done in a number of ways. In many professional groups, for example, the staff may be supported by a number of technicians some of whom may have computing skills. It is not uncommon, for example, to find a group of scientists with programming support enabling them to develop systems to meet their own professional requirements. In other circumstances the user may turn to external software consultants to advise them and to help them develop systems. In practice it is frequently the case that systems developed in this way can be effective for the users. The development is small scale and involves a close relationship between a user, who is only concerned with his own requirements, and a technical specialist, who similarly has a limited specification to work to and it is often successful.

The problem with systems of this kind is that users may make unrealistic demands because of their ignorance of the technology and the designers, for reasons of their subordinate role, or because they are being employed temporarily to do the work, are unable or unwilling to encourage the users to be more realistic. Nevertheless, as an approach this one shows signs of being able to meet user requirements.

Within a business context there is a particular problem associated with the development of small-scale systems in this way. If every department in an organisation seeks its own solutions for its information handling, it could lead to a profusion of different manufacturers of equipment, different software packages, and different ways of handling information within the organisation. The effects of cheap micros in this environment have led to suggestions that we may be in for a form of 'computer anarchy' in which everybody goes their own way with the consequence that there is no integrated policy or integrated system with respect to computing within an organisation. This may be of no consequence if two departments have no task interdependence, i.e. they can engage in their own tasks without having any kind of impact upon one another. However, if there is a degree of task interdependence and department A has to provide information which is fed to department B to act upon, it is clearly quite serious if the two departments operate incompatible systems and cannot exchange information. The drift away from centralised, integrated systems may therefore be regarded as a serious matter with respect to overall performance by the organisation. Many management services departments are currently expressing concern about this kind of development. One may regard this as an important expression of concern for the health of the organisation or as a group worried about losing their traditional control over computing but, nevertheless, in the examination of the organisational ramifications of systems development, it remains an issue to be considered very carefully.

One solution currently being advocated is to encourage the development of small-scale systems but within the controlled framework of a centralised service. The creation of Information Centres (Bird and Firnberg, 1984) is an IBM-inspired solution in which companies establish a centre which can hold a variety of microcomputers and offer an array of facilities. Users can visit such a centre and be shown the array of facilities available, can select those which best meet their requirements, can be taught how to use the facilities and can perhaps have developed on their behalf special programs to run on these machines. The facilities may be operated in the Information Centre or perhaps the users can purchase the facilities for use within their own department. This kind of structure offers a sheltered environment in which the users can develop systems to their own unique specification but also provides the organisation with an opportunity to control the profusion of different kinds of equipment and systems within some overall policy. It remains to be seen whether these twin objectives can be achieved in this way.

Conclusions

This review of system design practice has looked at five different types of design process from the perspective of managing organisational change. The evidence is overwhelming that the traditional data processing approach is inadequate in its treatment of these issues and has led to many failures. However, the design community is already moving away from this approach for many reasons and it is more important that we assess the potential of current methods for managing the organisational issues. Structured design methods which are the modern way of developing complex, centralised systems have a structured way of creating roles for users which could provide a way of managing organisational issues. Unfortunately these methods are devoted to the design of technical systems and give little recognition or support to the range of organisational changes that have also to be designed. They also give little support to the user who is trying to influence and assess the technical system and it is likely that the technical system will not in fact meet user needs when it is implemented. There do exist participative design methods specifically designed to give emphasis to the organisational design side of systems development. Unfortunately these are not well integrated with the technical system development methods that are widely used and, as a consequence, they are little used and little known methods outside the research community.

The principle ways of developing systems are not therefore meeting the users' needs very successfully, especially not the needs of the local end-user who may not like the systems planned by senior management in any case because they may represent an attempt to exert more central control over them. The changing nature of the technology means that many end users are seeking their own salvation by developing their own systems. This is often successful but poses two kinds of problems. Firstly, because they lack technical expertise, users may choose the wrong system or may find themselves having to devote large proportions of their own time to systems development. Secondly, the system may meet the narrow needs of a specific user but not the broader interests of the organisation. Systems development has to recognise the legitimacy of both individual requirements and the corporate needs of the organisation as a collection of interrelated individuals, and find a way of satisfying these conflicting requirements.

There are therefore problems in managing the human and organisational side of information technology applications whichever systems design approach is taken. With these methods in mind and the problems associated with them we can now begin the quest for ways of coping jointly with information technology and organisational change.

Chapter 4
Towards the Socio-Technical Design
of Information Technology Systems

Introduction

The preceding chapters have led to two conclusions. The first is that we are unlikely to achieve real benefits from information technology unless we find ways of designing for the human and organisational changes that are needed as well as designing the technical changes. The second conclusion is that examination of systems design processes suggests that current methods do not systematically address these issues. The implication is that we must seek ways of compensating for the current emphasis upon the technical side of the change process. This chapter offers an overall strategy for accomplishing this purpose and provides the framework for the subjects addressed in the remainder of the book. The chapter is structured in terms of a set of propositions which (1) establish the objectives we are seeking to achieve and (2) specify the conditions which must be met if we are to achieve these objectives. The propositions then provide the criteria by which we may examine the specific ideas and methods discussed in later chapters.

The Objectives

Proposition 1: The successful exploitation of information technology depends upon the ability and willingness of the employees of an organisation to use the appropriate technology to engage in worthwhile tasks.

Information technology does not produce benefits independently: it needs people to exploit its capabilities before it produces organisational benefit. It is necessary therefore to ensure that the staff are both willing and able to use the technology. This depends upon them viewing the work they are asked to undertake as worthy of their effort and viewing the technology as a valued and usable tool for undertaking these tasks. There was a time when perhaps the implementers of new technology could afford to ignore the question of whether potential users valued their own work or the tools they used. Where there was a concern for these issues it was usually because the management of the organisation held values which stressed employee well-being as well as pro-

44

ductivity. This is now no longer just a question of holding humanitarian values — that we should all care about the quality of working life we create for others. The technology is now seeking to serve professional and managerial levels of staff who have considerable discretion. If they are confronted by a system they have difficulty in using or one which devalues the work they do, their response can be, and is, to reject the system. More junior levels of staff also have many active and passive ways in which they can undermine the success of a technical system if it does nothing to promote their personal and work objectives.

Proposition 2: The design target must be to create a socio-technical system capable of serving organisational goals, not to create a technical system capable of delivering a technical service.

If the technical system design is treated separately from organisation issues the result may be a splendid system that may not serve its users. This may also mean the neglect of the organisational changes necessary to allow staff to exploit the technology. Similarly the independent development of organisational structures and policies to serve organisational objectives would be counterproductive if it did not consider the possibilities and constraints of the technical system which will provide the tools to do the job. The need is for the joint optimisation of the interdependent social and technical sub-systems; for the design of the socio-technical systems. This proposition was first proposed by Emery and Trist in 1962 who produced a body of theory which although created to explain, for example, failure of mechanisation in coal mines, is directly applicable to the design of information technology systems. In the coal mining studies (Trist *et al.*, 1962), the investigators found that the optimisation of a technical system for cutting and removing coal did not lead to the productivity gains expected. The reason was that the organisational changes made to accommodate the technical system were stressful and inefficient. When a workable social system which was compatible with the technical system was found the productivity gains were achieved. The other seminal study in the history of socio-technical systems was the study by Rice (1958) of the introduction of semi-automatic looms in an Indian weaving mill. In this case also the new looms failed to give the expected increase in production because the enforced organisational changes prevented employees from working effectively. Rice was able to design a new form of organisation which did enable the staff to use the new technology and the gains were forthcoming. These two studies were instrumental in demonstrating that the doctrine of 'technological determinism' was false. This is the concept that a technical change leads irrevocably to a specific set of organisational changes. These studies showed there was organisational choice and that some forms matched the technical system better than others.

This pattern is the one we now see being repeated with information technology. Implementing an optimal technical system and forcing a social system to become sub-optimal must create sub-optimal overall results because the two sub-systems are intimately interconnected. With information technology it is sometimes possible to rescue the situation as in the coal mining and weaving examples by changing the social system after the technical change so that it is compatible with the new technical system. However, there is not always a matching organisational option available or, because of the discretionary nature of the members of the organisation, it is not possible to implement it. It is much better, as Mumford (1983a) suggests, to treat the technical system as a set of options to be matched with organisational options in an attempt to choose a socio-technical system which achieves overall individual and organisational goals.

Proposition 3: The effective exploitation of socio-technical systems depends upon the adoption of a planned process of change that meets the needs of people who are coping with major changes in their working lives.

It is not enough to implement a socio-technical system even if it has high potential for serving its objectives. It may be possible (although highly unlikely) to switch on a technical system and quickly have it running at the required level of performance but social systems cannot be 'switched on' in the same way. The people who fill the roles in the social system need time and opportunities to adjust to the changes, develop the skills and learn how to work in new ways with their colleagues. Their acceptance of the new procedures will also depend in large measure on the degree to which they have been involved in their creation and have identified with the need for the changes. The processes by which the changes are brought about are therefore as important as the changes that ultimately result.

The Achievement of Objectives

In the realm of information technology implementation we can offer a number of propositions about the way in which these socio-technical objectives can be achieved.

Proposition 4: The design of effective socio-technical systems will depend upon the participation of all relevant 'stakeholders' in the design process.

The identification and development of socio-technical systems which can serve the future needs of an organisation needs a wide range of knowledge. The effective use of the system needs the whole-hearted commitment of the staff concerned. The knowledge required will include the technical knowledge of information technology, strategic knowledge of the market of the organisation, detailed knowledge of how specific tasks are undertaken, etc. The whole-hearted support of a system comes best from people who have examined their future options and concluded that the system being introduced is going to give them advantages in pursuing their individual and collective interests. The arguments for bringing relevant knowledge to bear and for winning active support both lead to the conclusion that systems must be designed by the participation of all relevant 'stakeholders'. This is a term made popular by Mitroff (1980) to designate all those who have an interest in the change that is being pursued. It is usual for proponents of participation to be advocating user participation and it is indeed the case that users from all levels, from different functions, the rank-and-file users and their representatives, all have a stake in the change. However, this concept also forces us to recognise that technical system designers also have an important stake as do the clients and suppliers of the company making the change. If important stake-holders are not able to participate in the design process we may confidently expect them to engage in counter-implementation strategies. Obviously if there are many interested parties design could easily degenerate into chaos and it is therefore important to manage the participative process effectively. Chapter 5 will examine how this may be accomplished.

Proposition 5: Major benefits will only result if the socio-technical developments are directed at major organisational purposes where there are opportunities to be taken or problems to be resolved.

It is tempting to introduce change in a small way or to copy the changes that others have made. However, these changes may well be divorced from the major questions which confront any organisation. If information technology is really to have a revolu-tionary impact, it will have to be directed at the heart of organisational affairs. The definition of these central issues and the development of strategies for dealing with them is not something that can be safely left to outsiders or to those who understand the technology leaving line staff to get on with day-to-day work. It is essential that the key organisational staff get involved in defining the future in which they will work. The processes of identifying opportunities for change and specifying systems to meet these opportunities is the subject matter of Chapter 6.

Proposition 6: The specification for a new socio-technical system must include the definition of a social system which enables people in work roles to co-operate effectively in seeking organisational purposes and provides jobs which encumbents perceive as worthwhile.

The principle resources by which any organisation achieves its objectives are its human resources who, even with the wonders of modern technology, are the most versatile and adaptive resources available. The capability of these resources can easily be reduced by forms of collective organisation which are rigid or inappropriate to the task so that expertise is not available in the right place at the right time. It can also be reduced by forms of individual job design which do not allow the person to use or develop their capabilities and skills or demotivate the person so that the skills are not fully available to the organisation. The problems of designing an organisation and designing its component jobs are examined in Chapter 7.

Proposition 7: Information technology systems must be designed to serve the functional needs of the organisation by serving the functional needs of individual users in a usable and acceptable way.

The information technology system must obviously be a cost-effective way of serving the overall interests of the organisation. However, it must do so by serving the interests of the individual members of staff who collectively pursue the organisational purposes. This puts the onus on the system to be a good tool for each user. A common finding in information technology impact research is that a system serves some users well but neglects or makes work more difficult for other users. If the organisation depends on all its staff for its effectiveness this is a dysfunctional way to proceed. If the system has to have the hallmarks of a good tool it must not only serve a useful function but it must also be usable and acceptable. As we have noted in Chapter 2 many would-be users are senior, discretionary people who will be intermittent users of any technology. These people must have very easy-to-use systems if they are to be able to exploit the functionality put at their disposal. The design of technical systems to meet these objectives is discussed in Chapter 8.

Proposition 8: The effective exploitation of information technology requires a major form of organisational and individual learning.

It is easy to see that information technology cannot be fully exploited until its operators have learnt what it can do and how to make it do it. Much information technology training is devoted to these ends. There are many other forms of learning that are also required, however. What is the best way to exploit the new tools in relation to the range of tasks that have to be undertaken? If the social system has changed, by what new ways is it appropriate to work with other people? What new opportunities now exist for furthering the interests of the organisation? These are the kinds of learning that are necessary to ensure exploitation of a new socio-technical system. There are also the forms of learning that are necessary if people are able to participate effectively in the process of specifying the systems that are to be developed. The theme of constant learning on many fronts will recur throughout this book but is brought to a focus in Chapter 9.

Proposition 9: The exploitation of the capabilities of information technology can only be achieved by a progressive, planned form of evolutionary growth.

We noted in Chapter 3 that the model for the technical system development is 'one-shot implementation', i.e. specify — design — implement — disband design team. However, it takes time for individuals to learn and it takes even longer for the collective learning to occur that can carry an organisation forward. There seems little purpose in great leaps forward in technical innovation when the organisation can only move forward gradually. This seems to be an invitation to have a lot of expensive equipment gathering dust. A form of technology which is as heavily dependent upon the skills of its users as information technology can only move forward at the rate at which its users can cope with the change process. An even more significant reason for evolutionary development is that we want the users to choose and plan the developments — which they cannot do without an understanding of the options and the potential they provide. This implies a growth in knowledge and experience before major investment decisions are taken.

These factors suggest that the appropriate model for system implementation may be an evolutionary one as depicted in Figure 4.1. In this case technical system development goes hand in hand with the individual and organisational learning process so that users are able to plan the next stage of technical development. This is not to say that there will not be significant stages of 'one-shot implementation': to achieve the next plateau on the curve it will be necessary to freeze a specification for long enough to design and implement a solution. The overall process, however, must be one of

Figure 4.1
The evolutionary development of information technology systems

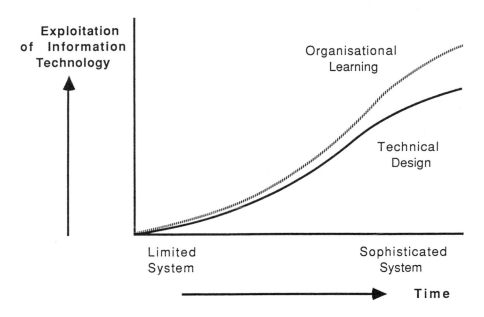

constant revision and growth. In all probability the model of 'one-shot implement-ation' was always a myth because the rate of introduction of new products has always made a system dated as soon as it was implemented. This rationale recognises, however, that individuals and organisational forces demand an evolutionary approach. The concept of planned evolution with the corollary of learning and evaluation is developed later in this chapter and detailed in Chapter 10.

Proposition 10: To be successful, socio-technical design concepts must as far as possible comp-lement existing design procedures and organisation change practices.

The concepts advanced in the earlier propositions may sound revolutionary, foreign and even idealistic to many currently working on the implementation of information technology. If this is their ultimate conclusion it is unlikely that many of these concepts will find their way into normal design practice. The final proposition therefore recognises the need, in developing these ideas, to do so in a way which can make them a practical adjunct to methods already in use within organisations. We recognise that people taking on information technology need to do so in an evolutionary manner so that they can gradually assimilate the new needs and opportunities. We must also recognise that people engaged in design processes need gradually to take on board the notion of *creating* socio-technical systems rather than *designing* technical systems. Thus technical staff need to retain their existing skills and procedures and explore how they relate to the new methods necessary to deal with human and organisational issues. Similarly, there will be procedures within any organisation to deal with organisational change; management decision procedures, personnel policy procedures and industrial relations machinery, etc., and these need to be more closely integrated with the plans for technical change.

There is a tendency for anyone offering a different perspective on the design process to produce a comprehensive and systematic strategy for engaging in design as though to invite designers to give up existing approaches and switch to the new one. In our experience this is rarely what happens; in practice people take what looks beneficial and practicable and mould it to their own use. If they take the whole approach, as many are doing with structured design methods, they still tend to reshape it to suit their own purposes. This process of personalising new ideas is an important way of internalising them and relating them to existing concepts. We have explored it more fully in Klein and Eason (1989). It is also an important process because it allows generalised methods to be shaped to the specific and perhaps unique circumstances of each organisation.

Recognising this process, the explicit aim in this case is not to offer a full and systematic strategy. Rather the aim is to accept that an organisation has ways of managing many features of design and to produce a series of ways of attacking problems which might otherwise be neglected, dealt with inadequately, or which appear too late in the design process. This is a 'toolbox' approach to design: to offer a series of concepts and techniques which can be applied in different ways in different contexts. Many of them we have used within the context of existing design processes and there are surprisingly few areas of incompatibility. There are, however, two overriding features of the design process which have to be present in some degree if it is to be possible to introduce these ideas, and both are represented in the propositions presented above. The first is that there has to be some acceptance of the importance of participation because it is the only way the full range of socio-technical issues can be brought into the design process. The second is some recognition that change is an evolutionary process. If the design process is driven by a series of technical deadlines that presuppose a complete specification at a very early stage, user participation will be very difficult and the whole design process will be forced into the familiar sequential process of technical design followed by organisational accommodation (or technical rejection).

Figure 4.2 summarises the propositions and their relationships as a prelude to examining some of the implications of adopting this approach to design.

In summary the propositions start (1) from the recognition that IT technical design is not enough because benefit can only come if these systems are effectively harnessed and exploited by their users. The achievement of this involves the creation (2) of compatible social and technical systems to (5) serve some important organisational purpose. This in turn means (6) the design of a social system to serve this purpose and (7) the creation of a technical system which will support the users in the social system. The design process by which this is achieved requires (3) a process of planned change which not only creates the appropriate system but creates in the users a motivational and knowledge state where they are able and willing to exploit the technical capabilities. This involves (4) the participation of the stakeholders in the design process and (5) individual and collective learning processes. Since organisational change and human

Figure 4.2
Ten propositions for the successful creation of information technology systems

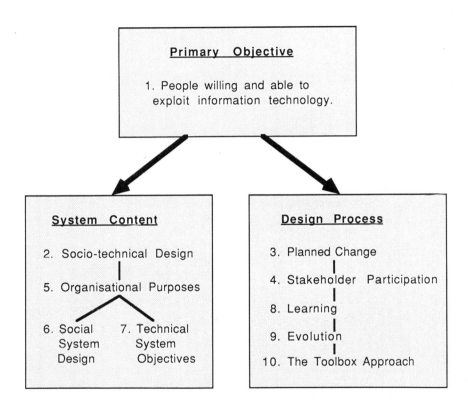

learning take time an important requirement (9) is evolutionary development so that decisions are made on the basis of mature reflection. Since there will be existing procedures for system design the pursuit of these objectives is most likely to be successful if (10) techniques are offered in the form of a flexible 'toolbox' which can be matched to existing practice and local circumstances.

This discussion has been presented as a set of abstract statements and the rest of this chapter explores their practical implications. In the next section we examine the topics that have to be addressed in socio-technical systems design of information technology systems and begin the exploration of stakeholder participation in relation to them. It is only too easy to slip into a 'one-shot implementation' way of thinking about these topics in the design process, i.e. they are addressed in sequence as we move towards the implementation of the complete system. The next section therefore examines how to deal with these topics in evolutionary design. Finally, an outline of the tools in the 'toolbox' is given as a prelude to their detailed consideration in subsequent chapters.

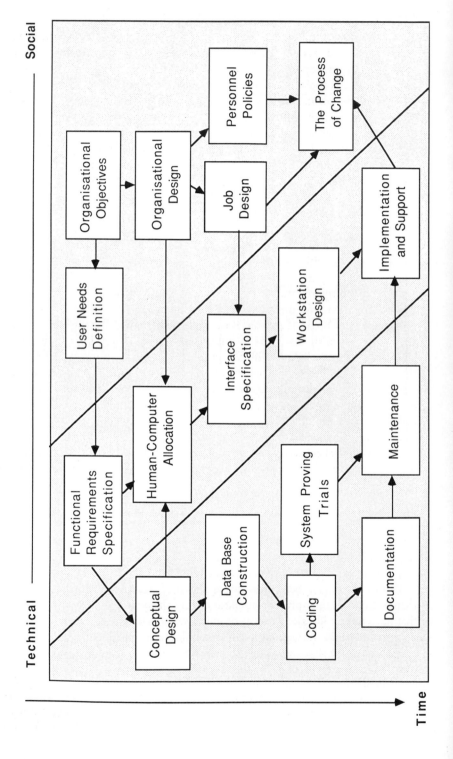

Figure 4.3
Design topics in the socio-technical systems design of information technology systems

Design Topics in Socio-Technical Systems Design

To give substance to abstract propositions it is necessary to identify the topics which would need to be examined in socio-technical systems design. This section provides an overview of these topics which will be treated in more detail in subsequent chapters. Examples of the topics are provided in Figure 4.3.

This diagram includes some of the major activities necessary to design a socio-technical system although it is by no means comprehensive. On the left-hand side are the activities necessary to specify and construct a technical system, the type of activities detailed in most systems analysis and design texts. On the right-hand side are the activities necessary for the organisation to define its objectives, specify the social structure necessary to achieve these objectives, to define its needs of a technical system and to prepare its staff to work within the new structure. Some of these activities may be found in management texts but it is rare to find them in the same text as the technical issues. This is the fundamental problem for socio-technical systems design; the two sets of activities are not treated as closely related. The central area denotes another set of activities which link the technical and the social sub-systems; that define the functional requirements for the system to meet user needs, that specify what will be done by computer and what by man, that specify how man and computer will interact and then implement the system and support the users when it is in operation.

There is a broad sequential flow to these activities although in practice many proceed in parallel. As befits a system all the parts are interconnected but the connections that are indicated in the figure are of particular significance to the design of the system. The activities on the left are predominantly technical matters which are the province of technical staff (provided they work to the user needs specification) and the activities to the right are the province of the user (although some of these activities demand an appreciation of the technical options and plans before they can be undertaken). The central topics where the technical and social issues interact must be an area of mutual concern. This description of the design topics can therefore be used to map out a plan for the allocation of responsibilities in systems design between users and technical staff.

Evolution, Iteration and Customisation

It may be noted that whilst Figure 4.3 attempts to show how social and technical design can proceed in parellel, it still shows signs of 'one-shot implementation' thinking, i.e. it proceeds through a full analysis phase to a full design phase (both technical and social) and into a single implementation stage. Where is the room for user learning in this process such that, after some experience of using a system, they may feel confident they know what is needed? We still have to build the concept of evolution into this process, and there are two ways in which this can be achieved:

1. *Prototyping for Iterative Specification and Design.* Within the large-scale design process there can be many small-scale design processes which go through the full problem solving cycle for the purposes of exploring options and developing a fuller understanding of requirements. The advent of rapid prototyping languages makes it possible

Figure 4.4
Evolutionary systems development using prototyping and pilot systems

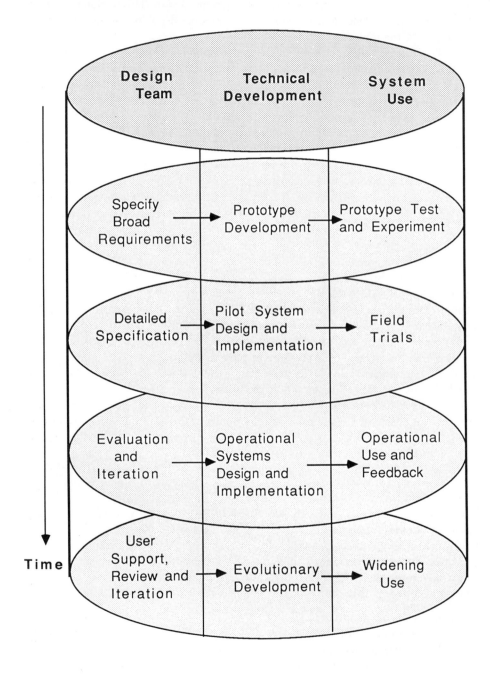

to create early versions of the facilities and interfaces which users may experience. These may be used to help users establish the strengths and weaknesses of different possibilities before any major investments are made. Many of the topics in the design process may be treated in this way. It is possible to examine the implications of different technical strategies, different types of interface, different job structures or different implementation strategies, in each case giving users some experience of the options so that they have a sound basis for their judgements.

Figure 4.4 depicts the major stages of a programme of evolutionary design in which the guiding principle is the creating of opportunities for learning from practical experience before major design decisions are taken. It is an extension of the phase model presented in Eason (1982) and contains separate prototyping and piloting phases before an operational system is introduced.

In this model there are three separate specification, design and implementation cycles. In the first one the design team and the users generate a broad specification of system requirements and, by the use of rapid prototyping techniques, a prototype system is created. This can then be used as a vehicle for users to examine and test in order to revise and detail their specification.

In the second cycle a pilot system is developed as a response to the detailed specification and this is then the subject of field trials. The aim in this case is to test the solution for refinements but to keep the solution if possible and make it the basis of an operational system. It is important to note the distinction being made here between prototype and pilot systems which is in line with the distinction made by Harker (1987a, 1987b) and by Janson (1986). The prototype is created to help specify requirements and is not expected to be used in the main implementation. The pilot system is an answer to the specification created to enable a full test of this solution. If it is successful it becomes the basis of the main development. The roles of prototypes and pilots are further explored in Chapters 6 and 7.

Following the field trials the operational system can be developed and progressively implemented. If evolution is to continue the full system should also be subject to regular review in the expectation that further developments and iterations will occur.

By this process major commitments to technical developments are not necessary until the users have had considerable opportunity to see and test what could be provided, thus enabling them to arrive at a specification with some confidence. Examples of developments with these characteristics are to be found in Gower and Eason (1989) and in Shackel *et al.* (1989). Presenting a comprehensive model of this kind is not to argue that every development must go through all of these stages: it is to argue that if users are uncertain about their requirements and major, irrevocable investments have to be made, it is only prudent to proceed via these learning stages before making major commitments.

2. *Nested Design for Customisation and Evolution.* Prototyping and piloting provide learning opportunities in the systems development process but most of the learning will still come after an operational system has been delivered. What can then be done, in the longer term, to stimulate and use this learning? A related issue is that within a

large organisation it may be necessary to establish long-term objectives and to make major investments in computer hardware and software development. At the same time it may be desirable to deliver services to an end user which can be customised and amended as the user's experience grows. How can these simultaneous demands for stability and change be reconciled? Figure 4.5 suggests an approach which depends upon nested design processes in which flexibility at the higher level permits lower level autonomy. An important concept in socio-technical systems design (Cherns, 1976) is the concept of minimum critical specification. The idea is that designers should only fix what they have to fix and should leave flexibility wherever possible because it is this flexibility which creates choice for the people who must operate the system.

It may be appropriate within a large organisation, for example, to establish a broad IT strategy which determines the types of applications to be given priority, the centralised data bases upon which major corporate activities depend and the main supplier or suppliers who can provide compatible equipment. These policies will be subject to review and change but in a period of years rather than months. Provided this policy is implemented with flexibility in mind it should be possible for a series of local

Figure 4.5
Nested design for local adaptation and evolution

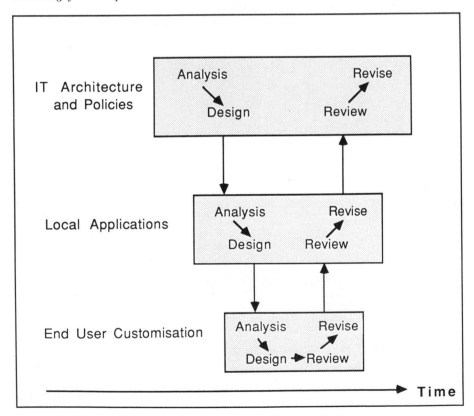

applications to be supported which provide particular services for defined groups of users. This level of activity is a full socio-technical design process facilitated and to some degree constrained by the overall policy. These applications can be reviewed and revised over a shorter time-scale than the overall policy. With the advent of flexible services delivered, for example, on personal computers to the end users, the design process can also be repeated at the end-user level. If the system provides a lot of functionality and allows control over the way this functionality is delivered, the end user can start with a limited service over which he has little control and, by a process of iteration, can develop to a fuller service over which he has considerable control, and which has been customised to his needs.

The Functional Specification of User-centred Techniques

In order to be more user-centred in the design process there is a need to develop the techniques on the right-hand side of Figure 4.3 (the social dimension) and to integrate these techniques with the methods used to create the technical system. However, the problems to evolution, iteration and customisation mean that none of these issues will be dealt with once and for all in the design process; rather they will be revisited a number of times at different levels and for different purposes. It would make the study of the design process much more straightforward if it were possible to create a flow chart of the component processes in a well-structured linear sequence. It is then possible to treat each in turn and show how it relates to the whole. Most textbooks on systems design have this structure. Unfortunately, concepts like iteration, nested design processes, evolution, minimum critical specification and customisation do not leave us this luxury. The aim of early passes through the design process must be to leave scope for later passes through the same processes. The problem of describing these processes means there is a difficulty in defining and describing the user-centred techniques necessary to support them. It will be apparent that even if a technique has a specific function it must take different forms each time that activity is addressed in the successive passes through the design process. The process of job design might start, for example, with a broad strategy for the allocation of tasks throughout the organisation. Subsequently, it may mean the allocation of duties within this strategy to a group of employees in a particular department, and, on a day-to-day basis, it may mean tactical changes in responsibilities to cope with changes in workload and work pattern.

Given these strictures, how can we best present the design process and at the same time address the creation of user-centred design processes? The approach adopted here is to treat the design process as a collection of design processes, each with the problem solving elements depicted in Figure 4.6.

Each activity in the overall design process can be regarded as a design task in its own right in which there is a need to specify requirements, identify solutions and implement them with a variety of feedback loops that can serve to change the solutions or to redefine the requirements. This task is accomplished by design resources, which includes the design team and the design tools it can bring to bear on the task. This structure is obviously relevant to the design of technical parts of the system but it is

Figure 4.6
The elemental design task

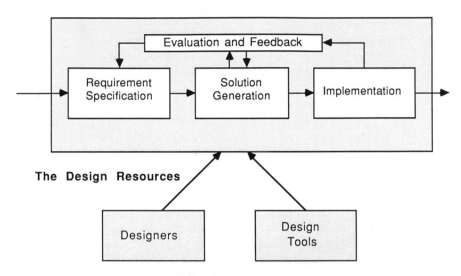

just as relevant to the treatment of human and organisational aspects, and will be used as a basis for describing all the techniques presented in this book.

The elemental structure also provides a way of describing the user-centred techniques that will be addressed. The aim is to cover the range of techniques that are normally under-represented in systems design, i.e. largely to ignore the purely technical aspects of design and to concentrate upon those that have the most direct relevance to users. These can broadly be described as specification techniques, design and testing techniques, and implementation strategies with associated evaluation procedures. Separately we have to know how to 'design' the design team process to undertake these activities.

In the list that follows, a brief description is presented of the function of techniques under each of these headings. Each heading refers to a subsequent chapter in which techniques for this function are discussed.

1. *Designing the Design Team and its Design Process* (Chapter 5). The purpose of these techniques is to plan who is to be involved in the design process and the responsibilities they take in the process. This includes the important issue of user participation.
2. *Specifying Requirements* (Chapter 6). The aim here is to examine techniques whereby requirements (for a socio-technical system) can be identified and evaluated, and is particularly concerned with the problem of users who have difficulty knowing what they need and assessing what is available.

3. *Creating and Designing Solutions* (Chapters 7 and 8). A major set of techniques is concerned with the processes of arriving at solutions which will meet the requirements specified. These have been divided into the creation of social systems (Chapter 7) and the design of technical systems (Chapter 8) because they are different processes. The term 'design' fits well the activity of fabricating a technical system but creating a new social system often has more to do with planning an evolutionary progression from existing structures.

4. *Implementing Systems and Supporting Users* (Chapter 9). The process of introducing a new system creates its own special problems for which techniques are needed and, for many of the users, this marks the start of a process of learning and adaptation which requires an ongoing source of support.

5. *Evaluating the Impact* (Chapter 10). The process of iteration and evolution is only likely to be effective if the progress made by users, individually and collectively, in exploiting the new capability is carefully monitored and fed back to a reviewing authority.

Each of these chapters takes a wide ranging functional requirement in the overall design process and one which will be approached at different levels a number of times during an iterative, evolutionary process. Each chapter will therefore be structured to provide an overview of the issues and possibilities before examining the variations needed to cope with the demands at the different levels.

Chapter 5
Designing the Design
and Implementation Process

Introduction

One of the most crucial aspects of designing and implementing information technology systems is the vehicle which takes responsibility for these activities. It is conventional to establish some kind of project team and the composition, reporting structure and methods of working of this temporary organisation are vital to the success of the project. The purpose of this chapter is to review the issues involved in setting up project teams and to present and evaluate alternative forms they can take. There is no single correct form for these structures because they must vary with the application, the size of the organisation, the level of information technology already implemented, the culture of the organisation and a host of other issues. The construction of an appropriate structure has therefore to be treated as a genuine design process.

Customers and Experts

The underlying aim with which we are concerned is the implementation of information technology which may change the technical and social basis upon which work is undertaken in a specific organisational setting. The creation of this change is going to require specialists in the relevant areas of expertise and the consequences of the change are likely to be of concern to the people currently working in the organisation. This gives us two important kinds of contributors for the design process; experts and customers. It is useful to broaden the concept of customer to include not only those who are actively seeking the change but all who will be affected by it. Mitroff's (1980) concept of stakeholders is useful here because it includes all who have a stake in the change being considered, those who stand to gain from it, and those who stand to lose.

As we saw in Chapter 3 it is now common to think of systems design as being based upon a customer–contractor relationship in which the customer commissions a contractor with the relevant specialist expertise to provide a system to meet the customer's requirements. This is a role distinction which is very useful in understanding the dynamics of systems design, but it is deceptively simple and needs developing before we can use it to examine alternative ways of setting up a design team. It is, for example, easy to conclude that all the expertise lies with the contractor and all the

Figure 5.1
Role contributions to the design process

Roles	Contribution	
	Knowledge	Stakeholding
Technical Experts	**1.** IT Skills Organisational skills	**2.** Skill advancement and Power Base
Customers	**3.** Organisation specific knowledge Task specific knowledge	**4.** Living with the consequences of the change for tasks and jobs etc.

'stakeholding' lies with the customer. This is the concept embodied in boxes 1 and 4 in Figure 5.1 in which technical experts contribute their skills to the creation of a system whilst the customers as stakeholders are concerned with the world they will have to inhabit after the change, both in terms of how they will be able to undertake their tasks and for more personal matters such as job security and the nature of their jobs. However, as boxes 2 and 3 indicate, both the technical experts and the customers have more to contribute. The customers have a wide range of knowledge specific to the way the organisation functions and the tasks it undertakes, which is vital to the construction of a system to serve organisational needs. They are the experts on these issues. Conversely the technical experts are not neutral suppliers of a service but have a stakeholding in what is supplied. At the very least they will want the system to help them advance their own design skills and they may have other interests in the system chosen. In the present climate, for example, with the proliferation of microcomputers in many organisations, internal data processing teams may prefer to see a mainframe-based solution because it maintains their control of computing power within the organisation. The structure of the design team therefore has to recognise the fact that both specialists and customers have expertise to contribute and vested interests in the solutions adopted.

To complicate matters still further we cannot assume that the only kind of external specialist skills that are necessary are information technology skills. If the analysis presented earlier in this book is correct many of the problems of design relate to organisational analysis, the design and implementation of social system change, and human adaptation to new working practices. It may be thought that the expertise the customers possess with respect to their organisation means that they will be able to manage these issues for themselves. As we shall see it may be right that they play a leading role in these matters but they may well need specialist help from organisational analysts, psychologists, ergonomists, trainers and others.

In summary, therefore, we need a design team structure which has two properties. It needs to bring people (whether specialist designers *or* potential customers) into roles where they can contribute their relevant expertise; it also has to provide an opportunity for people to understand the consequences of planned changes for their legitimate vested interests and to argue for design solutions that would meet their objectives. This statement encapsulates the basic problem of the process of systems design: it is both a technical problem-solving exercise and it is a political process. Technical processes are normally conceived as rational and logical methods used to search for the optimal solution whereas political processes are engaged in by people with different goals and values who seek to find a commonly acceptable solution. Many specialists in information technology would prefer the former to be the full story and textbooks on systems design tend to present only this perspective. Unfortunately systems that have consequences for a wider range of people cannot escape from the arena of organisational politics. To leave these issues outside the design team, as is often the hope and intention, is to leave them to surface at the time of implementation and (as discussed in Chapter 3) they often surface as counter-implementation strategies. We have then to construct a design team that can manage technical design and social process.

Options for the Construction of a Design Team

Let us suppose that we are the management of a company considering a major venture into information technology. What options have we as to how to assemble a team to do this work? Figure 5.2 provides three broad alternatives for us to consider.

Each of these options specifies responsibilities of the technical specialists and of the customers. We will describe each of these options and some of their principal variants before evaluating their effectiveness.

In the technical, design-centred approach specialists in information technology are given responsibility for the analysis of requirements, the design of a system and its delivery into the organisation. This has been the typical pattern of design in data processing applications. The customer obviously has to commission the system and ultimately will accept or reject the delivered solution. There are also likely to be contacts with the technical design team as the system is developed. Typically these consist of consultations with individual users during analysis to specify requirements, and communications to inform potential users of the progress of the design. Initially

Figure 5.2
Alternative design team structures

Options	Contributions	
	Technical Specialists	Customers
1. Technical Centred Design	Analyse, Design, Deliver	Commission and Accept Informed, Consulted and Trained
2. Joint Customer-Specialist Design	Analyse, Design, Deliver	User Representatives in all stages of Design
3. User Centred Design	Technical Service to Users	All Users Contribute to Design

this may consist of newsletters and general meetings, but as the design nears completion, it may include demonstrations of all or part of the system. When the system is ready for delivery it may also include formal training to prepare users for system use.

One way of characterising the technical design approach is to see it as a closed technical group doing the design with occasional references to the outside world of the customer. Increasingly there is a move to bring some potential users into the detailed design work. This is accomplished by having user representatives seconded to the design team to work with the technical specialists. There are many variations in the way this is done. It can consist of training some users in system design techniques and seconding them full time to the team so that they can contribute fully to technical design issues. At the other extreme it can consist of sending users on a part-time basis to review and assess design solutions prepared by technical specialists.

User representatives provide a way in which users can play a more comprehensive role in system development but, in user-centred design approaches, it is carried much further with the analysis, design and delivery being undertaken by the users themselves and the specialists cast in the role of technical advisers. In some schemes, such as

Mumford's (1983a) ETHICS, the aim is to involve all potential users in the process. In other variants where the aim is 'end-user developments' design may proceed without any recourse to technical specialists.

In broad terms these three options provide us with an opportunity to give the user community a progressively more dominant role in the construction of systems with a complementary change in the role of the technical specialists. We will now examine the merits of moves in this direction.

Evaluating Alternative Design Team Structures

In order to evaluate these alternatives we need a set of evaluative criteria. These are summarised in Figure 5.3. Some of the more obvious judgements of the three options in terms so these criteria are also included in this table.

The first two of the eight evaluation criteria in Figure 5.3 refer to the need to be able to feed appropriate specialist expertise into the design process. Obviously there are specialist contributions that can be made by information technologists but, if a large part of the design concerns human and organisational change, there may also be a need for specialists in human and social sciences. The next two criteria refer to the expert contributions that can be made by potential users. Detailed task knowledge will be necessary to specify the requirements for a technical service. Broader knowledge of

Figure 5.3
Evaluative criteria for design team structures

Evaluation Criteria	Options		
	1	2	3
a. Specialist technical skills where needed	✓	✓	X
b. Specialist social skills where needed	X	✓	✓
c. Users able to contribute task knowledge	X	✓	✓
d. Users able to assess organisational effects	X	✓	✓
e. Stakeholders able to negotiate interests	X	X	✓
f. All users develop feelings of ownership	X	X	✓
g. Practical use of resources	✓	✓	X
h. Acceptable to the organisation	✓	✓	X

organisational functioning and plans for the future will be necessary to specify the implications of the intended changes. The next two are concerned with the vested interests brought to judge the design solution by different stakeholders. The first criterion refers to the extent that stakeholders are given the opportunity to negotiate matters of concern to them. The second recognises that participation can have the effect of helping users to feel that it is their system and they want to use it, i.e. it can have a strong motivational effect. Finally, any scheme must be practical and acceptable to the commissioning organisation. It must be practical in terms of the resources the organisation can deploy whilst 'keeping the shop open', i.e. normal business must be continued whilst plans for the future are being laid. It must be acceptable in the sense that the forms of participation must be reasonably in harmony with existing practices in the organisation.

The judgements made of the three options in Figure 5.3 are based on our experience with many applications, mostly within the United Kingdom. The ratings may be changed by the way the option is implemented and may also be influenced by the nature of the application and the organisation. The ratings provide a basis for making some broad comments about each option but it is advisable to make separate ratings for a specific application.

The Technical Design-centred Approach

This approach emerges from this evaluation as a means by which specialist technical skills can be delivered to design and which is regarded as practical and acceptable in most organisations. Since it conforms to the status quo in most organisations with a data processing history this is hardly surprising. It is an approach in which design is conceived as a matter of technical system construction rather than about socio-technical design so it provides few opportunities for specialists in human and social sciences, except perhaps after the technical system has been delivered, when there may be difficulties adapting the organisation to accommodate it.

The technique by which user knowledge about task and organisational issues is captured in this approach is by systems analysts consulting users during the analysis phase and perhaps demonstrating solutions towards the end of the design phase. In practice the techniques used for these purposes are oriented to technical issues such as structuring the data base and sizing the system and are not intended to capture the reality of organisational life. As we shall discuss in Chapter 6, users can find it very difficult to respond meaningfully when they are consulted by systems analysts. The process of consultation is one whereby the user might influence design decisions which are in the province of the technical specialist. It is therefore unlikely that this process will adequately capture user task and organisational knowledge — which is no doubt a major reason why so many systems designed in this way produce a poor match with user requirements.

The technically-centred design process is also unlikely to allow the user stakeholders to see that their interests are fully considered during design. Since the technical staff are making the decisions it is quite likely that their stakeholder interests will be met by the system. The process normally allows for regular communications of progress to users but does not invite debate about design alternatives; any negotiation of user interests will probably take place during implementation when the technical system is a *fait accompli*. Similarly, the lack of direct involvement by users will mean that at best they will be well informed about a system designed by other people but they are unikely to feel strongly identified with it.

In summary this approach is likely to give emphasis to the rational process of technical design and any social processes are likely to be pushed outside the design forum and into the wider domain of normal organisational processes when attempts are made to implement the technical system.

Joint Customer–Specialist Design

This approach provides a potential forum for meeting most of the criteria. In theory joint decision-making by specialists and representatives of the user community should mean that a wide range of knowledge is available. Specialist skills relating to the technology remains available and the representatives should be able to bring task and organisational knowledge to the debate. If the design forum is broader it may also be possible to introduce specialists in human and social disciplines.

This kind of arrangement has become very popular as organisations see it as a practical and worthwhile investment to second some of their staff to work with specialists on future developments. The main limitations are that the users are seconded to design bodies to work within an agreed design strategy but this leaves little room for wider debates on the desirability of different types of system. There is also the very significant problem that the user representatives tend to become enthusiastic and committed to the system but their colleagues, who remain in their normal positions, may not share this commitment.

The extent to which the potential benefits are attained or the limitations overcome is very much dependent upon the particular way in which this strategy is implemented. Since in most cases the concept is that there are specialist design teams to which user representatives are attached, we can examine the alternatives by looking at the different ways of dealing with user representatives.

1. *User Representatives as Full-time Trained Members of the Technical Design Team*
   One solution is to find appropriate candidates among the staff to be sent for training as systems specialists who can then join the team as full-time members. This approach has the great advantage that the organisation gains a trained systems professional with insider knowledge of organisational tasks and practices. Banks tend to favour this approach on the principle that their systems will be designed by people who are bankers first and systems staff second. It is a strategy which also offers some protection from the very high turnover rates among technical specialists who are able to move freely among organisations with their sought-after expertise.

   There are, however, some serious disadvantages to relying completely on this approach. The people who enter design teams in this way are unlikely to return to the user community because of their investment in new and valuable skills. If they were willing to accept this opportunity the chances are that they were not highly dedicated to the user role they were occupying. They may become excellent system designers but be very poor user representatives. This tendency may be heightened by what Hedberg (1975) has called the 'hostage effect'. When a user joins a design team composed of technical specialists to work full time it is usually not very long before that person has acquired not only the skills but the ambitions, values and attributes of the team. This is a positive outcome if the planned role is to be just like the rest of the team but is a major disadvantage if the person was expected to represent the user viewpoint and, on occasions, challenge the views of other designers. The worst scenario is when the designers believe they have all the user knowledge they need in their own user representatives and do not bother to consult widely in the user community. The 'hostage' is a very convenient source of information but may become increasingly less reliable with the effect that the designers may complete their work confident they are meeting the users' needs to only find the real users have very different ideas.

2. *User Representatives as Part-time Members of the Technical Design Team*
   It may be that training users to be full-time system staff should be thought of as a way of adding to the technical resources of the organisation and not as a form of user representation. It appears that to remain a good user representative, a person needs to maintain a stance independent of the technical specialists and in keeping with the needs and views of the people being represented. This may be better achieved by seconding the representative on a part-time basis and not providing a training in technical systems design. This makes it difficult for the person to contribute directly to technical design decisions. It is very useful to make such people the guardians of user requirements and the evaluators of proposed design solutions against these requirements. Such a role is essential to the customer–contractor relationship built into structured design methodologies in which it is necessary for the users to 'sign off' each stage of the design process to signal their acceptance that it is in accordance with their requirements. Such a role is very important but remains a difficult one to carry out. The untrained user is not in a good position to appreciate the meaning of technical presentations or to appreciate whether they will meet user expectations. The problem is compounded by the fact that there has in the past been very little to see to indicate design progress except complex flow charts that even the professionals have difficulty understanding. In addition to this problem the user has the difficulty of knowing the views and needs of those he is supposed to represent. Many user representatives are asked to undertake normal work most of the time and to represent the users' interests in the occasional meeting. If this role is to be undertaken effectively a large part of the representative's time must be spent being briefed by colleagues about their needs and feeding back to colleagues the design as it progresses so that their evaluative comments can be fed back to the design team. If this two-directional feedback loop is not created there is a danger that the design work will continue in a closed group and the majority of the user community will be unaware of its progress and unable to influence it.

The user representative has all the problems of other kinds of representatives and the forms of role conflict to be found in this situation are reminiscent of the role conflict experience by worker directors who often find it difficult to understand the technicalities of company management and find their attempts to represent worker interests conflicting with their responsibilities as directors. They also have a duty to maintain contact with the people they represent and can often find themselves explaining and justifying company policy to their colleagues at the risk of being accused of betraying their roots. In its own way the user representative role in systems design contains all the same problems, and people occupying this role need help to fulfil it effectively.

3. *User Representatives in the Design of Social Systems*

The role of ensuring the user specification is adhered to in technical design is the main role of user representatives in modern system developments but there are other roles that can and should be played. The analysis of topics to be addressed in socio-technical systems design demonstrates that there are many more issues to be addressed than the technical system design and many of them involve design exercises within the user community itself, i.e. job design, workstation design and office layout and training design. User representatives can have an important and direct design role in relation to these issues especially if, through their work with technical system designers, they have a detailed knowledge of the planned technical system. In effect they may be able to play the vital role of holding together the social and technical sides of the development.

4. *User Representatives in Planning of Strategy*

Thus far we have considered the role of user representatives in the detailed design work necessary to establish and implement a system. There must, however, be a higher level activity which sets the objectives for the design work. Current practice at this level varies considerably. There was a time when senior management, having agreed to a technical development, simply left it to the computer department to implement the system. Most managements with experience of computer systems implementation now recognise that the process is not simply a technical exercise but has widespread implications and needs high level planning and monitoring. Ideally the senior management of the user departments to receive the system need to meet regularly with the leader of the design teams to establish technical and social goals and review progress. In one study (Shackel *et al*., 1989), we found it necessary to work in some detail with the Board of Directors of a Company because the planned system had considerable ramifications for the way they would be able to develop the Company in the future and they were initially unaware of these implications. Where the planned system is a large-scale integration of many company activities, it will almost certainly have profound consequences for management. There will be different ways of designing and implementing the system which will have different ramifications and these need careful examination at the highest level. When the system is of this level of significance it is inappropriate to speak of user representatives because it should be the duty of senior management to represent the customer's interest. However, it may well be that, because of the pressures on the time of such people, a senior assistant needs to act as a user representative at the strategy level in order to brief senior management about options and their consequences.

If a system has consequences sufficient to involve senior management it almost certainly will be of concern to the work force of the organisation. Since it is their futures that are at stake they could reasonably claim to have a right to a voice in the debate of future options. How this is handled depends very much on the culture of the organisation and the nature of its industrial relations and industrial democracy machinery. In some countries, for example in Scandinavia, the right of the work-force to take part in discussions of technical change is enshrined in law and elsewhere it is often a clause in the New Technology Agreements negotiated between unions and employers. The process of consultation could be conducted by asking elected representatives of the work-force to join a steering committee or by full information about plans being forwarded to the normal industrial relations machinery. We shall subsequently be discussing the techniques available to help management and user representatives understand and review strategic options and it is worth noting that if the role of employee representatives is kept separate from the management review they too will need support in considering the implications of strategic options. If people are not helped to see the issues they may respond negatively because of uncertainty — even when there is no reason for concern.

The process of involving employee representatives in the determination of technical change is a contentious one because the changes may have important implications for both management and employees. There are many managements who feel that the time to involve employee representatives is when the system is ready for implementation and the terms that have to be negotiated are clear. Among other reasons a frequent argument for this approach is that, when plans are still under discussion, many options may be examined with wide consequences for staff which are in fact subsequently rejected by management. Why cause alarm among staff unnecessarily? The problem with this argument is that it then leaves staff to be informed when the plan is a *fait accompli* and it invites a defensive negotiation stance rather than a mutual problem-solving approach. This approach has been the reason why many systems have had problems. We have encountered a number of cases where design has taken less than six months but implementation has taken two years or more because of the protracted negotiations that ensued.

The sequential strategy of design and negotiation is particularly damaging to any attempt to design new social structures. Two examples we commonly encounter will serve to illustrate the problem. One of the aims of job design is to construct jobs that will be satisfying for people to perform. There can be few things more calculated to damage the morale of a user group who have worked hard with designers to design future jobs than to have management and unions negotiate at the time of implementation to fix job numbers and demarcation lines between occupational categories and so ride roughshod over the plans already laid. A more specific example concerns the practice of negotiating work–rest pause regimes at the time of implementation. The concern about the stress caused by continuous use of visual display terminals has led many unions to establish norms for the length of time a person may use a terminal before being given a break. If such a rule is to be applied it must be included in the job design process, not introduced afterwards when the unions are brought into the debate.

These examples demonstrate that a process of socio-technical design, which is then followed by negotiation, is likely to lead to hasty and damaging changes in the socio-technical system and possibly to long delays in implementation. It is better to accept the reality of conflicts of interest from the beginning and to seek an outline agreement of how the process will be managed with the important stakeholders. Within this framework it will be possible to seek solutions with everybody's interests in mind. This is not to suggest that conflicts will not remain or that there will not have to be hard bargaining but it is to say that this process must be undertaken in parallel with systems development so that designers and user representatives are sure of the objectives and constraints within which they are working.

We have now examined four different strategies by which there can be customer representation in the design of a system. The four strategies make quite different contributions and may all have a vital contribution to make if the technical system is to be what is wanted and the social issues associated with it are to be effectively managed. The role of the representative is a pivotal one in holding the social and technical sides of the design together and obviously the choice of representatives is a crucial one. What criteria are relevant to the selection of a representative? There are some common criteria that are worth examining.

The danger is that the principle criterion is 'who can be spared?' The person who can be spared is often the least able member of the work team and this may mean placing a responsibility of great significance in the weakest hands. It is unfortunately the case that the person most relevant is the one who is most able within the user environment and is least likely to be spared, that this person will be most knowledgeable about user issues and probably most committed to them.

Another common belief is that the user representative should be the one with most interest in computers and probably the first to volunteer. This is appropriate if the plan is to train the person to be a full member of the design team who will pursue a career in systems design. If, however, the person is intended to represent user interests, it may be better to send someone sceptical about the value of information technology but who is willing to be convinced.

Another common statement is that the representative should be the most senior person concerned. This is certainly true for discussions of a strategic nature because an appreciation of the implications of potential systems is needed at the most senior level and it may be necessary for a senior person to mobilise debate among his colleagues and to provide resources to pursue the implications of system plans. However, the practice of sending user managers as representatives in detailed design work is of more limited value. Management are often somewhat distant from the day-to-day operations and may not appreciate the significance of many design decisions. The person needed here is someone with considerable experience of the range of circumstances with which operational staff have to cope who can point out the limitations of design proposals.

There may be a belief that the representatives should be elected representatives of the work-force. This is certainly necessary when there are issues to be negotiated but can be inappropriate in circumstances where user task needs are to be specified or design solutions evaluated for their service to tasks. Employee representatives in these circumstances may have no more detailed knowledge of the user task world than the management and the representation should be by those with knowledge.

It is important that representatives are chosen to cover the different user departments and the different levels and types of staff to be affected by the system.

A final criterion arises from a phenomenon we have noted in many applications. People who become user representatives rarely return to the job they did before the system was introduced. Often they take on duties of a user support nature, helping their colleagues understand and use the system and acting as liaison with the technical staff. This is a valuable and necessary role and the experience of being a user representative during design is a very good training for it. The selection of user representatives should therefore bear in mind that the person may in future be taking on these responsibilities.

A related issue to selection is the question of whether representatives should be rotated, especially if the design process is likely to take some months or years. There will be a temptation to do this if it is hard to spare key individuals or if the organisation is trying to give its staff a range of work experience. It is also a way of countering the hostage effect; i.e. introduce a new face just when the representative has 'gone native'. However, there are strong counter-arguments. It takes quite a long time for the average user to understand the processes of design sufficiently to be able to make an effective contribution and rotation may occur just at the point when this learning is about to pay dividends. Also, if the representative has been able to build a relation with colleagues whereby information about needs is collected and design progress fed back, much of the value of this channel of communication may be lost if the representative is changed. The future role in user support may also be lost. On balance then, in most situations, it is better to seek continuity in representation throughout the design process.

In summary the strategy of sending representatives to engage in joint systems development with technical specialists has much to commend it but it is obviously a structure to be organised and staffed with care so that the right people have the right roles. The user representatives, even in the right roles, will need considerable help to be effective and the support they can be given will be a major theme of subsequent chapters.

Total User-centred Design

One of the weaknesses of the user representative strategy is that it leaves the bulk of the potential users outside the design process, dependent upon the user representative for consultation and information. If the hostage effect becomes significant it may be that the remainder of the users are consulted less than they would have been had there been no user representative. There is therefore a danger that reliance on the user representative strategy will not allow all the users to contribute their knowledge and to ensure consideration is given to the issues that concern them. They are also unlikely to feel the same kind of commitment and ownership of the system that the user representative might experience. This factor can lead systems staff seriously to misjudge the mood of users towards a new system; user representatives may be very enthusiastic but, at implementation, there may be hostile reaction from the rest of the users.

Given these considerations there is a serious case for a strategy that seeks to involve all of the potential users in the design of the system. As Figure 5.3 indicates this is a strategy which seeks to make use of the knowledge of the range of users, to enable them to make their views known as stakeholders and to develop commitment towards the system. The major problems are the practicality and acceptability to the organisation of getting everybody involved and the role of the technical specialists if the users are given a greater say in the process.

We can usefully differentiate between two different forms of total user-led design. In the form of total participation reported, for example, by Mumford (1980) and Hedberg (1980) the aim is for the users to plan the organisational structures within which they will work and the jobs they will do and from this target to specify the technical system they require to support this form of organisation. Examples of this approach in the literature have usually involved users being given the support of organisational specialists, and technical specialists have been available to provide the technical system that is specified.

The other kind of user-led strategy is the 'end-user development' approach, described in Chapter 3, in which a group of users acquire one or more microcomputers and either develop their own applications or obtain a technical service to develop it to their instructions. Such applications are usually developed for a small group of users and as such are a form of total user participation. Wroe (1986) provides some examples of this kind of strategy being used in small building firms.

There can be little doubt that these approaches can develop a strong commitment on the part of the users, a commitment which will cause them to work to overcome all manner of subsequent teething troubles. A well-designed system can fail because the motivation is not there to make it work but a system that is not so well designed can succeed because its users are determined to overcome all its deficiencies. There are, however, a number of problems to overcome in adopting this strategy.

The first is that it is not too difficult to involve all users when the system is small and the users are few, but when a system is large the problems escalate. The case studies provided by Mumford (1980) and Hedberg (1980) involve less than 100 users. One way we have used to handle the problem of scale (see Gower and Eason, 1989, Shackel et al., 1989) is to establish different opportunities for participation so that ultimately everyone is involved. The underlying concept in this approach is that people should be involved in design issues upon which they have some knowledge to contribute or a direct 'stake' in the outcome. We would not therefore try to get everyone directly involved in broad strategic decisions about organisational or technical design but would leave these decisions to user representatives working with management and technical specialists. However, if the minimum critical specification strategy is employed there will be considerable flexibility in the system provided and many local decisions to be taken about the form of social and technical system to be operated in a given site. Thus there can be matters of job design, technical system service, office layout, and implementation procedure to be determined by working groups of local users.

A second problem is the knowledge the users require in order to participate effectively in the design process. If it is difficult to help user representatives to become effective members of design teams it is going to be even more difficult to help everybody. This is to some extent resolved if people are working on issues where they have relevant knowledge but there is a need to create methods where they can acquire the knowledge that is missing in the act of participating in the decision-making process.

A third set of problems relates to the power structure within which the system is designed. If all the users are involved might they not be pulling in different directions such that no effective system can be defined? This problem can manifest itself in a number of ways. Senior management may worry that separate user groups will develop different systems which will not permit central co-ordination and control. Technical specialists may be anxious that they may have to create a system serving different and conflicting objectives or that they will be left with a technical system impossible to maintain and develop because it contains incompatible sub-systems. In a hospital case study (Eason *et al.*, 1989), a powerful user group created a specification which could only be met within the financial constraints by the technical specialists at the expense of technical goals such as flexibility and maintainability. In the long term the failure to meet these technical goals meant the system could not be modified as user needs changed.

If these problems emerge it is usually because the project structure has not given sufficient attention to genuine management and technical goals and has slipped too far in the direction of specific end-user requirements. There will be conflicts of interest and the central steering group for the project has to find ways of managing these. One of the major requirements is for the steering group to establish the degree of autonomy within which specific working groups can do their work. Seeking the participation of all users is not to say that everything is possible but that there is considerable choice within established limits. For practical purposes there is very little difference between managing an information technology project and any other project requiring close co-ordination between a number of activities. It is necessary for the central management of the project to establish the terms of reference, composition and time-scales of sub-groups charged with parts of the process.

Establishing a Project Structure

The three strategies presented above are often seen as alternatives but in practice elements of each of them are necessary if an effective system of any size is to be designed and implemented. If the system involves a major technical change, especially if it includes bespoke programming, there will be major parts of the process which have to be dominated by technical specialists. If there are a lot of users with different requirements who will need to feel satisfied that the change is in their best interests before they will find it acceptable, some form of participation for all users will be necessary. If the total system is large, user representatives will probably be necessary because not everyone can or will want to be involved in the detailed work to construct the system.

To establish a project structure therefore requires a mixture of these strategies.

The appropriate mixture is likely to be different for different organisations and applications but we have found that the general structure depicted in Figure 5.4 is useful when fairly major changes are being considered.

In this structure the oversight of the project is with a project steering group which consists of senior management, technical specialists and user representatives chosen for their ability to represent the interests of their user group rather then their knowledge of user task needs. This group should be led by senior user management to express the fact that the technical system is being constructed to be a service to the users and to ensure there is awareness at a senior level of the kinds of organisational changes that may be necessary. The user representatives should be able to represent the interests of all the different user departments and the levels of staff who will be affected by the system.

The project structure is essentially a temporary organisation created for the duration of the project and it must relate to the normal and ongoing management

Figure 5.4
A typical project structure

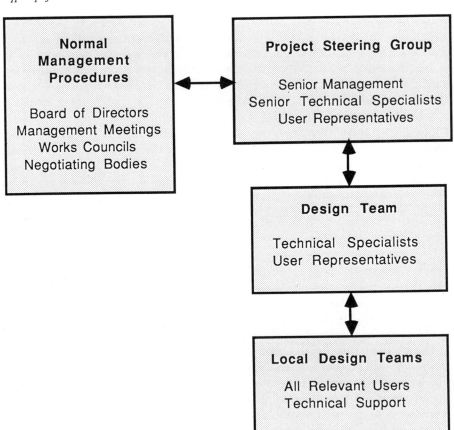

procedures of the organisation, i.e. it must report regularly at an appropriate level of management, perhaps the Board of Directors. It must also report progress to the representative and negotiation bodies of the organisation and provide technical support for any negotiations that are necessary.

The main design team should report to the steering group and will vary in size and composition depending on the scale of technical and organisational work to be done. The technical specialists will include information technology specialists but may well need organisational change specialists in addition. User representatives will be needed in the design team who have detailed task knowledge of the user domain and there should be sufficient users to cover the user departments to be affected.

The design team should work on the principles of delegating as much design work as possible to local design teams. This is one way of implementing the concept of minimum critical specification. If the design team concentrates upon agreeing the technical and organisational strategy that has to be common across the organisation it can then establish the terms of reference within which others can contribute to the design. The extent of co-ordination varies with the type of application and the degree to which different parts of the organisation have to co-operate in its operation. An airline or hotel booking system, for example, requires detailed co-ordination across many sites because the application depends upon the agreed, real time data base and becomes meaningless if each site does not play its part according to agreed procedures. On the other hand the provision of microcomputers for scientific purposes across a Research and Development organisation may need very little central co-ordination and a lot of local developments to meet different scientific purposes. In most applications there is considerable scope for local developments.

Local design teams can be organised by location and by the topic to be examined. They may, for example, be concerned with job design, the definition of specific applications, the conduct of user prototyping exercises, the design of office workstations and layout, the arrangements for implementation and training, etc. They are the opportunity to involve as many users as possible on issues of direct concern to them but the users will need relevant technical support if they are to perform the design tasks effectively. Some of these tasks may need to be undertaken in parallel with the work of the main design team, for example prototyping exercises, but many of them can be undertaken subsequently, for example before implementation or, when new local applications are being planned, some time after the system is operational. Where freedom and flexibility have been preserved there remains the possibility of subsequent development work.

The link between the main design team and the local design teams is one where the user representatives can be most important. They provide the route by which local users are consulted on issues being considered by the main design team and can act as the communications route by which local users hear of the overall design plans. They can also help to create the local groups that are necessary to make the best use of the overall system being planned and can support the people concerned in their work because of the knowledge and experience gained in the main design work.

It is interesting to note that this structure mirrors the structure to be found in many industrial democracy schemes where local representatives are active organisers of the people they represent as well as members of the central representative body. It is also a structure which finds favour with most members of staff. Wall and Lischeron (1977) undertook a study in which they asked local authority staff about decisions taken 'locally', for example about day-to-day deployment of staff and resources, and 'distantly', for example about negotiations with other organisations, decisions about offering new services, etc. Staff wanted more involvement in both kinds of decisions but they sought direct, personal involvement in the local decisions whilst looking to a system of user representatives to take care of their interests in the distant decisions. The same 'local' and 'distant' distinction can be made about system developments provided the central decisions leave sufficient freedom for the local decision-making process to be significant.

Towards Effective Team Work

If a structure is employed which brings users and technical specialists together there are likely to be a lot of circumstances in which people are gathered together who are unfamiliar with one another, where they do not understand the roles and contributions of the others and are not sure how to make a contribution themselves. The structure may have the potential to create an effective system but the potential can only be realised if the people concerned are able to work well together. We have, in Chapter 3, examined the general problems users experience when participating in systems design. Figure 5.5 lists the common problems that users and technical specialists have in attaining effective communication.

There is frequently a pressure for user representatives to be able to report details of the user world (for example, how and why certain tasks are undertaken, how frequently, how long they take, etc.). The user may be an expert at undertaking these tasks but may have great difficulty reporting how they are done. The designers of expert systems are continually encountering the problem that the expertise may be locked into the expert in a form that is not easily verbalised and user representatives have the same problem. Even when reporting such objective data as how many telephone calls are made each week or how much time is spent in meetings can lead to wildly inaccurate judgements. If this kind of information is important in the systems design process, users should be given an opportunity to collect information and consult colleagues in order that they can make a considered response to the question.

An even more difficult question the user is often asked is what future needs there may be for an information technology system. This is in part difficult because the user lives in a changing world and predicting future trends sufficiently to specify future needs is a problem. It is also a problem because the user is not a specialist in the technology and therefore cannot be sure what is possible, and what is needed must be coloured by what is possible. Ideally, before being asked to respond to questions of this kind, the user should be sufficiently familiar with the technology to be able to make a judgement but this brings us to another problem. Users frequently have difficulty understanding the technical language of information technology and of systems design. The jargon can seem impenetrable and this can render all attempts to discuss

Figure 5.5
Obstacles to effective participation

---

1. Users reviewing rather than doing

2. Users predicting future needs

3. Understanding technical language

4. Predicting and evaluating alternatives

5. Managing status and occupational differences

6. Getting time to consult

7. Coping with instant deadlines

---

options a meaningless exercise. It is very important to note that this is not a one-way process. The 'technical jargon' of the users, the way they describe the work they do, can be equally confusing to the technical specialist. This is one advantage a fully trained designer who has a user background can bring to the design team. The problem of misunderstanding technical terms can also undermine attempts to present and evaluate proposed design solutions. If the users have difficulty in understanding the proposal in technical terms, they will find it impossible to evaluate the effects it will have on the tasks and jobs of fellow users. Before embarking upon major decision-making activities it is important for the different disciplines to try to help one another develop an understanding of the technical worlds they each inhabit.

In addition to technical differences there may be other differences present in the team which can be obstacles to effective working. It is not uncommon for a design team to be composed of people with very different backgrounds and educational standards and different status levels within the organisation. Under these circumstances it is very difficult for someone who feels of inferior education and status to the others and who, used to getting on with a job all day, feels uneasy with a group discussion process, to make a contribution to the debate. Conversely it is very easy for the person who is of high status and familiar with systems design processes to dominate proceedings. If this happens the value of the user representative approach is lost. Indeed if the person is left feeling there was no serious intention to allow participation, the result may be that the user representative becomes alienated and negative towards the planned change. The status differences can exist between users and technical specialists or between the different users involved in the process. If, for example, the team includes members of management and the work-force, it may be difficult for the work-force representatives to make their contribution freely. One particular problem can be when the management present the prescribed process, i.e. how the work should be undertaken. The members of the work-force might be aware that the actual process is somewhat different in a way which is significant for the design of the system. Unless there is mutual trust and confidence within the team, it may be difficult for them to report these differences.

Another set of problems relates to the time put aside for the team work. If users are acting as representatives on a part-time basis there will be a tendency only to provide the time for meetings. It is equally important that there be time for the user to consult and inform fellow users of the issue at stake. There may also be a tendency to plan the work strictly in terms of the time needed to take decisions which may not leave time for team building and the sharing of knowledge which will be necessary if good decisions are to be reached. Another very common time problem is that users are asked to give instant responses to systems proposals; a complex document arrives a day ahead of the meeting at which it will be discussed and approved. If this happens regularly it can create a feeling among users that the representative process is not serious and is a way of making sure they agree without allowing proper consideration and debate. The reason may be quite different, for example, the designers may have been struggling against a very tight deadline set by senior management to produce the proposal. However, the effect on the users is the same, a loss of confidence in the validity of the process in which they are engaged.

If these obstacles are to be avoided there are four key elements which should feature in the work of design teams; team building, the provision of time, the use of concrete examples and the teaching of techniques whereby users and technical specialists can work together.

Team building is a process which specialists in organisational development (see, for example, Bass and Barrett, 1981) advocate whenever a group of people come together and will need to work closely together over an extended period of time. Its purpose is to encourage each member to get to know each other member well enough to know what to expect of them in later work. At best it will lead to mutual trust and understanding, an acceptance of the role and contribution each can make and a spirit of common identity provided by the task they share. At worst it should indicate to each person what he can and cannot expect from the others which at least ensures a sense of reality in later debates. The process by which team building is accomplished consists of getting team members together without the pressures to take decisions. Their first task is to get to know one another, to hear from one another about their past, their roles and their aspirations for the present task. As this process develops they can work out the respective roles they might play in subsequent work and can examine what knowledge they need to exchange to work well together. A few early meetings devoted thus can save a great deal of misunderstanding and bad feeling subsequently.

The second requirement is time. Information systems development is usually undertaken alongside normal operational work and the need to 'keep the shop open' without recruiting extra labour often means people are asked to contribute to design work almost as a spare-time activity. If it is significant for the future of the organisation it needs and deserves more time so that users and specialists can get to know one another, properly consider options and proposals and consult other users about the plans. There is a requirement both for a significant amount of time to be set aside each week and for the elapsed time before reporting to be sufficient to do the job. The elapsed time is often a problem if the project is being managed on a 'one-shot implementation' basis because the need to keep achieving the technical milestones may mitigate against time devoted to reviewing proposals and changing them in the light of feedback. The last thing technical specialists want to hear when they are up against deadlines is that the users have some queries and want to make changes. The structure of the project has to permit some form of progressive or evolutionary delivery of new systems if it is to provide the time for iteration which is necessary if the user's contribution is not to be undermined.

If the communications between the members of the design team about needs, options, proposals and their consequences are to be rich and meaningful to all parties it is best that they be conducted in as concrete terms as possible. Many problems have risen in the past because participants are using an abstract set of concepts which have little meaning for others. We have repeatedly found that the air of mystification drops away if we can provide practical examples of some future option rather than the general concept. Users may make little sense of a flow diagram depicting a future system in terms of symbols indicating files, terminals and processing devices. They may react much more readily to seeing the dialogues and outputs that might appear on screens and can quickly begin to see the implications for the users and their tasks. As we shall see in the next chapter, the introduction of rapid prototyping systems is making the provision of concrete examples of what a system might look like much easier, with consequent benefits for the kind of debate that can take place between designer and user.

The final requirement is for a set of techniques whereby technical specialists and users can work on the issues that jointly concern them. At present the available techniques are for use by the specialists designing the technical system and give little help in the processes of defining future needs, planning organisational changes, evaluating the consequences of technical system proposals, etc. The remaining chapters of this book seek to fill this gap.

Conclusions

In this chapter we have examined a range of ways in which a project structure can be established which will be able to take responsibility for the design and implementation of an effective and acceptable socio-technical system. It may be that a technical system can be created by a project team consisting mostly of technical specialists but once the objective is broadened to an acceptable socio-technical system the expertise required to design it must include significant roles for the potential users of the system. The selection of an appropriate structure depends on two important distinctions:

1. *The Customer–Contractor Relationship.* There has to be a clearly understood division between the people who are requesting the system (and their rights and obligations) and the people who are meeting the request (and their rights and obligations). Creating a structure for the design of the technical system largely consists of getting the users into roles whereby they can specify what is needed and evaluate what is proposed. The position with respect to the changes in the social system is somewhat different since the users can in large measure be both specifiers and designers.

2. *User Representatives and Total Representation.* In an ideal world all users would have an equal say in the design of the systems they will use in the future. In large systems this may not be practicable and the main route for user participation in the overall systems is user representatives. However, this need not prevent the participation of all users because there can be significant design work to be done locally to ensure the system is adapted to local requirements.

A structure built on these principles may have the potential for effective sociotechnical design but the contributors to design still have to work together effectively. To help them, team building processes are necessary, the issues must be examined in as practical and concrete a way as possible and techniques are needed which are specifically created for these circumstances.

It may seem that it is a lot of time and trouble to create a structure that has these properties and then face the problems of making it work. The joint design of a system by specialists and users is certainly not an easy path to success. The alternative, however, is to design the technical system first and then face the problems at the time of implementation.

Chapter 6
Specifying the System

The Problem

Designers cannot build a system until they know what is required. Users have difficulty stating their requirements of a technology they do not understand. As a result agreeing a specification is often a source of contention in systems design and the inability to produce an adequate specification may lead to a system that fails by being neither functional, usable nor acceptable.

In this chapter we will examine a variety of methods of coping with the process of specification. We have already identified, in Chapter 5, some of the problems that beset user–designer relationships. We now need to restate and develop the problems that surround system specification.

1. *Knowing what is Desirable*. It is not easy for users to specify the purposes of an information technology system unless they have a clear view of the problems and opportunities that face their organisation and which an information technology system might serve. Ideally the implementation of information technology begins with an analysis of business needs. Too often it starts from a narrow technological initiative, i.e. a desire to be up to date and use the latest forms of technology, to appear modern or not to fall behind the competition. Drifting into system development without a clear view of the business benefits is a recipe for disappointment.

2. *Knowing what is Possible*. Many purchasers face the problem of stating what they require when they do not know what can be provided. The novice purchaser of an information technology system is faced by a baffling array of products and may be told that anything is possible. Establishing what is worth doing is often a creative process of matching possibilities and needs. It may produce a new objective that could not have been contemplated before the technical option was identified.

3. *Knowing the Future*. It takes time to implement a system and its operational life will extend well into the future. Specifying the system is not therefore about meeting current requirements but about forecasting what will be required in the future.

4. *Meeting the Designer's Need for Detail*. The technical specification process often moves quickly to a detailed level of analysis in which the designer is trying to state the requirements in technical terms, i.e. what will the data base contain, how many files will be required, how many transactions will be handled each day? These needs get transformed into a set of questions about how tasks are conducted, how often,

when information is transferred from one person to another, etc. Users faced with these questions and a need to respond quickly may give broad estimates that do not reflect the variety of the average day or the possibilities of major change in the future. There is a considerable risk therefore that the technical system may be specified on the basis of an over simple description of the task procedures it is designed to support.

5. *Users Agreeing among Themselves.* The target population for a technical system may be many and diverse and there is little likelihood that there will be agreement about the requirements for the system. There may be quite diverse task needs among the user population, different working practices and aspirations. As Stewart (1971) has remarked a major art of systems design is working through these differences and a major gain is often to have achieved some agreed and commonly understood way of proceeding. She was even moved to suggest that if an organisation got this far it may have got the main benefit from computerisation and may not need a computer!

6. *Assessing Conceptual Specifications.* The first stage in preparing a way of meeting user requirements is usually to prepare a conceptual proposal — an abstract statement of how the objectives of the system might be met. This is often a technical description based on flow charts and can be difficult for the user to understand. It is even more difficult for the user to assess the degree to which a proposal of this kind can meet the organisational objectives.

7. *Assessing Organisational Consequences.* One of the problems of technical systems is that they have many ramifications within the organisation. It is clearly desirable to identify these before the system is finalised and to plan how to cope with unwanted consequences, perhaps by changing the technical specification. However, if the user has difficulty understanding the conceptual proposal for the system, there is little likelihood of being able to identify unwanted consequences at this stage.

8. *The Coverage of the Requirement.* One of the consequences of the view that implementing information technology is a technical process is that the specification is usually restricted to technical requirements. It is rare, for example, to find a specification of the human and organisational changes that will be necessary for the system to work, i.e. the job changes, new skills needed, changes in organisational responsibilities, etc. Even the technical requirement may not cover the range of requirements important to the user. The technical requirement usually specifies what will be delivered in terms of information and information processing facilities but it may not say how these facilities should be delivered to users and it is the 'how' that in large measure determines the usability of the system; for example, a Decision Support System may deliver just the information a manager needs but if its operation requires the manager to learn a complex command language it will probably be unusable.

There are then many facets to the problem of specifying the user requirement for a system and of assessing the initial proposals for meeting the specification. The problem is compounded by the significance of user specification in the customer–contractor relationship. The contractor agrees time-scales, costs and resources on the basis of what he is being asked to supply and the user specification is this statement. If the contractor is an outside supplier, the specification is part of a legal contract between the customer and the contractor. Any change in the specification, or dispute over it, can become the subject of arguments about time-scales, costs and resources. It is very important to the contractor to get a clear statement of the requirement as early as possible. It is nevertheless very difficult for the user organisation to know what is wanted but this may become progressively clearer as design proceeds.

At present the importance of this problem is probably better appreciated by the contractors than it is by the customers and, in the view of many customers, the dice is loaded in favour of the contractors. Within the structured design methodologies, for example, the customer is asked to sign off each stage of the specification process and, once signed, the customer may have no redress, if he subsequently finds that he misunderstood what was being offered. The methods by which the user specification process is derived are also dominated by the need of the technical system designer to define the specification in terms which identify the technical requirements. The methods used tend to emphasise the rational analysis of existing task procedures rather than the debate about alternative future objectives for the organisation.

Principles for User Requirements Specification

The need for the contractor, whether an independent supplier or an in-house design team, to get an explicit and agreed statement of the technical requirement can dominate the early phases of systems design. If this occurs it puts a lot of pressure upon the user organisation which needs to spend time and effort at this stage examining and evaluating possibilities. We need a design structure and a set of system specification techniques which enable the user organisation to establish its requirements before the need for binding technical decisions becomes dominant.

The techniques presented in this chapter are designed to serve this purpose and are founded on three principles:

1. *Producing Technical Specifications from Organisational Needs Analysis.* If information technology is to be effectively harnessed we need to reverse the tendency to look for a way of using the latest type of technology; for example, what application have we got for an expert system? We need to replace this approach with one that begins by looking at organisational objectives and problems and then asks whether the technology has a role to play. A touchstone of whether this approach is being used might be the decision that to achieve a particular objective the technology is not appropriate. The aim is to serve the organisation — not simply to implement more technology.

2. *The Principle of Minimum Critical Specification.* Given all the problems listed at the beginning of this chapter it will be difficult for a user organisation to provide a complete technical specification of what is required at the beginning of the design process. The 'right first time' principle for specification may be convenient in technical and contractual terms but makes no allowance for the learning which users must go through in order to relate the possibilities of the new technology to

their organisational needs. Attempts at comprehensive specifications also have a tendency to rob people of the flexibility they need in order; for example, to make subsequent decisions about the form of technology they need to support changing job requirements, their aspirations to work in a different way, etc.

For these reasons the principle pursued here is that at each stage of design only a minimum critical specification of the technical and the social system is attempted in order to leave freedom for more detailed specification decisions to be taken at a later date. In many ways we are already familiar with this approach in organisational decision-making. Senior management will establish broad objectives and policies which line managers will then interpret in their own ways and they in their turn may well leave significant areas of autonomy for their staff within the general constraints of the company policies. The application of these principles to the technical specification should enable us to retain the requisite flexibility at the end-user level to support the autonomy being provided by the social system.

The effect of this principle is that instead of a full specification phase preceding any design work there are a series of progressively more detailed specification exercises related to different levels of technical design work.

3. *The Principle of Iterative Assessment of Consequences.* Whenever a proposal is offered as a way forward it needs to be evaluated for its impact. Most technical proposals are evaluated against technical and economic criteria. However, their ultimate contribution to the organisation will come from their interaction with the social system; from their usage by the staff. Technical proposals must therefore be evaluated for their impact on the organisation and its staff. The impact analysis should examine the ability of the proposal to meet the planned objectives and should also examine the consequences that could ensue for the functioning of the organisation.

As the design process is pursued at different levels of detail so progressively more detailed proposals will be prepared. Each of them needs evaluating for human and organisational consequences. At the top level, for example, it may be necessary to examine the socio-technical system implications of a proposed integrated manufacturing system. Subsequently, it may be necessary to examine the implications for a work group of a particular workstation layout.

It is possible to imagine a formal evaluation procedure perhaps based on a computer model of the organisation. The proposal could be fed into the model and out would come the consequences. This is a very deterministic view of cause and effect in organisations and would be misleading. The consequences of systems depend upon the motivation and influence of staff because they can use the new conditions created by the system to pursue their own objectives. We need to recognise that consequences occur because of an active rather than a deterministic process. For this reason the emphasis in these techniques is upon the staff of the organisation reviewing proposals in a structured way so that they can use their knowledge of the culture of the organisation to predict likely outcomes. Hirschheim (1985) has called this form of evaluation 'hermeneutic role playing' — asking people to put themselves in a particular role in a future scenario and use their ability to extrapolate from the current situation to predict outcomes.

User participation in proposal evaluation in this way also has another important benefit. The problem is not only to predict likely outcomes but to place a valuation on these outcomes; will different groups of staff view them positively or negatively? Staff reviewing proposals are in a good position to make these evaluative judgements and it will help them make explicit the criteria by which system proposals are to be judged. The process of specifying a system is as much about establishing and agreeing goal criteria as it is about appreciating the opportunities that exist.

These three principles can be applied at many stages in the design process. In the following sections we will examine their application in four different circumstances. In later chapters they will be used in relation to job design, workstation analysis, etc., but for the present we are concerned with broader forms of system specification.

The specification process described in Figure 6.1 has six stages:

1. *Analysis of Organisational Needs and Opportunities*. In this stage the objective is to undertake a form of analysis which will identify the directions the organisation should be taking in a way which will facilitate the identification of valuable roles for information technology to play.
2. *The Specification of Options*. If the overall direction has been established technological and other options can be matched to the organisational requirements in order to produce broad conceptual proposals for potential socio-technical systems.
3. *Assess Consequences of Options*. This is the analysis by role-playing techniques of the direct and indirect consequences of proposed socio-technical systems and their evaluation from the viewpoints of different groups of staff.
4. *The Analysis of User/Task Requirements of the Proposed Socio-technical System*. Within the broad conceptual specification that has been agreed it is necessary to detail the requirements of the users and their tasks for the social and technical systems to be designed.
5. *The Specification of a Prototype System*. The creation of a version of the proposed system (including both its technical and social elements) for the purposes of evaluation and refinement of the specification (not as an early version of the finished system).
6. *The Evaluation of the Prototype System*. The systematic analysis, perhaps through trial usage, of the prototype system in order that users can have realistic experience upon which to base their assessments and to revise their requirement specification.

These stages can be pursued in the sequence depicted in Figure 6.1, perhaps with iterations where the evaluations show that the proposals are not viable options. However, there may be many circumstances where the full sequence may not be followed; for example, if an organisation has a clear statement of its objectives this may be sufficient to begin specifying socio-technical options without stage (1).

In the remainder of this chapter we will describe some techniques for approaching system specification in this way. We shall concentrate upon the procedures for analysis (stages (1) and (4)) and evaluation (stages (3) and (6)). The remaining stages are about

Figure 6.1
The specification of user requirements

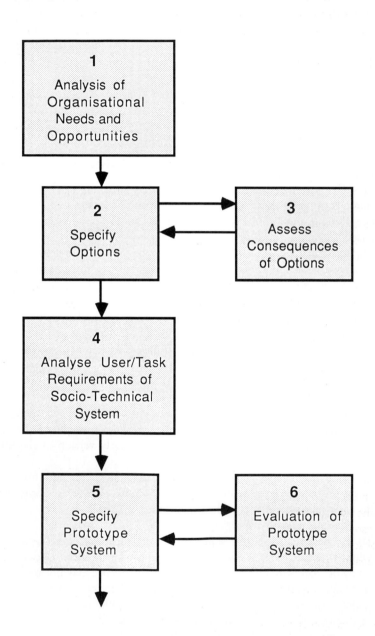

preparing solutions (stages (2) and (5)) and will be examined in greater detail in Chapters 7 and 8.

The Analysis of Organisational Needs and Opportunities

The objective of this stage is to develop a statement of organisational needs and opportunities that is in a form which will facilitate the search for socio-technical systems, including those making use of new forms of information technology. The problem for the user organisation is to stand back from the current round of problems and ways of handling them in order to see the underlying nature of the business, of how it is changing and what new opportunities the technology might offer them. If this detached and longer term view cannot be attained, the likelihood is that the technology will be used to sustain existing practices.

To obtain this view it is essential that analysis does not begin by examining existing information patterns and needs which is often the starting point for technical systems analysis. Indeed the analysis should not be too concerned with the current ways of undertaking tasks but should use this as evidence of the goals being sought and the problems to be overcome. The objective is to see whether there are other ways of achieving these goals or perhaps attaining new objectives.

A number of methods have been proposed for achieving this kind of view of an organisation. One of the most widely cited is the 'soft systems methodology' of Checkland (1981). Checkland refers to it as 'soft' methodology to contrast it with the 'hard' methodologies normally used in systems analysis which emphasise rational, quantitative descriptions of organisational processes. The 'soft' methodology recognises the more complex and fuzzy nature of organisational life where a variety of goals are being pursued and there may be many views of the reality with which staff have to deal. The methodology therefore concentrates upon building a rich picture of the organisation, encapsulating different and potentially conflicting viewpoints rather than seeking a neat, coherent framework for the relevant variables. From this picture the 'core characteristics' of the problem situation can be extracted and it is these that form the requirement in the search for solutions. In essence this is a methodology which supports an open, unstructured approach to analysis so that real needs can emerge and will not be overlooked because the analyst imposes an inappropriate and narrow frame of reference which limits the information that can be collected.

The approach adopted here employs a similar qualitative systems perspective but makes specific use from the outset of the concept that work is undertaken by a socio-technical system. The framework presented below owes much to the general principles of socio-technical systems analysis (see Cherns, 1976 for a useful summary) and to the analysis stages of Mumford's (1983a) ETHICS methodology (see Chapter 3).

Figure 6.2 shows the view of the organisation this form of analysis is trying to develop. It makes a fundamental distinction between a functional view of the system (what the organisation is required to do) and the work performing systems (how it currently does it). The problem the analyst faces is that the functional view is only to

Figure 6.2
A socio-technical framework for analysis

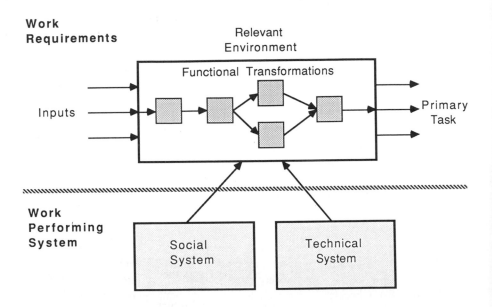

be seen in terms of the current work system so that it is necessary to look behind this surface structure to locate the deeper structure. This is done by adopting an open systems viewpoint and beginning the analysis from outside the system boundaries. An open systems viewpoint recognises that each purposive work organisation engages in transactions with its environment which involves acquiring inputs (raw materials, orders, recruits, etc.) and utilising resources to transform raw materials into some finished goods or services which can be exported from the system. If these are valued by the outside world it is likely that the system will be able to survive by maintaining a throughput of such transformations. The relevant part of the environment which affects the nature of the work throughput is likely to show fluctuations (for example, in the supply of raw materials), and the work system needs to be sufficiently adaptable to cope with both short-term fluctuations and long-term trends. The nature of the outputs that have to be produced constitute the primary goal of the enterprise and the process of making the transformations from inputs to outputs can be described as a number of functional steps, i.e. what is necessary (not how is it achieved).

An analysis of this kind is a very useful basis for considering the future of the organisation because it expresses the underlying, inescapable and enduring characteristics which any way of addressing the primary goal must consider. To produce this description when most of the evidence available to the analyst is about the current way of engaging in this work needs a way of collecting information that has the following characteristics:

1. Use a top-down approach; ask senior people about their objectives and responsibilities and then examine how these decompose to give the objectives and responsibilities of their subordinates. This will reveal the hierarchical nature of the goals and sub-goals within the organisation.
2. Concentrate on 'what' and 'why' rather than 'how'. This will keep the data collection focused upon goals and requirements and not upon current modes of operation.
3. Examine relations between functions; the structure of the transformations shows in the way in which different functions relate to one another. Broadly three kinds of relations can exist (Thompson, 1967):
   (a) sequential interdependencies where one function must be performed before another; for example, the letter must be written before it is posted.
   (b) reciprocal interdependencies where two functions pass the task back and forth between them, or share in its simultaneous execution; for example, two pilots flying a plane but controlling separate functions.
   (c) pooled interdependencies where two functions can coexist in an organisation without affecting one another except that they share a common pool of resources; for example, branch managers in different parts of the country.
4. Look for variations in demand, inputs and environment. Achieving organisational goals is made difficult by the changing nature of the goals to be achieved, differences in the input materials to be used and the changing environment in which the work is undertaken. The key to understanding an organisation is often to understand the variations it cannot control and which are critical to success; for example, the way a manufacturing organisation structures its activities will be different if it is meeting a regular market as compared with a highly seasonal demand such as Christmas.

Eason *et al.* (1989b) provide an example of this kind of analysis. The subject of this analysis was the engineering function of the District Office of an Electricity Supply Board which has the primary task of providing a continuous supply of electricity to its consumers. This task is performed via a number of largely independent functions such as maintenance, refurbishment, network control, emergency repair, network development, etc. Each function has its own largely sequential sequence of sub-functions to fulfil, i.e. emergencies involve collecting fault reports, locating the fault, correcting it, restoring supply, etc. The work can be critically dependent upon environmental factors (electric storms, for example, damage overhead lines and create major losses of supply).

The major thrust of this analysis is the functional character of the requirement to achieve this kind of primary goal. It should describe any organisation with this mission. It is also necessary, however, to create an outline view of the socio-technical system currently undertaking this work, the social structure responsible for different functions and the way in which technology is used to support the fulfilment of the functions. This is necessary because it is from this base that the organisation will move forward. The members of the organisation must be able to see the advantages of any proposal over the existing structure. There may also be constraints both social and technical which it may be difficult or undesirable to change. In a Scandinavian case study, for example, a major constraint on the development of information technology systems was that they must support the participative culture of the organisation. This was not a task or business demand but it was regarded as a vital way of operating in Scandinavian culture.

In the study of the District Office in Electricity Supply, Eason *et al.* (1989b) got respondents to state what they saw as the major problems in achieving work goals and the major opportunities they saw for development. These were not specifically related to the use of information technology but it provided a pool of ideas of worthwhile developments for consideration in the next stage.

A socio-technical analysis of this form provides both a statement of the core characteristics of the enterprise and a way of understanding the principle problems with which many organisations in this business must contend. There are some problems which are local and transient, the difficulties caused, for example, by an incompetent manager. But there are other issues which will recur because they are inherent in the structure of the business. You can keep firing the manager but the problem keeps coming back. An example of such structural 'conflicts' is the relationship between sales, which wants to be able to offer the customer whatever variety of the product he wants, and production, which wants a good long run of a specific version of the product. In the Electricity Supply example there were a number of such conflicts, which were to be found throughout the industry. The need, for example, to maintain central control over the electricity network for efficiency and safety reasons versus the need of the engineer, out in the field working on part of the network, to have control over that part of the network.

Another useful set of outputs from this analysis is an understanding of the critical relationships that exist between the work system and the outside world. This can be a source of perennial problems with which the organisation must find ways of coping. The need for the Electricity Supply Industry to cope with unexpected storm damage is a case in point. The analysis can also be extended to look at trends and forecasts in the relevant external environment and this may reveal future problems; for example, a reducing market for existing products, or new opportunities for products the organisation may be in a good position to provide.

In summary an analysis of this kind focuses attention on underlying business and organisational needs and opportunities and also reveals some of the features of the current form of organisation which will have to be considered if a change programme is undertaken. It is in the nature of problems and opportunities that exist between the system and the outside world and between major functions inside the system that the processing of information plays a major part in any successful solution and it is not too difficult to think of roles information technology could usefully play. However, the nature of this analysis ensures the focus is upon the search for socio-technical solutions rather than simply an information technology solution. A fundamental objective of approaching the analysis of business needs via a socio-technical framework is to ensure that the role of the social structure in mediating the information technology contribution to the business need is never overlooked.

Specifying Socio-Technical Options

The analysis described above has usually been conducted by an independent investigator although there is no reason why a member of the user organisation should not undertake this work. A significant point to note is that members of user organisations are usually worried that they will not be able to specify their requirements because they have little knowledge of the technology. By starting with the nature of the business we are playing to the strengths of the members of the user organisation and building their confidence that they know what they want even if they do not, at this stage, know how it could be provided. The next stage is to bring the technology to bear in seeking socio-technical options to meet the needs that have been identified.

In the participative style in which we have undertaken this work the next stage has usually consisted of sharing the results of the above analysis with a relevant group of managers and their staff and some specialists in information technology. It has rarely been difficult for this group to use the analysis to identify a range of potential information technology options. In the case of the Electricity Supply Industry eight opportunities were identified ranging from improved forms of communication between field engineers and control rooms to ways of scheduling resources to cope with the unexpected demands of emergencies.

The nature of socio-technical options will be explored more fully in the next chapter so there are only a few points to make before proceeding to the next stage of the specification process. The first point to make is that the solution to the problem or opportunity that has been identified may not involve information technology. It may, for example, need a major organisational change, and, even if it does warrant use of information technology, it may only need tried and trusted forms of the technology rather than the latest developments. The converse can also be true, however; the identification of a new application may reveal a gap in the technology which needs some development work and may lead to a new product range in the information technology spectrum. This kind of analysis is therefore of interest to suppliers intent upon being more user- and application-led in the development of their products.

Another point to make is that in addition to a range of application types being identified by this process, there are also likely to be a variety of technical ways of serving the application and a number of possible social structures. The technology is very flexible and there are many ways of organising people to work. Where there are many possibilities there is a danger that people will quickly adopt a 'satisficing' strategy (Simon, 1965), in which they reduce the number to be examined to a few by seeking those that 'will do' and which can be implemented with the minimum disruption. This may be an appropriate strategy but it should be consciously adopted rather than adopted by default. It may mean that potential high value solutions for the organisation are not considered because they look difficult to implement. With further examination it is possible that implementation could be achieved by a phased, evolutionary development which would not cause major organisational disruption.

Impact Analysis: Assessing the Consequences of Socio-Technical Options

We will now assume that one or more options have gained sufficient support to be examined more thoroughly and that a broad conceptual specification outlining the technical system and the way it would serve the social structure has been prepared. It might, for example, state that the technical system will provide a real-time data base for room bookings in a chain of hotels to be used by management, staff and agents to optimise the utilisation of rooms. It would not, at this stage, state in detail how the technical system would operate. Management is likely to evaluate such a proposal for its ability to serve its primary purpose and to make an overall cost–benefit assessment. What is usually missing is a systematic appraisal of the impact of the technical system upon the social system. This is a vital consideration because systems can have widespread indirect effects which many may regard as negative and block implementation. There may be other versions of the system which would be much more acceptable. An analysis of the impact at the earliest possible stage is therefore desirable because it will provide feedback before any major investment decisions are taken and changes are relatively easy to make. In this section we therefore offer a technique for making an impact assessment at the conceptual specification stage of system development.

The general form of this technique is shown in Figure 6.3. It is in essence a form of cost–benefit assessment performed separately for the different groups of 'stakeholders' so that different perspectives on the proposed system can be made explicit. It has been widely used to help groups of managers, user representatives and designers forecast the likely impact of the technical proposals on the table. It functions best when the people involved in the analysis have a close working knowledge of the relevant groups of stakeholders but it is useful even when this is not the case because it serves to identify areas of critical ignorance which will have to be rectified before design proceeds.

The aim of this technique is to map the outline of the proposed technical system onto the existing user organisation in order to make an impact assessment of the system upon its target users. These stages are summarised below and a fuller description is given in the Appendix.

1. *User Population Mapping.* The first step is to identify the users to be affected by the system. It is surprising how far many systems are developed with a relatively unclear vision of the target user population so this stage in itself often provides interesting insights. Often the design team has a vision of a primary user target, i.e. the people who are to be the full-time users of the system (for example, the hotel booking clerks) but they do not consider other users such as the managers who will receive outputs from the system, the travel agents who access the data base to check vacancies, or the customers who receive computer-generated booking forms and invoices. It is often helpful to distinguish different types of users:

   (a) Primary Users — the direct, 'hands on' users of interactive terminals who may be full-time users and who may need workstations dedicated to their use.

   (b) Secondary Users — the occasional users of interactive terminals or people who have to work directly with major output from the systems.

Figure 6.3
Assessing the impact on user groups

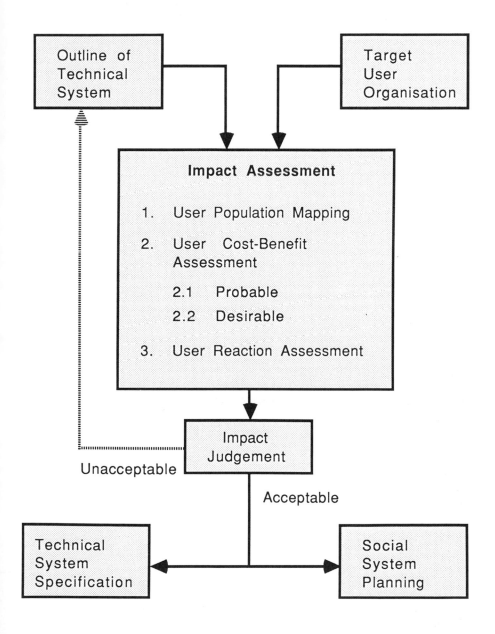

(*c*) Tertiary Users — people who are likely to be affected by the operation of the system but are not direct users of it. Customers and suppliers often find themselves in this category.

Producing a list of this kind can be helpful in reminding designers that there are people who may not be the main focus of design attention who are nevertheless critical to the success of the system and whose needs have to be understood and included in design considerations.

The next step is to map the proposed system facilities against the different groups of users. Who is to receive terminals, to be given access to which data bases, to be allowed access to computational facilities, etc? Again this can be an interesting exercise in its own right, especially when it reveals that some critical groups are to be left out of the system provisions. The stage of mapping provisions to user groups is a crucial one in revealing how a particular role is to be affected by a system and is a vital part of job design to be considered in the next chapter.

2. *User Cost–Benefit Assessment.* The core of the impact assessment is to consider the implications of the system for each of the user groups that have been identified and to estimate how they are likely to evaluate the changes that may occur. This is done by considering what is likely to happen to each of the groups in terms of the five types of impact that are often found in evaluation studies. These are:

(*a*) Job Security. This is made the primary consideration because, when it is an issue, it is bound to be the dominant concern within the user group. It should be noted that the impact assessment needs to consider not only whether there will actually be job loss in this group but also whether there will be fears of this outcome even when it is not intended. This can occur, for example, because there have been previous system developments which have affected job security among this group of staff or their colleagues. Negative views of systems can be generated out of suspicions that may have no basis in terms of the intended impact.

(*b*) Service to the Job. In this section the impact of the facilities to be provided by the system are examined. Will the users see these facilities as helpful in performing their work tasks more effectively? Will they see the access to facilities provided for others as threatening the work that they have to do?

(*c*) The Impact on the Job. The system may affect many features of the job, the content (the skills needed, the variety, the autonomy, etc.), the rhythm (the deadlines, the pacing, the workload, etc.) and the way people evaluate the job (stresses, job satisfaction, etc.).

(*d*) Organisational Changes. The system may create broader changes that affect the user group; it may, for example, introduce a greater degree of formality or standardisation into work procedures, it may raise questions of data privacy, and there may be changes in power and influence structures.

(*e*) Personnel Consequences. Finally, if there are any changes in the above categories, there are likely to be consequences for a variety of personnel policies (for example, payment, grading and other aspects of the reward systems, informal systems, career structures and industrial relations agreements, etc.).

The Appendix contains check-lists giving more details of these dimensions of impact. It also suggests a technique for rating likely user responses. This is based on a very simple view of how people respond to the new technological systems. First, we describe the change that may occur and then we evaluate whether users will see this as a benefit to them personally (will it help do their job, provide a more satisfying job, help them in developing their career, etc?) or whether it will be seen as a cost. The 'cost' may be financial but it may be a loss in other ways, a loss of job security, of valued skills or of power and influence; it may also be a 'cost' in terms of effort to learn and change or a fear of not being able to cope in the new situation. It will be noted that the check-lists provide for each dimension of change to be scored as both a benefit and a cost because often the outcome may have both elements; for example, valued skills may no longer be required but the new ones to be developed may have considerable market value.

Although it is not essential, many people who have used this technique have found it useful to rate the change in a dimension on a scale from major benefit, through a disinterested, neutral response to major cost. Ratings of this kind give a profile of costs and benefits for each group of users so that the positive and negative impact areas can be easily identified. It also provides a coarse way of calculating an overall 'score' for each group of users which makes it easy to detect the 'winners' and the 'losers' if the system is introduced. It can show, for example, that one group will benefit in service and job content whilst another group gets little service and becomes less powerful in the organisation.

One way this technique has been employed is to get different members of the design team to play the role of one of the user groups and to present a user impact profile to the rest of the team. By design team in this context we include everyone charged with some kind of responsibility for systems development which will include representatives of the user organisations. The team can then review the probable overall outcome of the implementation of the system. This process has to occur at a very early stage in the development of a system if the analysis is to have any affect in shaping the course of technical system development. Unfortunately this means the impact assessment may involve a lot of uncertainty; about the detailed plans for the system, the way it would actually be implemented and how users might respond. Despite these uncertainties the analysis ensures that a recognition of the range of possible impacts gets on to the system design agenda. It can also offer another form of analysis. Thus far the assessment has been in terms of *probable* impact. In making these assessments, however, many people find themselves saying 'but if we did "x" the impact would be different and users might find that much more acceptable'. The areas of uncertainty can therefore be turned to positive advantages and ways sought to produce a more *desirable* outcome for the user groups. Figure 6.3 therefore includes a cost–benefit assessment where an attempt is made to identify a more favourable set of outcomes for a user group. The Appendix provides a check-list for this purpose which contains the same impact dimensions but asks the rater to state the conditions under which the favourable impact may be obtained. These conditions may be about social system factors or implementation strategies (for example, no redundancy agreements) or may be about changes in the technical system (for example, new services that are required, the omission of some planned features or their allocation more widely among the user groups, etc.). The end result therefore is both a first approximation of the probable impact of the planned system and some ideas of more desirable alternatives.

3. *User Reaction Assessment.* Another step can be taken with this analysis before the overall position is reviewed. Using the impact profile for each user group it is possible to make a prediction of the likely response of the groups to the introduction of the system. This is useful in identifying the problems that may occur at the time of implementation but can also be a very potent force in preventing designers and their superiors from adopting a 'they may not like it but they will get used to it' attitude. It is very easy to concentrate upon current technical issues and leave user issues to the time of implementation which is the reason many systems have not been effectively implemented. It is therefore useful to use the impact profiles to forecast implementation problems, and the simplest way to do this is to take the groups that appear to be overall 'losers' and to ask how they are likely to respond if these plans are put into effect. The Appendix provides some guidance on how different kinds of user groups respond to different kinds of impact. In general people who see themselves as losers in a change process will use their power base to defend their position. Different user groups will have different degrees and types of power they can use. Some of the possibilities are as follows:

(*a*) A line manager with considerable formal authority may simply veto the development of the system or ensure his department makes no use of it.

(*b*) Managers or professionals with considerable discretion to determine their own work patterns may react by not using the system personally or by only using those facilities that provide a beneficial outcome, i.e. they can use their discretion to avoid the negative features.

(*c*) Non-discretionary users may collectively negotiate to mitigate the negative effects, in New Technology Agreements, for example, or they may demand compensation, in the form of higher pay or other conditions important to them, in return for the changes they will be required to make.

There are other kinds of response that are possible and a profile of likely impact together with knowledge of the possible ways a group could react provide a good opportunity to predict the problems that may lie ahead. This can provide the impetus for the design team to look for other alternatives which may be more favourably received by the user population.

When each of these steps has been undertaken for each of the user groups an overall assessment of the impact of the planned system can be made. It should start from the initial objectives of the system and, taking account of the impact on each group of users, make an assessment of whether these objectives are likely to be achieved. Usually, as we discussed in Chapter 2, the achievement of objectives is dependent upon change, learning and co-operation in user groups and the impact analysis can show the critical areas in which objectives may be in danger. The conclusion may well be that the present plans are unacceptable and the technical system needs to be reconsidered. The impact analysis, and especially the desirable impact analysis, may well provide guidance in the search for better alternatives. The manner in which this analysis has focused upon specific user roles leads to one particular way in which it guides the search for other possibilities. It focuses not upon what the system can do for organisational objectives but upon what the system can do for its users in order that they are better able to serve organisational objectives. It brings the users and the social system into the planning and this can often lead to new ideas about the way in which information technology could be harnessed to serve the unique characteristics of the organisation. If further technical options are identified they can be put through the same impact assessment procedure to see whether they produce more positive outcomes. It is important that they are analysed in this way because, even if they have been specifically introduced to overcome some of the problem areas, they could create more problem areas for other groups of users.

If and when the outcome of this process is a technical system outline which looks acceptable, the next stage is to detail the technical and social systems and plan a design process for bringing it into operation. These stages are the subject of later parts of this book but the Appendix includes some check-lists to help in the planning of these activities.

Analysing the User/Task Requirements of a Socio-Technical System

Having identified an outline system that looks acceptable the next stage is to detail the specification of both the technical and social aspects. This is often the stage at which users are confronted by questions about their requirements which they find difficult to answer, for example: 'We are going to give you some management reports, what do you want in them?' To answer the questions about detailed requirements with authority we need a user/task analysis which will reveal needs.

The technique to be described here is 'Open System Task Analysis', devised by Eason and Harker (1980) as a form of analysis appropriate for tasks undertaken by individuals or work groups which employs (at a more detailed level of analysis) the same concepts as socio-technical systems analysis. It enables us, therefore, to take those parts of the overall socio-technical system which will be most affected by the proposed change and to explore their requirements in greater detail.

The aims of this level of analysis are to provide a statement of the criteria whereby the social system of the future will be constructed and to do the same for the technical system; to state what functionality will be required and, in the light of the social systems criteria, to specify usability and acceptability criteria. An account of the open systems task analysis used for this purpose is given in Harker and Eason (1985) and an example used in the Electricity Council case described earlier is to be found in Eason *et al.* (1989b).

The boundary for this analysis may be more limited than for the initial socio-technical analysis, for example the transactions performed at the counter by a group of cashiers rather than the entire operation of a branch of a Bank, but the principles for the analysis are the same. For convenience the various stages of the analysis are numbered in Figure 6.4 and the stages are listed below:

Figure 6.4
An open systems task analysis for user requirements specification

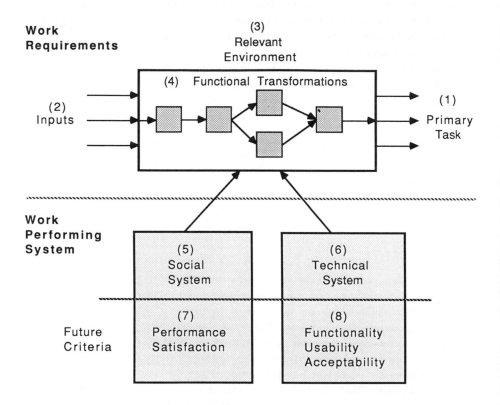

1. *Primary Task*. The analysis starts with a statement of the primary task of this particular work system, i.e. what is this person or group of people there to accomplish? This is not as straightforward as it might appear as there is usually a hierarchy of goals to be identified, and there are short- and long-term goals. An additional distinction can be made between task performance goals and system sustaining goals (i.e. make the product but not damage the equipment or the operator).
2. *Inputs*. The work system receives the materials, orders, etc. from outside the system and the character of these inputs frequently plays a large part in determining the way the system has to behave in order to achieve its primary goal. One of the main problems for an order processing system was, for example, that it had no control over the form in which the customers sent the order — it could be typed, handwritten or over the telephone. This socio-technical system had therefore to have the ability to cope with this range of inputs. The character, variation and predictability of inputs are important factors shaping the way transactions have to be handled.

3. *Environment.* As a mini-open system, the environment is likely to play an important part in establishing the work requirement. Since it is part of a larger work system much of the relevant environment may lie within the larger system and this may protect it from much of the external world turbulence. However, if the work system in question lies at the boundary with the outside world (for example, if it deals directly with the general public), it may have to cope with the full range of external conditions.

4. *Transformations.* Having established the external conditions it is next important to establish the functions that have to be undertaken to transform the inputs into out-puts fulfilling primary goal requirements. This is best done by an action/object framework, i.e. what are the objects that have to be transformed and what are the actions at each stage that can bring this about? For example, in a hospital the patient is the 'object' to be transformed from a sick state to a well state and per-forming operations, administering drugs, and conducting tests are the kinds of actions available to make this transformation. The analyst again has the problem that this analysis can be pursued to any depth, i.e. performing an operation on a patient can be described to the level of every cut the surgeon makes. In this context it is not appropriate to describe the current way of undertaking an activity in any detail but to concentrate on the purpose of the activity.

In addition to purposes other important information refers to the *relations* between activities, i.e. you have to pick up the telephone before you can answer the caller's query. The types of relations between functions that can exist are the same as described above for socio-technical analysis. Some activities may also be *time dependent*, i.e. there may be only a limited time frame in which an activity has to be undertaken if it it to be successful; a car driver, for example, must brake within a certain time frame before the red traffic light depending on the speed he is travelling. Perhaps the most important information to add to the description of the transactions is the *variations* that have to be taken into account in achieving them. In many cases the variations in the input conditions, or the pursuit of a slightly different goal, mean that a different set of rules must be applied in one case than another. For example, in the case described by Shackel *et al.* (1989) freight-forwarding clerks had to vary the way they completed the order form depending on the sequence in which customers were able to make information available. The human contribution to many seemingly routine tasks is often to adapt the content and sequence of the actions to fit the particular characteristics of this instance of the task. If the variants are not appreciated by the analyst, the system created to support the task may not be able to cope with the diversity of the task world.

5. *The Social System.* An examination of the social system that currently performs the work provides two kinds of information. It provides for a *role analysis*. It indicates the way the activities are currently allocated between individuals, i.e. what roles people play with respect to one another. As we will see in the next chapter on job design, the introduction of information technology usually changes this allocation whether or not it is the intention of designers. Understanding the current allocation patterns and their rules and rationale are therefore important parts of the analysis.

Secondly, the social system provides information for a *user analysis*, i.e. an exploration of the characteristics and qualities of the people who will ultimately become the users of the new system. There are many factors about users which may be relevant to the design of a system but the following are the main categories of information to be sought.

(a) Physical characteristics. Many of the terminal and workstation issues will ultimately depend on the sex, age and physical size of the user population.

(b) Skills and qualifications. Users who have typing skills, are already using computer systems or related tools (calculators, for example), will need to be treated differently from truly naïve computer users.

(c) Sources of stress and satisfaction. What is it about the current work system which provides job satisfaction and what is it that causes stress and frustration? A new system can succeed or fail to the extent that it facilitates the former and mitigates the latter.

6. *The Technical System*. The existing technical system may need analysis for two reasons. Firstly, the new system may only replace it in part and it may be necessary to ensure the new system is compatible with what remains of the old system and with the links that need to be made with other systems. Secondly, the existing *human–computer allocation* needs recording. This will indicate the degree to which the technology currently supports the users in the work they do and will show the degree of change that will be necessary if the new system is adopted. It is one important measure of the degree of change in the nature of work that is being considered.

7. *Criteria for a New Social System*. The information collected in the analysis can now be used to specify the requirements for the social system when the new technical system is introduced. The analysis provides a factual base for this process but it is essentially a judgemental activity in which users, both managers and their staff, need to consider what kind of social structure they want and need in the future. It will have to embrace criteria about the performance goals of the work system and the needs of the work-force for satisfying work. It is often the case that managers and their staff desire only minimal change in the social structure as the new information technology system is introduced. The processes by which people can participate in the design of jobs in this way are the subject of the next chapter. Suffice it to say at this stage that the task analysis described here is an important information base from which new options can be indentified and evaluated.

8. *Criteria for the New Technical System*. The task analysis also provides the work requirement that the new technical system must meet. It should, for example, serve to define many aspects of the functionality that will be required in the system. It will specify the information needed in any data bases, and the processing capability that will be required. The analysis of variations will also serve to specify the flexibility required in the system. It is not, however, a simple matter of matching the system to the task requirement. There are important matters of judgement to be decided such as the role of the technical system and the way its services will be allocated to members of the work-force. These issues will be examined in Chapter 8.

It is generally the case that the task requirement determines the functionality whilst the user analysis determines the usability and acceptability criteria for the technical system. It is the tasks which determine the information that has to be manipulated but the people who determine the way in which they will be able and willing to manipulate it. This is one reason why it is necessary to establish the criteria for the future social system before trying to establish the criteria for the technical system. The usability criteria will cover ease of use and ease of learning issues whilst the acceptability criteria cover the autonomy, control and responsibility issues, i.e. if it has been established that the future social system permits each person a certain degree of discretion in their work, this becomes a criterion to which the design of the technical system should adhere.

The Specification of a Prototype System

A few years ago it would have been necessary at this stage for the designers to put together a detailed conceptual solution, a theoretical vision of a technical system which could meet the requirements laid down for the system. The users would then need to judge this abstraction to determine whether it did indeed match their requirements and whether it had additional implications they did not want. The fact that the solution was only an abstraction, usually a set of flow charts, made this a difficult process for the users. With the advent of fourth generation computer languages there are now a variety of application generators available which can be used to 'rapid prototype' significant aspects of the proposed system. Using these tools, for example, it is possible to create screens and dialogues in the form that might be used in the real system and to allow users to interact with these to test whether indeed this form of technical system would meet their requirements. This provides a much more concrete version of the future system and there is growing evidence that it enables users to identify the good and bad points of proposed solutions in a way that was simply not possible with 'conceptual walkthroughs'. From the point of view of helping users to specify their requirements there can be little doubt that the development of these tools constitutes a major advance in systems design methodology. It has been suggested (Gilb 1988, for example) that these tools will actually lead to a major change in systems design methodologies so that development proceeds iteratively through the design and testing of prototypes. We will limit the present debate to a consideration of the user implications of these opportunities.

It is beginning to be quite common for a prototype version of a system to be built early in the design process and used to seek user agreement that it represents the form required for the operational system. There are, however, a number of common mistakes that are made that can limit the usefulness of this procedure:

1. *Technical or Socio-Technical Prototype?* The first problem is that the capability for rapid prototyping can cause designers to rush into constructing a technical solution forgetting that what is needed is a socio-technical solution. At this level a socio-technical solution has to specify how the functions that have to be performed are to be allocated between man and computer and how the human functions are to be allocated between different members of staff.

Before embarking upon the development of a technical prototype it is important that a form of task representation is produced of the kind depicted in Figure 6.5. This is not a new level of task analysis but a statement of how the proposed work-performing system would undertake the required work. It is an overlay of the functional requirements as shown in Figure 6.4 with the social and technical system that is to do the work.

Figure 6.5 shows the decisions that have been made about the allocations of functions between various members of the social system and between the users and the technical system. It will show where there are interfaces between human and machine and, because these are for specific users, will indicate the properties the interface will have to exhibit to be usable and acceptable. For example, if user 1 is an occasional, naïve user whereas user 2 is a full-time, computer professional the interfaces (1) and (2) will have to exhibit quite different properties.

2. *Prototype for Specification or Operational Use?* With a clear allocation of function target to work towards, a technical prototype can be developed. It has a very important role to play in enabling users to see the detailed issues of adopting this approach and can be invaluable in confirming, changing or elaborating the specification. Unfortunately, in many circumstances designers and users see the

Figure 6.5
A task representation of the proposed socio-technical solution

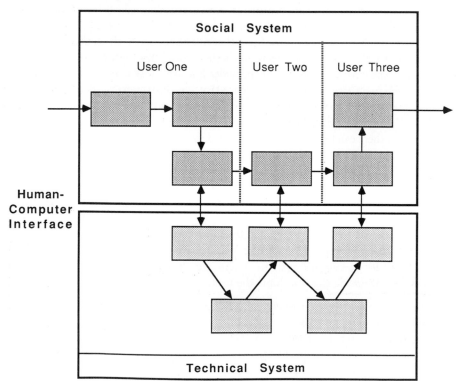

prototype as the early version of the final system and treat prototype evaluation as a proving trial. In these circumstances minor amendments may be tolerated but the realisation that the real system may have to be of quite a different character may be rejected. If the prototype is being used as part of the specification process it is better if everybody recognises that it will be thrown away before design work on the main system begins.

The Evaluation of the Prototype System

The main virtue of the technical prototype from the user's perspective is that it provides a means by which they can explore the reality of what having such a system in their organisation might mean. We need then a set of techniques by which to test the adequacy of the prototype and to explore its implications for the organisation. This is the detailed level equivalent of the impact assessment except that we now have an example of the technology upon which to base the assessment.

The power of the prototype to help users appreciate the consequences of the technical change is very great but unfortunately this potential is often lost in the way prototype trials are conducted. Frequently it is little more than a demonstration with the designers operating the system and then asking users for comments. The concrete reality of the system is usually sufficient to generate many valuable comments. The prototype reported in Eason *et al.* (1987) was used in this way and it led users to identify a number of ways in which the system would not have met their needs. However, this kind of trial does not make as much use of the value of the prototype as it could; in particular it does not help users experience potential usability problems. They need 'hands on' experience within a realistic task scenario before problems of this kind become apparent to them. There is therefore a need for an evaluation methodology which will enable users to test more fully the implications of a prototype solution and to revise their specification accordingly. The methodology described below and illustrated in Figure 6.6 is provided by Harker (1987a).

Figure 6.6
The conduct of prototype evaluations

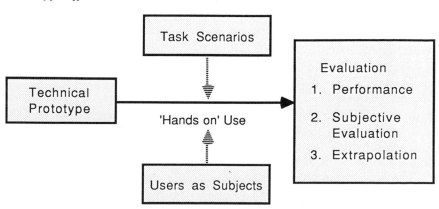

The general principle to be followed in user evaluations of prototypes is to provide a full and realistic experience so that users can make informed decisions about the specification. As Figure 6.6 illustrates this involves not only the creation of the technical prototype but the generation of appropriate task scenarios for a sample of users acting as subjects to work through in 'hands on' trials. This should provide experience which, if properly evaluated, should greatly enhance the user's understanding of the advantages and disadvantages of the system they could get. In what follows we will assume the prototype is being tested 'off line', i.e. in an experimental setting rather than being used by real users for real tasks.

The important feature of the technical prototype is that it should be a realistic representation of the likely operational system. As Harker says it should 'adhere to the design principles'. Since users respond holistically to the system they encounter there is little point mounting a screen format which conforms to the design criteria but putting it on a much larger screen than users will actually experience. Similarly a prototype based on a micro may achieve a very fast response time. There is little point in using this to prototype the dynamics of the system if the final system will involve the access of large data bases and will not achieve these rates of response. The prototype should be neither better nor worse than the expected system but a faithful copy of the characteristics to be expected. Unless this is the case users may be misled by the properties of the prototype which will not be in the full system.

It is important that users be given 'hands on' experience but they should not just play or try specific facilities. They will be able to make more informed decisions about their requirements if they work their way through a characteristic array of task scenarios. There might also be a case for doing a form of 'stress testing' of the prototype, i.e. trying an uncommon but real form of the task to see whether the user and prototype system can cope with the unusual as well as the normal demands. The people acting as subjects in these trials should be representative members of the intended user population in order that they have the characteristics of the ultimate users. The familiar and convenient procedure of using the designer at the next desk is not good enough; the designer is most unlikely to have the same characteristics as the ultimate users. The conditions of the trial should also be as close as possible to those expected in normal use. The subjects should be asked to take on the roles of the future users, usage should occupy the same time frame as the usage expected and, if training will normally be given, it should be given to the subjects.

It is possible to develop a programme of trials with all the scientific rigour of an experimental study, i.e. to test a variety of conditions (for example, different interfaces, different facilities, different tasks, etc.) with a large sample of subjects. Unless the results will influence major investment decisions it is unlikely that there will be the resources or the time to make such systematic studies. However, a great deal of valuable insight can be gained from a more focused study as long as the experience is valid, i.e. the technical prototype adheres to design criteria and is used for examples of real tasks by people who have the characteristics of real users.

User trials of this type can generate a number of kinds of information. The most obvious is the performance data of the subjects using the system, for example, the time taken to complete tasks and the errors made, etc. This data can be very helpful in assessing the quality of the interface, displaying gaps in the dialogue logic, poorly presented instructions, etc. Most of the interesting information, however, concerns the evaluations of the subjects about the degree to which the system would be able to cope with the real situation. This is why subjects with experience of the user situation are so important. These users will be able to say whether the procedures adopted by the system, the data it holds, the outputs it produces, etc. will match the needs of the real tasks and whether the use of the system is sufficiently easy for people to cope with under normal working conditions.

The prototype system also needs to be examined for the wider implications it may have within the organisation. It represents the detailed specification of the outline system assessed for impact earlier in the design process. It now needs examining again to check whether earlier assessments were correct, i.e. what will be the impact on job structures, power and influence, personnel policies, etc. Users who have acted as subjects and used the technical prototype generally feel more confident about making the assessments of impact (as contained in check list 1 in the Appendix) than they did at the earlier stage of design when there was a greater degree of uncertainty.

It would of course be preferable to mount a real trial of the prototype with real users using it for real tasks. It is then possible to see the direct impact and to try some alternative organisational arrangements (for example, different forms of job design). It is rare to have this kind of opportunity in part because prototypes usually have limited capability and can, for example, only perform part of the functionality required for the real tasks. However, we have worked on several projects where a system was used for real tasks as part of a specification process, i.e. at the end of the trial it would be withdrawn. It is quite common to run pilots and trials with systems before they are widely implemented but in this case we are only making a limited implementation for specification purposes. It is a process worth pursuing if the investment is going to be considerable because it provides the clearest evidence to all concerned of the value of the technical system and the organisational implications of its use.

Three examples can be given where this procedure was followed. In the freight-forwarding case (Shackel *et al.*, 1989) a trial was established in a branch and was used to explore several job structures within the branch. Subsequently the trial was extended to three branches to test the potential for inter-branch co-operation. This revealed the enormous organisational issues that would have to be undertaken and this part of the development was discontinued. Shackel *et al.* (1983) describe the BLEND experiment in electronic publishing which offered scientific workers this capability for a trial period. Again the trial revealed the many systems and organisational problems standing in the way of effectively harnessing the technology for this purpose. Finally, Pomfrett and Damodaran (1989) report the trial usage of an electronic mail system to link salesmen working from home with their regional office. Once again many system and organisational problems were encountered and the organisation concluded that the benefits to be gained did not warrant the development of the full system. In each case the study led to a fundamental rethink of the kind of system that would be relevant for the intended purpose.

Conclusions

The problems of establishing an appropriate specification for a system are considerable. The dangers of not getting it right are that a great deal of money will be spent producing a system which will not do the job for which it was intended or will be rejected by its intended users. The approach adopted in this chapter has been to proceed iteratively towards a more and more detailed specification. Each stage is informed by an analysis of the relevant task and user characteristics so that the target for the system is well established. The outline and prototype solutions established at each stage are expressed as socio-technical solutions in order to keep social and technical developments together and at each stage the impact of the solution is evaluated.

At the end of this process the end users and the designers have gone through a joint learning process and can be fairly confident about the specification of a system worth development. It is of course possible to carry the specification and evaluation processes into much greater detail. There are techniques available, for example, which will facilitate a fine grained representation of the tasks necessary to conduct the computer-based aspects of user tasks (for example, editing files, searching data bases, etc.), and of systematically checking the quality of technical systems designed to serve these tasks. The CLG (Command Language Grammar) method of Moran (1981) and TAKD (Task Analysis for Knowledge Descriptions) by Johnson (1985) are examples of such techniques specifically created for the design of human–computer interfaces.

Whether it is necessary or appropriate to carry the specification process to this degree of detail is dependent on the scale of the planned system and the investment that is involved. Similarly, whether powerful prototypes are developed and subjected to full systematic trials probably depends on the consequences of make wrong decisions. Whatever the effort put into deriving and confirming the specification, creating some opportunity to evaluate the potential impact is vital if the dangers of inappropriate systems are to be avoided.

The theme of this chapter has been specification which in most serial design methodologies comes neatly before the design of systems to meet the specification. By adopting an iterative and gradualist approach we have already begun to explore some of the issues involved in creating solutions. In the next two chapters we turn to a fuller examination of these topics. Since we have adopted a user-centred approach it is necessary that we consider design issues associated with the social system before we turn to the design of the technical system.

Chapter 7
Organisational Change
and Job Design

Introduction

The implementation of information technology leads to changes in the structure of jobs and other organisation practices. Frequently these matters are dealt with in an *ad hoc* way as problems arise and constitute a piecemeal and unsystematic way of changing from one form of organisation to another. It is a strange counterpoint to the planning of the technical system which is often highly structured and rational. The end result is often tension and conflict in the social structure and an under-utilised technical system. The aim of this chapter is to bring the job design and organisational change issues into the planning domain when information technology systems are being contemplated.

There are applications where it is obvious there will be major organisational change — where, for example, a major centralisation of clerical or secretarial staff is planned. Under these circumstances it is a case of finding appropriate techniques for handling a process that everybody recognises need attention. However, there are many other applications where the intention is to make a change in the available technology and organisation change is not on the agenda. Indeed in some cases it has been an explicit aim of the management to introduce the technology without disturbing organisational structures and procedures.

The social and technical sub-systems within an organisation are so tightly inter-related that a change in the technical system inevitably has knock-on effects in the social system. In circumstances where people do not want to make changes in the social system the result is often creeping pressures for change as the technology begins to be utilised. It is useful therefore to divide this chapter into two parts: the situation where organisational change is recognised and needs planning; and the situation where it is unwanted and unplanned. Lest any readers should feel they can skip this chapter because their system does not involve changes to the social system we will begin with this situation. We will first explore why changes in the social system are a necessary co-rollary of technical change.

From Technical Change to Organisational Change

We can look upon a work system as having a range of tasks to undertake to transform its raw materials into finished products and services. It is necessary to commit resources to undertake this workload. In organisational life this is done by a process of task specialisation in which resources are allocated parts of the workload. As Figure 7.1 illustrates, these resources are people and technology.

It is useful first to consider a finite workload divided between people and between individuals and their technology. What then happens when there is a change in the technology? The pattern that normally occurs, and has occurred throughout the Industrial Revolution, is that the technology plays a larger part in the undertaking of the work. From physically moving earth with a shovel the worker moves to earth-moving equipment which can cope with much larger loads than he can. From typing letters the secretary moves to a word processor which enables the work to be done twice as fast. In general there is a revised allocation of function such that the machine does more of the work. The effects on the individual are twofold. Firstly, if the workload remains the same, there is less to do. Secondly, the nature of the work changes; from direct 'hands on' the raw materials to be manipulated the person moves to a more indirect role, guiding and controlling the machine which acts directly on the raw materials.

What is the effect on these changes on the social structure? The change in the nature of the work means that different skills are necessary which means retraining or the selection of people with different qualifications. The decrease in individual workload means a reduction in the people employed or extra work being introduced from elsewhere. The extra productivity may be exactly what was wanted but its acquisition may cause disequilibrium in the social structure. If the person can do more

Figure 7.1
Changes in allocation of function as a consequence of automation

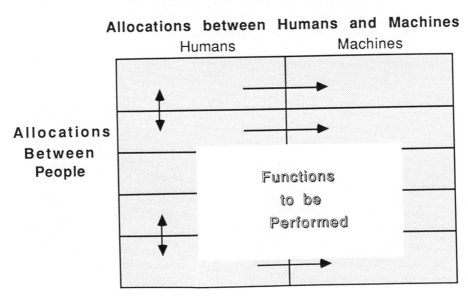

of the same without affecting anyone else, it may be possible for the system to continue as before. However, most organisational tasks are divided between people and when one part can do more or goes faster it affects other parts of the task chain. A common effect is that work is taken from some other job or that the greater productivity in one sector adds an extra burden to another sector that has not been aided by further technology.

Some examples may illustrate these pressures for change. In the City firm example Gower and Eason (1989) followed the progress of secretaries acquiring word processors when previously all long documents had been handled by a central word processing pool. Managers naturally preferred to have long documents done by their own staff and the extra power of the word processor enabled them to do this. But the firm wanted to keep the word processing pool. There developed a debate about what constituted a long document and arguments about a set of rules defining who does what. The effect is often that previous rules for allocating duties come under pressure when the technology changes. An obvious example is the way in which access to information technology means that journalists can submit their stories in an electronic form rendering obsolete the skills of the printers. In less obvious ways the same process is occurring wherever the spread of the technology gives people the opportunity to do for themselves tasks which previously required a specialist. If managers, for example, use word processing and electronic mail facilities for themselves, this obviously has an effect on the traditional role of the secretary.

Looking ahead a few years it is also possible to see that other common work relationships may be changed by the spread of the technology. What, for example, will become of the client–expert relationship when much of the expertise resides in an expert system directly available to the client? Whilst it would be foolish to suggest there will be no further need for the expert, there will obviously be a change in the nature of the work the expert is asked to undertake. Another interesting case is the system designer–end user relationship. Increasingly the technology puts the power to design systems directly into the hands of the end user; in what way does this change the role of the systems designer? This issue will be examined in Chapter 11.

Another example will show the effects of a knock-on in the task chain. In a Hospital case study, Eason *et al.* (1989a) found doctors able to make blocks of test requests because of a new system that made this process much easier than the manual, individually written, requesting procedure. The result was that the laboratories were overrun with test requests. They of course had received no additional technological support to cope with this unpredicted extra load and could not maintain the service the doctors relied upon.

Returning to Figure 7.1 the effects of the shift in individual allocations of function towards the technology is, in general, to put pressure on the allocations of work between roles in the same social structure. The rationale for the demarcation of roles is often undermined and there is a growing need to find a new set of rules. Since all work systems are open systems engaging with other systems beyond their borders there are also likely to be broader effects.

Recognising the Need for Job Design

Most information system implementations, and certainly small-scale changes, are planned as technical changes with no explicit intent to change the job structure. The outcome of a successful implementation, however, is likely to involve some degree of job change. If this is not to be fragmentary, unplanned and possibly dysfunctional there is a need for early recognition of the pressures and directions of change so that constructive action can be taken. Assessments of the likely changes can be made at two stages: (a) when the technical plans have been reasonably well laid, and (b) after implementation, when usage begins to grow and the impact begins to become apparent. We will look at what can be done to recognise job design implications in these two situations:

1. *Reviewing Technical Plans for Job Design Implications.* Let us assume that the plans for a technical system are well established and we know the equipment and software that will be available and to whom it will be made available. By using the structure depicted in Figure 7.1 we can trace the likely route of pressures for changes in jobs.

   Step 1: Examine the primary user roles to be affected by the technical system. What affect will the new allocation of function between the user and the computer have on the work to be done by the user? What will be the changes in work content and workload?

   Step 2: What will be the consequences in each primary work role of the shift in allocation of function to the computer? If, for example, the overall workload falls how is it intended that the vacuum will be filled? By reducing the number employed in the role, increasing the amount of work of that kind, or will the staff concerned (or their seniors) widen the work role to include other kinds of work?

   Step 3: What will be the consequences of any changes in primary role behaviour for related work roles? Look at the work roles that have task interdependencies with the changing roles and look for knock-on effects, i.e. if managers type their own letters, what happens to secretaries; if doctors order more tests on patients, what happens to the laboratory staff etc? The effects may spread through the task interdependencies into other sections and departments.

   As this analysis moves away from the allocation of function in the primary roles to the potential relations between other roles so it becomes more difficult to be sure of the effect. It will depend upon the behaviour of staff, choices made by management, etc. The analysis should be used to show the jobs and tasks allocated to jobs which will become problematic when the system is implemented and which should be the subject of job design debate and discussion.

2. *Reviewing Job Design Implications After Implementation.* In many cases the allocation of function in the primary roles only emerges after implementation. This is particularly the case when discretionary users (managers, professionals, etc.) are offered a range of technical facilities and it is a matter of their judgement which ones they choose to use and for what purposes. As their usage grows and takes shape so the implications for job design become apparent. This process may have all the

positive features of an evolutionary development in which people gradually learn to exploit more and more of the technical capability. However, it can be an unplanned form of evolution with unrecognised and possibly unwanted consequences for other roles, especially those of less discretionary users. A useful strategy in this situation is to make regular audits of the usage being made of the system and the inter-role impacts that are beginning to result. This is the procedure followed by Gower and Eason (1989) in following the evolution of usage of office automation in the City firm example. The steps are similar to those listed above but are now seeking actual changes:

Step 1: What allocation of function is emerging in the primary roles? How is this changing the work done and the workload? What kinds of plans do the staff have for further developments?

Step 2: Are these changes creating any anxiety among primary role holders, for example, secretaries in the City firm were becoming increasingly concerned that they were becoming word processor operators? What actions were staff taking to avoid negative effects?

Step 3: What were the implications of these changes for related roles i.e. how did the movement of the secretaries to becoming word processor operators affect the existing word processing pool?

A regular audit of the staff with most experience of system use can often show early signs of pressures for organisational change that will become much more widespread. It can function as an early warning system and can feed back information to policy-making bodies which can attempt to plan the organisational change rather than have it occur by piecemeal evolution.

The Process of Job Design

We have now identified three routes by which an organisation might decide a job design procedure is necessary. These are (a) where a major system is planned which will obviously include major organisational change, (b) where a technical change is planned but early analysis shows that there will be changes in job structure and demarcation and (c) where an evolutionary growth in usage is producing a gradual change in primary roles with consequent pressure on other roles. In all cases there is a need to plan future job structures if they are not to emerge in a haphazard and probably inefficient way. It is unusual to find this process a major item on the agenda of systems designers — possibly because technical systems designers would not see it as their responsibility or an area where they have expertise. It is therefore an area where the user community itself must take direct design responsibility. Two kinds of responses are possible.

1. *Maintaining the Status Quo.* It is possible to try to maintain the social structure as it is. This may be done because the current job structure is considered entirely satisfactory. It is more likely, however, that the designers concerned wish to adopt a minimum disruption policy and keep the development to technical change with

limited social system ramifications. It is important to note that, if this policy is adopted, it is not sufficient to do nothing about the social system; because of the interdependence between the technical and social system there will be knock-on effects and, if the aim is to keep the job structure, deliberate efforts must be made to sustain it in the face of the pressures for change. It may require efforts, for example, of the following kinds:

- The restriction of access to equipment or facilities on equipment to those who are officially responsible for the work that requires that equipment. The role of the photocopier operator, for example, became problematic, when everyone could use the photocopier. When journalists could enter their stories directly the role of the print workers was threatened.
- The restriction of access to information or the authority to change information. If it was your role to monitor information, and act on it, the role may be eroded if others, particularly your seniors, can do this without reference to you.
- The establishment of more precise rules about who does what in circumstances where access cannot be restricted, i.e. if everyone has access to a word processing package rules may be necessary to control who issues letters, reports, etc. In the City firm example there were debates about the length of documents secretaries should process, anything longer being the responsibility of the word processing pool.

Obviously actions of these kinds can be taken, but if they are needed on a large scale, the effect may be to create an elaborate structure which has no inherent logic to the user community who may find ways of subverting it. There have, for example, been cases of people making use of word processing surreptitiously in order to avoid the delays of the official procedure. Procedures which try to restrict the consequences of technical change can also have the effect of minimising the benefit to be gained from the technology. They make it difficult for the organisation to exploit the capabilities of the technology and contribute to its under-utilisation. What is needed is a way of safeguarding the interests and legitimate concerns of the user community without blocking useful progress. The process of participatory job design examines both individual and organisational needs in the exploration of alternative social structures.

2. *Job Design Procedures*. Job design is a process with an extensive tradition which has been widely used in manufacturing organisations. Davis and Taylor (1972) and Klein (1976) give many examples of this kind of application. Mumford has provided examples of job design applied to information technology systems in Rolls-Royce (Mumford and Henshall, 1979) and in ICI (Mumford, 1983b). Other examples are to be found in Eason and Sell (1981) and Hedberg (1980). Damodaran (1986) provides an example of building job design procedures into a structured design methodology.

In summarising these procedures in this chapter we will first examine the stages of the process and the roles people need to take in it. Then we shall look in more detail at the job design options that exist and the criteria for distinguishing between them. A presentation of some of the research of the impact of information technology systems upon jobs will then provide a basis for distinguishing between some of the job design options from the perspective of the job holders.

The general procedure for job design is summarised in Figure 7.2 and is broadly applicable whatever the scale of the organisational unit under consideration.

An important point of departure in this procedure is the selection of an appropriate organisational unit for the analysis. There is a tendency to choose a limited part of the organisation, for example, those work roles which are the primary target for the planned technical system. This can have the unfortunate effect of leaving out of the analysis the consequences of any change for closely related work roles. There are many examples of job design changes that could not be implemented because they encroached too much on other roles. The aim in establishing the unit of analysis should be to select that part of the organisation which is to be affected by the technical system and which is, to some degree, an autonomous whole, i.e. a unit serving a common purpose which it can accomplish without tight relations with other parts of the organisation. The overall socio-technical systems analysis procedure outlined in Chapter 6 will serve to identify such organisational entities and to show the links to related work systems which will have to be examined whenever a change is proposed.

Once the unit of analysis has been identified it is a question of eliciting design options, i.e. alternative ways tasks can be allocated to people to achieve work objectives. As we shall see later there are always many theoretical possibilities and the

Figure 7.2
Procedures for job design

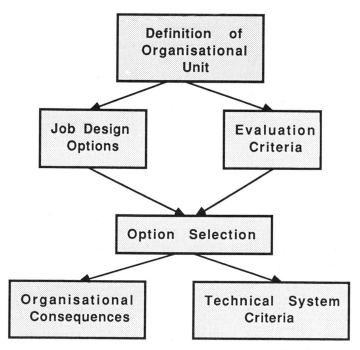

criteria by which the decision is made are particularly important. Different 'stake-holders' may place different priorities on the criteria and most job design specialists now adopt a participatory approach in which the relevant work-force play a full part in selecting an option which meets their requirements. Once an option has been agreed it will be necessary to establish the organisational issues to be settled before the option can be implemented, e.g. training requirements, pay and grading issues, agreements with trade unions, etc. There will be a similar range of issues with respect to the technical system, i.e. the computer system must be developed in a form suitable to support the planned social system.

The Job Design Options

People who are very familiar with a particular form of task allocation often find it difficult to think of alternatives. We will therefore examine two common work systems to illustrate the alternatives that are available. The first is an order entry system reported in Eason and Sell (1980) and summarised, as in Figure 7.3, in Eason (1984c).

This system is based on an analysis carried out in a company that had branches throughout the country taking orders from customers for its products. It had a paper-based system for stock control but it planned to move to an on-line entry system in which clerks could make a direct check of the availability of products, for example,

Figure 7.3
Alternative Job Designs in an Order Entry System, after Eason (1984c). (Reproduced from Health Hazards of VDTs?, *edited by B. Pearce, with permission of John Wiley & Sons, Ltd.)*

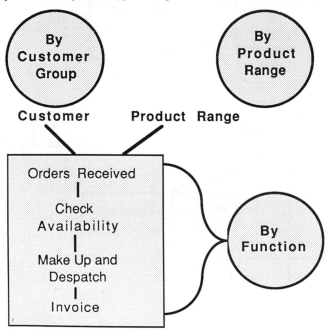

whilst the customer was on the telephone. It was apparent that this system would change the jobs of the people responsible for taking orders, making up orders and dispatching them and subsequently invoicing the customers. Figure 7.3 shows a simplified task description of the kind that would be produced by the methods summarised in Chapter 6 and identifies three different strategies by which job design could be approached:

1. *By Function*. The exisiting structure was based on a form of task specialisation in which staff undertook just one of the functions to be performed. Some staff received the orders, others checked availability, others dealt with invoicing and credit control, etc. Task specialisation is perhaps the most common form of job structure in industrial society.
2. *By Customer Group*. A possible structure is to ask each member of staff to deal with the orders from one customer or a small group of customers and to follow through all the stages necessary to fulfil the order.
3. *By Product Group*. The company offered a range of products which could be grouped by common characteristics. Another job design alternative would be to ask a member of staff to take care of all the orders for a product group and to handle the complete ordering cycle for these products.

It will be clear that these alternatives have different consequences for the organisation, its staff and the customers. However, before turning to the ways in which these alternatives might be evaluated, we will consider another example.

The second example is taken from the survey of text processing undertaken by Pomfrett *et al.* (1985). Figure 7.4 below shows the forms of work organisation associated with word processing.

Figure 7.4
Work organisation for text processing, after Eason (1984c). (Reproduced from Health Hazards of VDTs?, *edited by B. Pearce, with permission of John Wiley & Sons, Ltd.)*

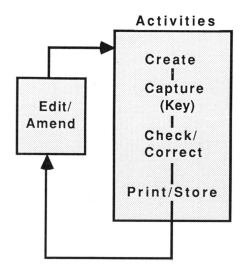

Activities

Create
|
Capture
(Key)
|
Check/
Correct
|
Print/Store

Edit/
Amend

Job Design Options

1. Author as Operator

2. Author-Operator
   Partnership

3. The "Pool"; Many Authors-
   Many Operators.

4. The "Pool"; Functional
   Sub-divisions

The functions required to process a document include its creation, typing it into a system, checking and correcting, printing and subsequent editing or amendment. In some organisations all of these activities were undertaken by one person (author as operator). In others the traditional manager–secretary relationship was maintained (the author–operator partnership). Another common structure was the word processing pool where many authors sent work to a group of operators and there was no personal link between the person creating the text and the person machining it. Finally, a number of functional subdivisions were found within some word processing pools so that different people did the first keying in, the checking, the printing and subsequent amendments. Again there are many options, some of which fragment the cycle of work and create task specialisms, and others which have one or two people responsible for the entire cycle.

In general where job design options are concerned there are usually three main ways in which work can be allocated: by functional specialisation; by product or service; or by orientation to the initiator of the work (the customer, supplier, manager, etc.). The degree to which these alternatives are followed produces different kinds of jobs and Figure 7.5 lists the main types which have been extensively studied in job design research.

Forms of Work Organisation

The alternative ways of combining tasks into jobs can be used to construct a number of forms of work organisation as illustrated in Figure 7.5.

If the main approach is to assign each person a specific function the result is a form of work organisation with task specialisation in which the overall task passes through a number of hands before completion — a very common form of work organisation. This approach means each person is engaging in a very small part of the total range of

Figure 7.5
Alternative forms of work organisation, after Eason (1984c). (Reproduced from Health Hazards of VDTs?*, edited by B. Pearce, with permission of John Wiley & Sons, Ltd.)*

1.	Task Specialisation
2.	Job Rotation
3.	Job Enlargement
4.	Job Enrichment
5.	Autonomous Work Groups

work and a variant which gives a wider range of work is job rotation in which staff rotate through the range of tasks that make up the total array, perhaps spending two or three hours on each specialist operation. Rather than rotate through the tasks another approach is job enlargement in which other tasks are added to the specialism to give a wider, permanent set of responsibilities. This is sometimes known as horizontal job enrichment because there is a tendency to combine unrelated tasks into the job. This adds variety but little extra meaning to the job. The alternative is vertical job enrichment, an approach developed by Herzberg (1968) an example of which can be found in Paul *et al*. (1969). A job is enriched vertically when the task array is enlarged by including all the tasks necessary to undertake the larger scale task. If a person has hitherto been putting the wheels on a toy car, the job would be vertically enriched if he were asked to assemble the entire vehicle and perhaps subsequently to test it for quality.

These approaches are all based upon concepts of individual job design, i.e. each person is assigned a specific array of task responsibilities. An alternative, most associated with socio-technical systems theory, is the semi-autonomous working group. In this case a large task is assigned to a group of staff who are given sufficient autonomy to allocate the component tasks among themselves. This is an old established form of work organisation. Trist *et al*. (1962) found that the traditional form of work organisation in coal mining was a group of self-selected workers, probably close relatives, who took responsibility for a particular coal face almost on a sub-contract basis and shared the income between themselves. There are now many examples of the deliberate creation of working groups of this kind, a well-known example being the Volvo Kalmar plant where the traditional paced assembly line was rejected in favour of separate work areas where work groups could assemble larger components of vehicles, for example, the whole transmission (Blackler and Brown, 1980).

It will be apparent that division of labour by function leads to a form of work organisation based upon task specialisation but that divisions based on product, service, customer, or supplier criteria are likely to produce forms of work organisation closer to job enrichment or semi-autonomous working groups.

Criteria for Evaluating Alternatives

When the introduction of information technology creates opportunities for rethinking the organisation of work many of the alternatives described above may become possibilities. How is one to choose between them? A list of the categories of evaluation criteria that might be considered relevant is given in Figure 7.6.

The criteria in Figure 7.6 are broadly listed in the order in which they are weighted in the design of most forms of work organisation. It is a common experience that decision-makers feel that all the criteria are important but that when decisions have to be made and trade-offs have to be found, it is the first four categories that dominate.

We will examine how these evaluation criteria relate to the work organisation options by using the two examples presented earlier in the chapter. Some forms of

1.	**Cost**
2.	**Productivity**
3.	**Technical**
4.	**Tradition**
5.	**Organisational Effectiveness**
6.	**Health and Welfare**
7.	**Satisfaction and Motivation**

work organisation are cheaper than others. For example, the reason often given for moving to a centralised word processing pool is that staff reduction can be made; a smaller group of central staff can cope with the same workload as a larger number of secretaries serving individual managers. The effect of making this decision on cost grounds is, of course, to produce more task specialisation and greater communication difficulties along the task chain. Efforts to achieve greater immediate productivity in terms of the numbers of key strokes captured, the number of enquiries processed, etc. can lead in the same direction. The best way to maximise the output of a particular function is to make it the responsibility of a particular person and make sure they are highly trained and highly practised. Technical considerations can lead in the same direction. If, for example, we want to minimise the number of terminals we want to purchase we will want a high rate of productivity from each terminal. We cannot have a solution therefore in which everybody has a terminal they use only occasionally. A terminal shared between a number of people might be possible but it is unlikely to achieve a high rate of productivity. This is because the individuals using it will not be as highly practised as a full-time operator and sharing produces scheduling problems which reduce productivity. In the study of Freightforwarding, for example (Shackel *et al.* 1989), having to share a terminal between three caused staff to have to create temporary paper records until they could get to the terminal.

The effect of traditional forms of work organisation also has a major effect. This may be because it enshrines the existing demarcation agreements and supports current policies on grading and payment. It may also be because it is what people are familiar with and reduces the degree of change and uncertainty they may have to accept. Since most existing forms of work organisation are based on task specialisation this tends to confirm this kind of approach. It may serve to accentuate the effect, as the need to fulfil the function 'data entry' is met by creating a new job called 'data entry clerk' rather than disturb any existing jobs by adding this function to them.

The first four sets of criteria in Figure 7.6 reinforce the existing tendency to adopt task specialisation forms of work organisation. The other criteria tend to encourage the selection of other options. If the objective is long-term organisational effectiveness as measured, for example, by the ability to develop good customer relationships, the flexibility to adapt to changing circumstances, etc. a form of work organisation is needed which develops staff as multi-skilled, flexible individuals who can adapt to changing demands. A form of work organisation based on job enrichment which allows an individual clerk to process the complete orders for a specific customer may, for example, be the best solution to the order processing example if the object is to enhance customer service. Work organisation structures which allow the individual to follow a complete cycle or, as in semi-autonomous working groups, allow groups of workers to agree their work patterns, creates multi-skilled and flexible staff who are then ideal resources for a flexible and adaptive organisation. It has to be recognised, however, that this kind of arrangement may involve short-term costs; to become multi-skilled, for example, an individual has to be trained in all the tasks not just the one in which they might specialise.

An important criterion in the working environment is the health and safety of the work-force but it might be a surprise to find this criterion related to the choice of work organisation. There is considerable evidence, however, that some forms of work organisation create more stress and health problems than others. Most of the reports of health problems in the use of visual display units (Pearce, 1985) come from circumstances where people are using this equipment on a full-time basis. The people who are at most risk are those who have a repetitive function to fulfil which ties them to the computer-based workstation for long periods in a constrained posture. The human body is not designed to be fixed in one position for a long period and using a visual display unit under these conditions produces visual fatigue, backache, neckache, etc. (Hünting, 1984). Designing the workstation and the environment to be a good fit with the characteristics of the operator can mitigate against these stress reactions but a more effective solution is to create a job which involves a variety of activities, some of which do not involve using a visual display unit. This kind of consideration leads therefore towards job rotation, enlargement and enrichment solutions.

The final set of criteria are those that concern the motivation and satisfaction of the employee. This is a complex topic because what gives satisfaction to one person may not give satisfaction to another. Researchers have devoted a lot of effort to trying to establish criteria for a 'good' job and some of the conclusions of this work are expressed in Figure 7.7. This list is the work of the Work Research Unit (Tynan, 1980) which is a group backed by Trade Union Council, the Confederation of British Industry and the British Government to develop recommendations for good work organisation practice. Although it has no statutory power this list is therefore as near as Britain comes to an official definition of the properties to strive for in job design.

Figure 7.7
Job design criteria (Tynan, 1980), reproduced from Eason (1984c)

TASKS SHOULD AS FAR AS POSSIBLE:

Form a Coherent Job

Make a Significant and Visible Contribution

Provide Variety of Method

Allow Feedback on Performance

Entail the Use of Discretion in Carrying out the Work

Carry Attributable Responsibility for Outcomes and Particularly Control of Work

---

The criteria are expressed as the way tasks should be combined to make up the job. The important elements from the job holder's perspective are that there should be a variety of tasks that relate together to form a coherent whole. The task performer should have a degree of discretion in carrying out tasks and should be able to obtain adequate feedback to assess and improve performance. Finally, completing the job should enable the job holder to make a significant and visible contribution to the performance of the overall work system and the performer should carry responsibilities for the outcomes of his work. These criteria cannot be used to fix the requisite amount of variety or discretion, etc., because these will vary from person to person, but they do express the dimensions that are important and they demonstrate, for example, that machine pacing is likely to be a problem because it removes discretion over timing from the job holder.

These criteria once again suggest that the task specialisation forms of work organisation will not yield the same degree of job satisfaction as those which give task variety and discretion, e.g. job enrichment and semi-autonomous working groups.

The fact that the different criteria would lead to different forms of work organisation being chosen lends added weight to issues of who makes the decisions and by what means. If there is no forum charged with responsibility for job design, the form of work organisation will emerge as a consequence of other decisions taken, for example, about technical and cost considerations and this will favour forms of task specialisation. If the forum making the decisions is predominantly technical designers the outcome is likely to be the same. It is often the case that designers will express the desire to create a solution that is, for example, healthy and satisfying for employees but will achieve a solution which is neither. Hedberg and Mumford (1975) demonstrated this in a study of the values held by designers in Britain and Sweden. The reason that these values are not expressed in the solution is either that other values took priority in the decision-making or that designers knew how to achieve technical goals but not human motivational goals. In either case it is important that the forum making the decisions is predominantly the managers and staff of the user departments who will have to make the work organisation function when it is introduced. It is also important that they use methods which make explicit the goals that are being sought and examine each option in relation to these goals.

The technique we have used for this purpose has the following stages:

1. The elicitation of work organisation options by a 'brainstorming' activity in which all alternatives are listed without evaluation. It is useful to start with the basic alternatives, i.e. division by function, product, service, customer, etc. and then look at the hybrid possibilities, e.g. some functions on some products. The reason for 'brainstorming' is that people have a strong tendency when an alternative is voiced to list immediately the reasons why it is not possible and this can quickly stifle creativity with the result that some potentially valuable options may not be suggested.
2. The identification of the advantages and disadvantages of the different options. Each option will have advantages and difficulties with perhaps different stances being taken by the different parties around the table.
3. Identifying and weighting the criteria. The process of evaluating each option throws up the many goals and values that are important and it can be useful to list these as criteria and try to give them weightings. When this has been done it is relatively easy to go back to the list of options and identify a short list of possibilities that are worth further consideration.

This process encourages a wide ranging debate of opportunities and works to prevent tradition and short-term expediency from dominating decision-making. Its function is to ensure that other possibilities get onto the agenda and are thoroughly considered. It may well be that the solution adopted is a form of task specialisation based upon the traditional work divisions in the organisation. It will have been adopted, however, as a result of comparison with other possibilities.

The Impact of Information Technology on Jobs

In order to evaluate the desirability of different alternatives it is necessary to be able to predict their effects. There have been many studies of the impact of information technology systems upon jobs and these studies provide useful information on the kinds of impact of different alternatives. The comments presented above of the consequences of the different alternatives were largely based on non-information technology studies and this research enables us to check the degree to which the findings are relevant to information technology systems.

The first conclusion from this research is that whilst information technology systems do lead to job changes there is no 'technical determinism', i.e. the changes may be of many different types. Although the diversity is large there is one distinction which offers a way of summarising many of the changes and this is presented in Figure 7.8.

Two views of the likely impact of information technology upon jobs have been promoted. The first is the 'deskilling' hypothesis which says that computers take work from people, rob them of the opportunity to use their skills and leave them performing routine, monotonous duties. The second is the 'enrichment' hypothesis in which the computers take the routine aspects of the work and leave the people with the creative work and a powerful information handling tool to help them with their work. These hypotheses could not be more different and there is evidence to support both of them.

The 'deskilling' approach is represented by the left-hand column in Figure 7.8. There are a number of examples of cases in the literature which show most of the characteristics in the column. Wainwright and Francis (1984) give an example of an insurance company and Fallik (1987) describes a system used by the United States Internal Revenue both of which are organised in this way. The objective which most characterises this approach is that the organisation was looking for a way of bringing a work process under closer control and either getting a higher level of productivity or managing the workload with fewer people.

If this is the objective the information technology may be used as an agent to control the work process. It may do this by providing a means of engaging in the work process which structures the work, renders it repetitive and requires little skill. It can also be used to pace the work, for example, by feeding new work to a person as soon as the previous work is completed. The work may be so centred on the computer system that there is no reason for the member of staff to leave their workstation and this can lead to feelings of social isolation. Finally the computer can be used to monitor performance. Since the work is being undertaken on the system, the computer can log what is done, down to every keystroke if necessary, and performance assessments can be passed on to superiors. Alternatively a supervisor can 'look in' and see what each member of staff is doing at any time. This kind of monitoring can be done so that the member of staff knows when it occurs but it can also be done without the knowledge of the person being observed. The practice of monitoring has become very common in the USA to the extent that white collar unions are working to ban at least the undeclared form of monitoring (Congress of the United States 1985).

In nearly every respect this form of job fails the test of the job design listed in Figure 7.7 and it is not surprising to find that staff treated in this way report dissatisfaction. They also report being stressed by the degree to which they are controlled, paced and isolated, apart from the stresses caused by continuous engagement with repetitive VDU operations. The effect on the organisation is often that a higher degree of productivity is achieved or a smaller resource pool is necessary. This may be achieved, however, at the expense of creating a formal and inflexible control system

Figure 7.8
The impact of information technology upon jobs

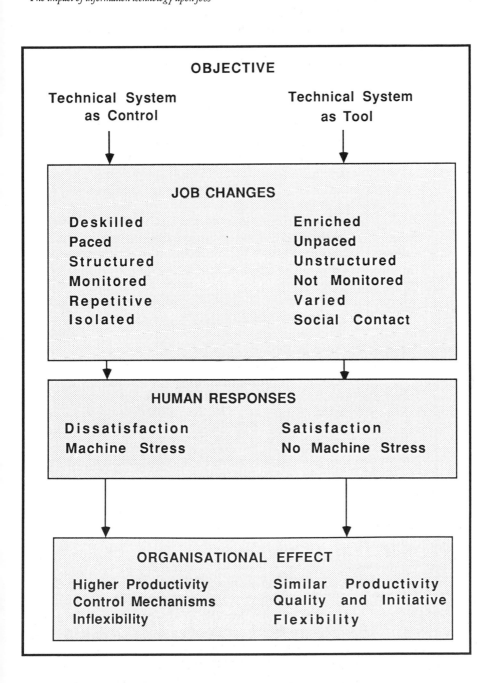

OBJECTIVE

Technical System
as Control

Technical System
as Tool

JOB CHANGES

Deskilled	Enriched
Paced	Unpaced
Structured	Unstructured
Monitored	Not Monitored
Repetitive	Varied
Isolated	Social Contact

HUMAN RESPONSES

| Dissatisfaction | Satisfaction |
| Machine Stress | No Machine Stress |

ORGANISATIONAL EFFECT

Higher Productivity	Similar Productivity
Control Mechanisms	Quality and Initiative
Inflexibility	Flexibility

and of reducing staff to resources of limited capability who are neither willing nor able to respond to change.

Fortunately this black picture of the effects of information technology refers to the minority of applications. Most studies of the impact of information systems upon job satisfaction report increases. Bjørn-Andersen *et al.* (1979), for example, reporting a multi-national survey of the impact of computers upon bank clerks, concluded that the dominant effect was an increase in job satisfaction because their jobs had been enriched. Other studies have shown that the most common characteristic of systems which have this effect is that they are perceived by their users as a tool to help them engage in their work and their work takes them beyond the system to serve the customers of the bank, to arrange holidays for customers, to handle the accounts for clients, etc. Where the system serves as a tool in this way it usually offers users a choice of service and method, does not pace them and provides no performance monitoring. The outside world is the stimulus for a variety of work and for social contact. The usual reaction to questions about the effect on job satisfaction is that the new, more powerful tool allows the work to be performed more effectively which is a source of satisfaction. None of the sources of stress associated with full-time repetitive use is mentioned although there may well be stresses caused by the demands of those for whom the work is undertaken, especially if their expectations rise because of the introduction of the computer system.

For the organisation the effect of having a system which changes jobs in these ways does not greatly improve direct productivity, although it would be unlikely to decrease, but it may well lead to better quality work and may enable staff to show initiative in extending the capability they bring to their work. One way of expressing what can happen is that the information technology system does the lower level functions of sorting, storing and processing information, thus enabling the human partner to operate at a higher level in planning what needs to be done, examining new possibilities, dealing with the unusual, etc. This may well mean the organisation acquires more flexible resources capable of responding well to demands for change.

It would be wrong to cast every application in the 'deskilling' or the 'enriching' category. Clearly many have elements of tool usage as well as elements of control. In some cases the effect may be different for different groups of staff; it may provide a tool for managerial and professional staff but be a control system for clerical staff.

Preparations for Organisational Change

One view of information technology is that it is a way of enabling us to contemplate alternative organisational forms freed of many of the constraints that have defined existing forms. We do not, for example, have to have secretaries, typists, etc. if everyone can perform these activities for themselves. The problem is that greater freedom always makes choice more difficult and drives people back to basic questions about what is worthwhile achieving and what has priority. The examination of the research evidence about the impact of information technology upon jobs shows that the implementation of the technology presents some stark choices. It can be character-

ised as an alternative between tight control and minimal resources (with the consequences of human stress and organisational inflexibility) and the introduction of
powerful and flexible tools which might lead to innovations in the business and the
greater use of human potential (at the cost of considerable organisational change and
human learning). This is an over-simple dichotomy but gives an indication that an
organisation seriously contemplating the use of the technology will have to look
deeply at the goals and values it espouses.

It is not the purpose of this book to advocate a particular set of goals and values
which should drive this decision-making process, although the extreme forms of task
specialisation and tight control are so stressful for job holders and inflexible for the
organisation that they must be challenged as inhumane and counterproductive. Many
other alternatives remain, however, and selection among them must be made by the
informed stakeholders of the organisation.

Once consensus has emerged on the strategic direction to be taken when the
technology is implemented there will be many preparations to be made for the
necessary organisational changes. The implementation of the changes will be discussed
in Chapter 9 but Figure 7.9 lists the important issues to be considered in developing
the plan for organisational change.

Figure 7.9
Preparing for organisational change

Detailing the Organisational Structure

Establishing Responsibilities
Allocating Tasks
Defining Communication and Control Systems
Establishing Manning Levels

Facilitating the Change

Definition of Skills and Knowledge
Training, Recruitment and Team Building
Physical Space Provision
Pay and Conditions
Job Evaluation, Grades and Career Progression
The Costs of Transition

Managing External Relations

The Impact on Other Work Roles
The Impact on Other Departments, Customers, etc.
Industrial Relations Agreements

The broad strategic form of the proposed organisational structure has first to be developed in detail. This involves the identification of the specific work roles and the establishment of the responsibilities associated with each role. Within these responsibilities it becomes possible to identify the particular set of tasks which each work role will undertake. The relations between work roles can also be specified and the strong relations should accord with the areas within the task structure where strong interdependencies exist. The relationships to be defined include monitoring and control procedures and also communication procedures to facilitate collaboration between roles. An important part of the process is the establishment of manning levels; i.e. how many people will occupy each of the work roles.

The process of establishing the organisational structure holds within it a particular dilemma. If the designers get enthusiastic they may define the structure in great detail so that it is rational and comprehensive. There will be a desire on all sides to do this so everyone can know what is planned and uncertainty can be reduced. However, taken to extremes this process destroys later discretion; it gives neither managers nor staff the opportunity to develop the structure in their own ways, to experiment and change the structure with experience. A fully detailed work role specification may well rob the holder of the autonomy which makes it worthwhile as a job and the organisation of flexibility it needs to cope with the demands of change. The process of establishing the organisational change has therefore to be governed by the principle of minimum critical specification. In effect this means that responsibilities and tasks should be specified without detailing how they should be executed. The boundaries of discretion should be defined without establishing how that discretion should be executed. It is perhaps more important to establish the relationships between work roles than it is to detail the content of the work role. If a structure based on individual work roles is being defined, the relationships can be made explicit. However, if the intention is to create team working within the philosophy of the semi-autonomous working group, even this level of detail is too great because, within the working group, there must be discretion to establish roles and relationships. The planners of working groups should be more concerned with the boundaries of the groups, the relations with management and other groups, than with the internal working of the group.

Once the structure has been developed the procedures necessary to facilitate the introduction of the change can be identified. An obvious requirement is the establishment of the skills and knowledge needed to fulfil the new work roles and, following from this, the development of a training programme to equip staff with this expertise. It may be necessary to design a recruitment policy if new staff are needed to fill some of the roles. The obvious need to specify the operational skills required should not obscure the need to help people develop the ability to work in the new structure, i.e. team building exercises may be necessary where the occupants of new roles are given the opportunity to explore the nature of the role and to build relations with those who will occupy similar and related work roles. Such exercises can ensure that when the new organisational form is implemented, the job holders have a clear idea of what is expected of them and what they can expect of others.

Facilitating the new organisational form also involves a consideration of the physical space it will occupy, the furniture it will require, etc. Many a new organisational form has foundered because, for example, it was not possible to get all the people who were supposed to work closely together under one roof. The geographical structure has to reflect the organisational structure. There are also particular problems when the new structure creates new demands for communication. In Sweden, for example, the enthusiasm for shopfloor semi-autonomous work groups created a demand for meeting rooms within the shopfloor because you cannot hold planning meetings effectively in the middle of a noisy machine room.

The new organisational structure may also lead to changes in many personnel policies. The new jobs with their different skill requirements may, for example, score differently on job evaluation criteria when compared with the existing jobs. If this is the case there may be demands for changes in grades, pay structures and other conditions of employment. The new structures may also change traditional patterns of career development in the organisation, the consequences of which will have to be examined for manpower planning purposes.

Finally, the change process has to be facilitated by developing an implementation strategy which examines the cost of transition. A strategy of this form seeks to specify the activities that must occur to move the organisation from its existing form to its new form and will include a timetable for all the issues described above as well as the technical changes that must occur. The nature of the implementation strategy will be examined in Chapter 9. The need at this point is to outline the strategy so that the existing structure can be phased out (which may include issues of redundancy, transfer and early retirement) and the new structure can be phased in. In most situations this has to be accomplished whilst normal business is being undertaken. The costs of this process are often underestimated with the result that the change takes a lot longer than planned and people are underprepared for the new ways of working. One consequence of making the transition whilst working normally, for example, is that extra staff may be needed on a temporary basis so that other staff can be retrained. This is often a difficult concept for management to grasp if the overall objective in the longer term is staff reduction.

In preparing for change within the target user organisation there is a natural tendency to concentrate upon the effects within the unit. This unit does not exist in isolation and therefore the preparation also has to look at the impact upon external relations and establish policies about any changes that may be necessary.

The first requirement is to look at associated work roles that may be changed. It is common in job design work to discover, for example, that changing the nature of the jobs of operational staff changes the work of managers and supervisors. One of the consequences of job enrichment on the shopfloor, for example, has been 'the erosion of the role of the foreman'. If more responsibility for organising work passes to the individual worker what becomes of the person who previously scheduled the work? Where this kind of change has been introduced the role of first line management has usually changed from organising and instructing to facilitating and training, i.e. ensuring staff have the resources to do the work and have developed the skills to complete it. This is often a major role change and requires its own training programme. Other roles that may be changed if a job enrichment approach is adopted include quality control, maintenance and planning (where elements of these activities may be undertaken by operators). Other kinds of changes may have other influences and a mapping of the effects is essential if the change programme is to go smoothly.

There may be other, broader influences that need recognition and action. The user department may change the demands it makes on other departments of the organisation which may cause those departments to resist the change. The effects may be indirect, for example, a change in a grading of some staff because of job changes may cause unrest among staff in other departments who have previously been treated as comparable to the staff undergoing the change. The effects may stretch outside the organisation to involve suppliers, agents and partners. Frequently the customer may experience a significant change, as, for example, when the public are offered banking services via cash dispensers. All of these changes need early identification and the development of policies on similar issues to those discussed above. Many of the changes may affect the existing industrial relations agreements in the organisation and it will be necessary to take the proposals to the relevant negotiating bodies at an early stage. One of the most common reasons for protracted delays in implementing systems is that agreement for changes has not been procured through industrial relations machinery, often because there was no clear view of the job changes that would result until the technical system had been designed. One good reason for dealing with organisational change at the same time as technical design is that the industrial relations consequences can be recognised early and the due process entered into at an early stage.

Conclusions

Job design is not a topic that will be found on the critical path of many system development methodologies. As a result organisational changes issues are usually dealt with in an *ad hoc* fashion late in the development process. At best this leads to delays in implementation; at worst it leads to rejection of the system. This chapter has presented a process which looks at the options and the goals early in the process and begins work on the policies necessary to bring about the selected forms of organisational change. It is not a process that belongs to the technical designer but a central process that user management and end users need to undertake if they are to establish the future work practices they need and want.

In this chapter we have not considered the technical consequences of the organisational changes, apart from noting the way in which technical innovations lead to organisational change. If we start by planning the organisational change there will be many consequences for the design of the technical system. We need a system which will support the job structure we seek to implement. The issues this raises for the selection and design of the technical system are the subject of the next chapter.

Chapter 8
Designing the Technical System for Human Use

Introduction

The selection and design of an information technology system will inevitably involve many technical issues but it must also meet user and organisational requirements. An effective socio-technical system depends upon the compatibility of the two sub-systems. In this chapter we will look at the demands the social system places upon the technical system and how they translate into design criteria. The accent upon human issues will produce a set of criteria which are different from the normal set a technical specialist may use when 'shopping' for a system, for example, cost, reliability, compatibility with existing equipment, capacity, speed, etc. The aim in this chapter is to add to the normal list rather than to replace it and thus to ensure that systems are chosen and developed that are both technically sound and will fit the organisational context.

It is convenient to classify the set of criteria to be examined under four broad areas that have already been presented as human and organisational requirements:

1. *Functionality*. The technical specification must cover the functions the system will have to be able to perform in order that it can support the required range of organisational tasks.
2. *Usability*. The system must offer its functionality in such a way that the planned users will be able to master and exploit it without undue strain on their capacities and skills.
3. *User Acceptability*. The system must offer its services in a way which its users will perceive, as a minimum, as not threatening aspects of their work they hold to be important, and, ideally, they will perceive it as positively facilitating goals they wish to pursue.
4. *Organisational Acceptability*. The organisation at large has goals, policies and structures and the system must not only serve immediate task needs but must not impede other aspects of organisational functioning. Ideally it will serve as a vehicle to promote wider organisational goals; as a minimum it must provide an 'organisational match'.

In general these criteria reflect the fact that, like any newcomer, the technical system has to serve the specific tasks for which it is introduced but also has to fit the wider, pre-existing context in which it has to operate. Many of the topics that will be discussed are already matters of concern to people purchasing and developing systems but are couched in general terms such as 'it must be user friendly'. If it is not possible to be specific about terms of this kind, or to illustrate how much better one system is than another on this criterion, the factor is not likely to weigh heavily in purchase decisions in comparison, for example, with measurable criteria such as cost and capacity. In examining these issues, therefore, it is necessary, as Bennett (1979) and Shackel (1984) have pointed out in relation to usability, to operationalise these goals as assessable criteria. In this chapter we will be presenting these issues and examining how they may be operationalised.

It will not be possible in one chapter to offer solutions, i.e. to state how the criteria might be met. This is because there are many ways of technically meeting a criterion and developments in the technology continue to offer new and better solutions. It is also because, as Harker and Eason (1984) point out, the way of meeting a particular criterion is often 'contingency dependent', for example, what is easy to use for one set of users in one situation is hard to use for a set of users somewhere else. The criteria will need interpreting according to the user and task specifications developed by the methods described in Chapters 6 and 7. There is a growing body of human factors literature describing standards, guidelines and other formulations of knowledge that offer specific solutions for different criteria. Reference will be made to this literature as each criterion is examined.

Functionality

The single most important feature of a system to its user is that it should provide a way of serving the user's task needs. If it does not do this all other issues become irrelevant. The functionality provided by the system is therefore a primary consideration. Figure 8.1 identifies some of the major issues in meeting the need for functionality.

The requirement for functionality emerges from the task analyses described in Chapter 6 totalled across the relevant user population. One way of serving these task needs is to provide a facility to match each need so that when, for example, the airline check-in clerk calls up the flight details the facilities presented should be an exact match with the tasks that have to be undertaken. This is the ideal for the user; the system does exactly what is required, no more and no less. This is appropriate and possible for *well structured tasks* of a clerical nature but is more difficult when the tasks vary considerably from one user to another and from one occasion to another. This must be the case with the ill-structured tasks of discretionary users but can also be true of seemingly well structured tasks. What appears to be a routine activity often has many subtle variations which the human operator adapts to but a pre-programmed machine does not. There are many examples in the literature of attempts at exact matches which have misfired (for example, Buchanan and Boddy 1983, Eason *et al.*, 1989b, Shackel *et al.*, 1989), with the result that the user has to engage in compensatory activity and extra work to meet the task need. Exact matches with the task world are probably best attempted when the nature of the task world can be acceptably determined for the user, possibly

Figure 8.1
Meeting user needs for functionality

Analysis	Task Variables	System Criteria	Consequences
Task Analysis	Well Structured	Task-System Match	Prototypes and Trials
User Population Analysis	Ill Structured	Flexibility Adaptability Customisation	User Support Customisation Support

because the user is unfamiliar with the task—a member of the public using a computer for a consumer service, for example. Where attempts are made in design to create screens and dialogues to match the needs of well-structured tasks it is important that prototypes are created and user trials undertaken to ensure that the assumptions made about the structure of the tasks are valid.

Developments in the technology and the recognition of the variety of specific user task needs that have to be met have led to the creation of much more flexible systems. These systems have a wide range of available functionality and give the user many facilities whereby the work of the system can be matched more exactly to the specific needs at the time. Where there are many users to be served or the needs of the user are not stable, i.e. where the tasks are *ill structured*, this would seem to be the best solution. It is, however, a route leading to many problems. There is a tendency for supplier and purchaser to go for the system with the widest range of functionality; to choose the system with the longest 'tick list' of functions. The current development of multi-functional workstations is one manifestation of this phenomenon. If you can have every facility in one system as a flexible capability you do not, in theory, need to bother with detailed task analysis, because it is more than likely the system will be able to do whatever the user later decides is necessary. The problem is that the flexibility is gained at the cost of complexity which makes the system difficult for the user to use. Too much functionality is gained at the expense of usability.

There is now considerable evidence of what users do when confronted by systems that offer them a lot of functionality. In one example (Eason, 1989) a study in branch banking showed that, of 36 on-line functions branch staff could use to obtain information about a customer's account, five accounted for 75% of usage. Half of the functions were rarely used although each of them was designed with a common banking task in mind. In a similar study Hannigan and Kerswell (1986) reported that of 25 functions available on advanced private automated telephone exchanges (PABXs) 10 facilities accounted for 83% of usage. Reporting a similar phenomenon in the USA, Smith (1984) notes that under-utilisation is particularly striking among users of multi-functional workstations. Even the computer professionals are not immune from this effect. Sutcliffe and Old (1987), for example, report the usage made of UNIX, a powerful and sophisticated operating system, by computer specialists in an academic environment. Of the 256 publicly available commands on the system 50% of users used 25 or less. Each of these studies also demonstrated that there was much more functionality in the system that the users could use with benefit, but they were not making use of it.

Users seem to respond to systems that offer a lot of choice by cutting down the range of options they consider. It is like being confronted in a restaurant by a very lengthy menu with many interesting variations. How many diners, faced with the daunting task of choosing, ultimately turn to the short list of recommendations at the front of the menu? The development of easy-to-use systems will make it easier to cope with a sophisticated system, but nevertheless the extension of choice must increase the effort to use — if only because there are more options to consider and choose between. It is frustrating to be faced with many more choices than you need and it appears that many users avoid this situation by only dealing with a sub-set of the system, no matter what benefits might lie in store within the unknown section of the system.

The implications of this phenomenon of under-utilisation are that selecting a system because it contains more functionality than another is not the best way of serving the user's interests. It would be better to use the task analysis to identify the required range of functionality and the flexibility necessary to use it and ensure that what is delivered to the user has a high probability of usefulness.

Where the tasks to be served by a system are ill structured or vary across the user population, a major set of criteria, as indicated in Figure 8.1, will be the establishment of the requisite level of functionality and the system flexibility to enable the user to locate the function required. There are two associated criteria of importance. User task needs are rarely stable over time and this is especially the case where the tasks are ill structured and the users are discretionary. In these cases users frequently learn from their early use of a system and as a consequence redefine their tasks and therefore what they need from the system. In this situation it is important that the potential exists in the system for it to be adapted and elaborated so that it evolves as the user's needs evolve.

Many systems allow a great deal of choice not only about the functionality but also about the specific form in which it is offered, the format in which reports are generated, etc. This offers users the opportunity to have the system tailored to meet their specific requirements and, therefore, this customisation feature of a system is a very important property in meeting user needs. Unfortunately this implies that the user will be able and willing to operate the system to customise it to meet a unique set of requirements. In practice, users tend not to do this and, where it is intended that this feature will be used, it will probably be necessary to provide support for custom-isation when the system is installed (see Chapter 9).

In summary we have identified two routes by which the functionality of a system may be determined. One route, which has been typical of data processing applications, is to establish a direct match between what the system provides and the tasks the user has to perform. This works best in circumstances where the tasks are, or can be, well structured but the creation of prototypes and user trials are necessary to establish that the assumptions about the task structure are valid. The other route, more typical of generic office products, is to provide a powerful range of functions from which the user can select that which is required. This route is more suited to ill-structured tasks which will require different services on different occasions. The criterion here should be requisite rather than maximum functionality; too many irrelevant options will serve only to make the system more complex than is necessary. Where this approach is taken adaptability and customisation may also be important. The effect of this approach is that the power and sophistication of the computer is placed in the user's hands but at the cost of the system not being matched to the user's specific needs. This may mean the users will need support *in situ* to use the customisation facilities to create a unique match with their task needs.

Usability

Once a system has the functionality the users require the next step is to ensure that it is delivered in a way the users feel able to operate. It is in this domain that the importance of 'user friendliness', 'ease of use' and 'ease of learning' are normally emphasised. In general what we seek is a way of interacting with a system which fits our capabilities and skills for processing information. Some of these properties are universal to human beings but most have to be modified according to the specific properties of the users in question, i.e. their knowledge and skills, the language they use, etc. Therefore, in determining what will be usable, we need to make use of the data obtained in earlier user analyses.

Discussions of usability are often presented in terms of technical system properties, i.e. the properties of an easy-to-use keyboard. However, we wish to move from the user analysis to the required properties of a system and we are therefore going to structure this account in terms of human properties. Whilst some of these properties may be unique to a user population in a given application there are some broad ways of categorising users which are very useful in determining usability. A simple but powerful classification is presented in Figure 8.2.

Two kinds of expertise are relevant to the effective use of an information technology system. System knowledge refers to the expertise needed to operate the technical system whilst task knowledge refers to the expertise needed to use the system in a specific application domain. A computer specialist may understand the technical basis of a system to support investment decisions, for example, but may be unfamiliar with the investment decision-making process. By contrast the investment analyst will be familiar with the task domain but be unfamiliar with the use of the system to support this application. There is a growing army of users who are professionals in their fields, discretionary in respect of their tasks and only ever likely to be occasional users of a computer-based system. This group of users poses a particularly awkward set of usability questions because they are demanding and knowledgeable about their task

Figure 8.2
Dimensions of user expertise

		Task Expertise	
		Low	High
System Expertise	**Low**	The Public	Occasional, Discretionary, Professional Users
	High	Computer Specialists	Full time Application Specialists

world but do not expect to have to learn much about the system in order to use it. A familiar group in data processing applications is the full-time user of a specific system, for example, a data preparation clerk, who becomes very practised in the task area and in the use of a specific system. At the other extreme, members of the public may encounter computer systems in the high street for which they have neither task knowledge nor system knowledge. Obviously a system which the computer professional finds usable may not suit the needs of the public in the high street.

With this brief look at some of the important user dimensions we will now turn to an examination of the properties a system requires to be usable. These are divided into three broad areas; properties that relate to how human beings give and receive information, that relate to how we represent the world to ourselves, plan actions and take decisions and finally, how we learn and develop.

The first, and most traditional, area covers the properties required to allow the user to get inputs into the system and to be able to receive outputs. For these purposes the system has to match the motor skills capabilities of a human being, i.e. the way we use hands, feet, speech, etc. to communicate and act on the world, and our perceptual characteristics, i.e. the way we use our eyes, ears and other senses to capture information from the world around us. Figure 8.3 lists as criteria some of the most important properties a system will need, and gives examples of some of the potential ways of meeting these criteria.

Figure 8.3
The perceptual-motor skills match

	Criteria	Potential provision
General Factors	Transfer of Training	Match Existing Equipment Standarisation Population Stereotypes
	Natural Motor Skills	Keying, Speaking, Touching, Pointing, eg. the Mouse
Input	Feedback and Error Correction	
	Input Tolerance	Intelligent Interpreters
	Input Minimisation	Automatic Identifiers, eg. Card Readers
Output	Perceptual Discrimination	Legibility, Image Stability, Formatting
	Perceptual Cueing	Icons, Colour, Alarms
	Task and Media Match	Numbers, Words, Graphs, Pictures, Video, Speech
	Response Speed	Fit with Task Completion Pattern
Control	Interaction Control	Suspension Facilities, Multi-Tasking and Backtracking, eg. windows, freezing and undo.

The most general requirement is for people to be able to transfer the skills they have already developed to the new situation. This may mean that the new computer system operates according to the same rules as those in current use, for example, has keys in the same places on the new keyboard, follows the same procedure for logging in, etc. Unfortunately the lack of consistency between information technology systems often means that people find that their existing training is an obstacle rather than a help. Sometimes different user groups will have existing but different skills. A skilled typist, for example, will be able to use the normal QWERTY keyboard but an accountant may be more familiar with a calculator layout. On a wider basis users may be familiar with various population stereotypes, for example, red means stop or danger, turning a control to the right increases whatever it controls, etc. A system that obeys these stereotypes is much easier to adapt to than one that creates new rules to be learnt. Adults have devoted many years to developing knowledge and skill with which to interact with the world and a usable product uses that background rather than demanding a new round of learning.

The qualities of input devices need to match the existing motor skills of the user. There is a movement away from the ubiquitous alpha numeric keyboard but it is important to remember that a section of the population has well developed skills with this input device and it would be foolish not to make use of this skill where it is appropriate. If the users are non-typists there are a wide variety of alternatives on the market or under development, for example, touch screens and the mouse, which allow the user to point at a specific area of the screen and initiate actions. There are also rapid developments in speech recognition which, because it is a well-developed skill in most people, may prove to be an important input medium in the future. Current limitations, however, mean that the error rate is high for continuous, unrestricted vocabulary from a variety of speakers and practical applications are restricted to isolated words from a restricted vocabulary.

A word of caution is appropriate here. There is a tendency to believe that the next development in input devices will be the universal panacea, the answer to a well-known bottleneck in human-computer interaction. It is rapidly becoming apparent, however, that each input device has a limited range of application; it will be the best way for some users to engage in some tasks. As Waterworth (1984) points out, for example, continuous speech recognition may sound like the ultimate solution but because it is a serial medium and we have limited short-term memory, we may find it quite difficult to use in many situations.

Whatever the input device there are two features which are worthy of specific mention. One is the provision of immediate feedback, for example, a click as a key is pressed, because motor skills depend upon knowledge of results, i.e. being able to connect the action and the result. The other feature is provision for the avoidance of catastrophic errors. The most common problem is when the key next to a frequently used key leads to a dramatic and irreversible action, for example, the SHIFT key next to the CLEAR key. Where an action can have major consequences it is important that it has to be taken deliberately—for example, it requires two keys simultaneously or requires the user to confirm the action.

A problem which has infuriated many computer users for many years is the rigidity of many systems which must receive literally everything in the right place before they will respond, i.e. the syntax demands that every comma must be present and in the right place. Since people are rarely exact, especially the occasional user who will have great difficulty remembering complex syntax rules, it is important that systems are tolerant of a range of inputs. There are many ways in which a system might check inputs against a lexicon of possibilities and confirm its choice with a user. It is part of the same development that provides spelling checkers to support the accuracy of the user's work.

Finally under input, the occasional user in particular is likely to be slow and error prone when providing input. Automatic identifiers such as card readers, for example, may avoid having to remember and enter complex and deliberately non-meaningful security codes.

The provision of good quality displays is also an area where human factors standards and guidance is well developed (see, for example, Cakir *et al.*, 1980). The user has first to be able to discriminate the characters that are being displayed which is affected by the size and shape of characters, the contrast between the figure and its background, image stability and the flicker rates, etc. The format of screens can be improved by the use of layout principles—such as the constructive use of space to avoid clutter etc. (Galitz, 1981). There may be a conflict here for the systems designer who wants to get as much as possible on a screen to minimise the number of screens to be transmitted. Pushed to its extreme this philosophy can create very dense fields of data which may be impossible for the occasional user to decipher. The full-time user, by contrast, may prefer a dense screen to searching a number of screens because the practised eye is quickly able to see a pattern or select the vital item of information.

In recent years there have been many developments which help the user in perceptual cueing, i.e. finding that which is relevant and understanding what can be done with the system. Instead of a list of complex word commands, the user may see a set of icons, i.e. symbols which characterise each function in an instantly recognisable way. The best-known example is the use of a waste paper basket for the 'erase' function, an analogy which is extended in some systems to the extent that items placed in the 'waste paper basket' can be retrieved at the end of the session because it is only 'emptied' when the session ends. This kind of aid appears very useful for the occasional user but irritates the regular user who is familiar with a wide range of word commands. There are several varieties of cueing aids which can be used for attention-getting purposes and for enhancing the structure present in a display (for example, colour, blinking characters, reverse video, audio alarms, etc.). All of these methods can be used to add valuable variety but if they are over-used they can cause confusion and annoyance.

Perhaps the most significant development to come in the display area is the ability to use and integrate a variety of media in one system. In normal engagement with a task, for example in a meeting, we may use speech, the written word, graphs and tables, pictures, video, etc. to communicate and further the task purposes. In human–computer interaction we have been largely limited to one medium at a time which has artificially constrained how we handle the task, i.e. we may spend a lot of time interpreting a complex table of data when a graph would have displayed the significant trend instantly. The availability of options will provide new opportunities but poses the problem that the selection of the medium will have to be linked to the task purpose and to the way the users wish to represent the task themselves. Eason *et al.* (1987) describe a system for use by electrical engineers which used graphics and text for separate functions in order to match the way the engineers worked on a range of tasks. The arrival of media options for human–computer interaction places greater emphasis upon user and task analysis to reveal the most useful way of using these opportunities.

The final aspect of the perceptual–motor skills match concerns the dynamics of the interaction. Human skill develops a finely tuned rhythm with rapid bursts of inputs and outputs as the user moves purposively towards the goal. The sustaining of the rhythm is important if the person is not to lose the coherence of the thought process. The rhythm of the work in human–computer interaction is linked to the response speed of the computer which can be very disruptive if it is too fast or too slow. Whilst a speed of a few seconds is normally recommended, the actual speed required depends upon the stage of the task. A practised typist in the middle of a word needs to be able to complete the word within milliseconds if the skill is not to be disrupted whereas the timing of the response to 'PRINT' may be much less critical. Advice on appropriate response times for different tasks is widely available (see, for example, Damodaran *et al.*, 1980, Shneiderman, 1986).

A related issue to the rhythm of the interaction is the control the user has over it. In early systems, once embarked upon a task, the user had to move through the options it provided or exit from it altogether before other tasks could be entertained. There are, however, many real world environments where this single-minded approach to a task is not realistic, where the user may be interrupted and have to go to another task, or may want to go from one part of the system to another and check some information and then come back to continue the first task etc. As the technology develops so there are more opportunities for the user to control these aspects of interaction, to 'freeze' the task and return to it later, to undo what has recently been undertaken and return to an earlier point, to use 'windows' to engage in several tasks simultaneously and to have the system perform 'background' tasks such as printing and filing whilst still continuing the interaction with the user. Whether these facilities are desirable or just add to the complexity with which the user has to deal depends upon the nature of the task environment and the expertise of the user.

As the degree of co-operation or mutual dependence between the human being and the computer deepens, it is not the input/output facilities that constitute the main problem area but the central processing undertaken by the communicating partners. At its worst engaging with a computer can seem like dealing with someone who not only speaks a foreign language but also thinks in an entirely alien way. If a system is to be usable it has to exhibit ways of operating that are compatible with the normal cognitive processes of a human being. Achieving a cognitive match of this kind depends upon our understanding of human cognitive functioning which is a difficult and relatively young area of research which we are only recently beginning to translate into guidance for human–computer interaction (see Allen, 1982 and Gardiner and Christie, 1987 for useful summaries). Whilst much of the work in this area is theoretical and may influence long-term developments in forms of human–computer interaction, there are some more practical implications that can be applied to the development of applications on existing technology and four such areas are listed in Figure 8.4.

The first requirement is that the operation of the system should appear natural to the user, i.e. the way it behaves should match user expectations. A popular way of expressing this is to say that the system should conform to the 'user's model'. This expresses a fundamental feature of human cognition, that we function by creating a representation of the part of the world with which we interact and this representation enables us to make predictions, consider our actions before making them, etc. This representation is the distillation of previous relevant experiences and, although it typically contains gaps, inconsistencies and even illogicalities, it is the basis for our action. A new user of a system attempts to gain an overall understanding of it, to discover what general principles apply to it. This usually means 'What have I previously experienced that is like this?', or 'Is this device like a telephone or like a typewriter?' If the system does behave according to a set of principles the user has already developed for another purpose there can be a rapid transfer of training and new learning can be as rapidly attained. Ideally, the new system should signal what it is like and have a vocabulary of system commands, a syntax for interaction, a set of inferences underlying its operations, etc., which will be internally consistent and consistent also with equipment and systems already known to the user population. Hannigan and Kerswell (1986) describe a study which demonstrated that, of two new telephone interfaces, subjects found it much easier to relate to one that most closely resembled the

Figure 8.4
The cognitive match

Criteria	Potential Provision
1. System Matches Cognitive Expectations	Match with 'user model' of system; common vocabulary, syntax, inference structure for system operation.
2. Task Compatibility	Match with 'user model' of application; common application vocabulary and dialogue flexibility for task needs.
3. Navigability	Status, direction, 'road maps' and indications of location and options.
4. Transparency	Explanation of task inferences with protection from system 'housekeeping'.

traditional telephone. It is not necessarily the case that the new system can or should copy the principles of existing equipment. It may be better that it copies the principles of the working practice with which users are familiar. There has, for example, been considerable interest in building systems based upon 'the desk-top metaphor' to mimic the way office workers structure their work environment. The principles of windows and multi-tasking have in part developed as ways of providing the computer equivalent of working simultaneously with several untidy piles of documents on the desk-top.

It is often important to separate the user model of the technical system and its mode of operation from the user's task model and the degree to which it is compatible with the task model built into the system. Whilst a novice in a task domain may be content to learn a task model from the system, a task expert will have many expectations about the way the task will be handled; the technical vocabulary, the relations between variables, the legitimate actions that can be performed upon variables, etc. When task experts reject systems designed for their use it is often because they do not accept that the system behaves in valid ways. They are particularly prone to reject 'expert' systems on this basis because these systems contain explicit rules that govern relationships in the task domain. If the users do not agree with these rules, they cannot use the system. It is as though two experts in the same area have found themselves in disagreement and one has decided it is not therefore possible to work with the other one. In evaluating a system, therefore, it is particularly important to explore how far its version of task reality conforms with the views of the target users — another justification for prototype trials.

A complex system can seem like a nightmarish n-dimensional space to users in which it is difficult to know where you are and how to get where you want to go. For some users 'getting lost' in a computer system creates as much anxiety as being lost in a real forest and is probably one reason why people stick to the safe but limited 'highways' that they know rather than exploring the unknown. As systems get larger and one system allows access to other systems, *navigability* becomes progressively more important; the system needs the equivalent of road signs and road maps. It needs status indicators to show where the user is and what the system is doing and it needs constantly available lists of options to show what is possible from that point.

The final issue is the way in which the user can learn what the system is doing and why. In many respects the average computer user is like the average motorist, there are many things going on 'under the bonnet' that you do not want or need to know. A good system hides most of its technical 'housekeeping' from the user but provides ways of revealing it to the technical specialist. However, the user will need to know what the system is doing in respect of the task and this part of its operation must be *transparent* to the user. The user, for example, needs confirmation when something has been filed, it is useful to know when a message has been read by a recipient and, when a lot of processing is taking place, it is useful to know the computer is working and how long it will take. Many a user has been left wondering whether anything is happening inside the black box! A good example of transparency is the growing practice in expert systems of providing the user with a facility for asking the system to report the logic by which it arrived at a recommendation. If you are surprised by the recommendation you get from an expert, you ask for an explanation. Users have the same need of expert systems.

Many of the usability issues discussed above are ease-of-use issues but there is a closely related set of issues about ease of learning. Inasmuch as a system can be built which behaves in a way consistent with the user's expectations of the world and can be used with the skills the user already possesses, the need for new learning is minimised. However, there will always be new learning to attain if the user is successfully to exploit the system. Figure 8.5 introduces further criteria which are necessary if the system is to provide a good learning environment for the user.

The conventional way in which new technology is introduced into an organisation is to precede implementation with a training programme so that users are fully equipped to utilise the new system. We shall examine the issue of training more closely in Chapter 9 but we should note here that there are many reasons why users of information technology systems are unlikely to be fully proficient before they start using a system. One reason is that they may be intermittent users who will forget the detailed operational procedures they have been taught before they get round to using them. Another reason is that many systems provide multiple functions and it would be a very long training course to cover them all in detail. Finally, occasional, discretionary users see very little reason to spend a lot of time learning a system which will make only a marginal contribution to their work. A one-day familiarisation course may be the

Figure 8.5
Creating a learning environment

Criteria	Potential Provision
1. Explanation/Redundancy Trade Off	Multi-level Dialogues
2. In-System Training	On-line demonstration, practice opportunities
3. In-system, point-of-need Support	Help facilities, 'pop-up' menus, explanatory error messages
4. Documentary Support	User oriented manuals, cards, posters etc.

maximum that is possible. As a consequence the ability of the user to exploit a system depends heavily on 'learning-by-doing'. This puts a premium on what we have termed the 'point of need' support facilities associated with the system, i.e. the sources of help and advice users can turn to when they are in the process of using the system. The criteria listed in Figure 8.5 are directed to this end.

The most obvious way in which a computer system can teach its user is for the main dialogue screens to structure the interaction for the users and to provide all the necessary information for choices to be made. Systems for public use, such as automatic cash or ticket dispensers, typically adopt this strategy. The aim is to ensure that the user needs no other source of information to undertake the transaction. The main problem with this approach is that, if the user repeats the transaction, the structure and explanation rapidly become tedious and restrictive. People learn very quickly and, when they have the knowledge, they need a fast and uncluttered way of achieving their purposes. There is therefore a conflict between the 'easy to learn' and the 'easy to use' objectives, the beginner needing a self-explanatory form of interaction and the practised user a terse form of dialogue omitting redundant explanations.

Where the user population are all beginners, or are well practised, this conflict of objectives is not a problem but unfortunately most user populations contain both the beginner and the experienced user. A popular solution in this case it to have *two or more levels of dialogue*, a self-explanatory mode and a terse or 'fast' mode for the expert. The self-explanatory mode may give structure by using menus or form-filling techniques whereas the fast mode may pass control of the interaction to the user by responding to commands or combinations of commands. In some cases intermediate modes may also be useful. If the multi-mode approach is adopted it is important that there is consistency between the modes so that what the user learns from the explanatory mode provides the basis for operating the faster modes.

It is tempting to think that users will either be beginners or experienced but in fact most people will be a mixture of the two. This is especially the case with multi-functional systems where any user tends to be an experienced user of some facilities and a beginner with respect to the rest. One user may therefore need both modes of interaction. This raises the question of how the selection of dialogue mode is made. The practical solution is usually to give the user the option at the beginning of each period of interaction. The development of adaptive computer systems, however, raises other possibilities for the future. If the computer was able to monitor and log the usage patterns of a user it would know the extent to which the user had knowledge of each facility and could automatically provide an appropriate level of dialogue. This is a tempting proposition but creates an image of an intelligent computer taking decisions outside the user's control and may well not be acceptable to a lot of users. The adoption of this kind of practice needs considerable research before it is widely implemented.

The explanation provided by a system does not have to be in the main dialogues. It can be provided by *in-system support* in the form of help screens, explanatory error messages, on-line manuals, demonstration routines, etc., all easily accessible at any time from the main screens. In theory this should provide a very supportive environment in which a user could learn about a facility before using it and, at any point in its use, could obtain more information. There can be little doubt that the extensive intro-duction of this range of in-system support made systems much easier to learn but the quality of the support is often a disappointment. In evaluation studies we regularly ask about the use of in-system aids and a common response is that they are not useful because 'you need help facilities to explain the help facilities'. In providing explanatory information systems designers often resort to the technical language they themselves use and this adds to the confusion of the user. The provision of in-system support needs as much attention as the design of a training course and requires the expertise of specialists in training. Too often it appears to be a peripheral chore for a technical designer struggling to meet a deadline.

The traditional medium for the provision of point-of-need support is the manual and other forms of *documentation*. The computer manual is the butt of many jokes among users and is often the most unusable feature of the entire system. A standard question for evaluation studies is the usefulness of the manual and it often gets the most negative of responses. Often the question leads to users hunting their offices for the manual buried deep in piles of documents which does not, of itself, suggest a high degree of usage. Many users say they follow a strategy of on-line experimentation and use the manual as a last resort. This suggests that on-line support facilities may, in time, usurp many of the functions of the manual. There remain, however, many good reasons for good documentary support. It can, for example, be studied off-line and away from the system, and, despite our best software design efforts, a paper-based document still provides the most flexible and easy to search medium for complex material.

Many of the problems of manuals arise from poor design. Document creation has been the poor relation of systems design which has often resulted in complex technical documents that attempt to provide a comprehensive guide to the product. As a result they are often not very well suited to end users who need a quick source of reference in which they can find the specific piece of information expressed in non-technical terms that they need for their current task. Advice on the designing of complex documentary material is widely available (for example, Wright and Lickorish, 1983), and can do much more to improve the accessibility and readability of manuals. They need to be well indexed and to enable the user to enter from a task or trouble-shooting perspective as well as from the perspective of an organised top-down description.

One of the most popular forms of documentation among users is the simple *aide-mémoire*; a card or poster that lists the vital information, i.e. the log-in procedure, the names of the main facilities, the telephone number to call for help, etc. Designers who are enthusiastic about in-system aids are apt to forget the user still has to know how to start the system which can make this kind of aid available.

There is then a lot a system and its associated documentation can do to provide a supportive, learning envrionment for its users. However, there are likely to be limits. The system can explain itself, the purposes of its facilities and the way it operates, etc. but the creator of these forms of help does not know the particular circumstances of the user and the task that is being attempted. If the user's problem is that he does not know whether the system can assist his task or how to frame his task so that it can help, he is unlikely to find the in-system facilities of direct assistance. In these circumstances we find repeatedly that users seek human help, from their colleagues or the technical staff who support the system. These human 'point of need' support mechanisms are discussed in Chapter 9.

User Acceptability

Having created a system which serves the user's functional needs and which is usable, given the user's knowledge and skills, the next question is whether the user will find it acceptable, i.e. what motivation the user will have to use or not use it. A user's motivation will largely be established by the job design processes described in Chapter 7. Now we have to ensure that the technical system actually supports the user in the conduct of the job. For a discretionary user acceptability criteria are critical because non-use is a relatively easy option; if it does not positively help the user to do the job, it does not get used. For the non-discretionary user acceptability criteria are of less obvious importance but, because a dissatisfied user can find many ways of thwarting the intentions of others, they are of considerable practical significance. Figure 8.6 lists two groups of factors which are major contributions to user acceptability of a system. This list is derived from separate lists created by Eason (1981), Bjørn-Andersen (1985) and Henderson (1985). In each case the authors were taking the general needs of people at work and exploring their implications for the design of information technology systems. They take, for example, the job design criteria provided by Tynan (1980), as listed in Figure 7.7 in Chapter 7, and relate them directly to working with visual display units.

Some of the factors listed in Figure 8.6 relate to the way in which a technical system is used within an organisation but others depend upon the technical properties of the system. Others are the product of the two factors; the technical property facilitates one kind of usage and makes another difficult to implement. It is difficult, therefore, to pinpoint where in the design process responsibilities for the acceptability of the system might reside. It is important that every stage of the design process considers the acceptability implications of its work. Suppliers, for example, need to ensure they provide systems with the flexibility to be moulded into acceptable forms in organisations and, within organisations, implementers need to use the flexibility of the technical system to serve the job design goals established by the methods described in Chapter 7.

The factors in Figure 8.6 are in two groups: control, and discretion and growth. In many respects the control group are issues which can lead to non-acceptance of a system. They represent factors which can take control of work and working life away from the user and will therefore evoke negative responses. The discretion and growth factors are ways of positively promoting acceptability. They constitute the kind of factors which may be perceived by users as giving them more discretion over their work than hitherto and of providing opportunities for personal development.

Some of the control variables were discussed in Chapter 7 as factors which have been shown to cause stress and dissatisfaction among users. The discretion and growth factors will be necessary to promote the positive kinds of job design described in Chapter 7.

Figure 8.6
Criteria for user acceptability

Control	Discretion and Growth
Access	Servant or Master?
Reliability	Levels of Choice
Confidentiality	Intuition and Informality
Monitoring	Assuming Knowledge
Pacing	Supporting Learning
Health and Stress	Co-operative Work
Social Contact	

1. Control

The first group of factors relates to the user's need to feel in control of events when using the system.

Access to the system is a basic requirement if users are to undertake their work — a fact that seems so obvious that it should never be a problem. However, in many surveys it has been found to be a major constraint — usually because users have to share access to a terminal. Sharing is usually the result of load assessments which show that none of the users needs to use the system more than 50% of their time. Therefore, if their terminal is not to stand idle, two or more users can share it. Unfortunately this logic assumes all users can schedule their work around the availability of the terminal, but this is rarely the case. Users often have to access information at a particular point in time and if they cannot log information as it becomes available they may have to record it manually for later entry into the computer system. Shackel *et al.* (1989) found that three freightforwarding clerks experienced frustrating delays even when the total util-isation of a terminal was only 30% because there were peak periods of activity during which they all needed the terminal. Another access problem associated with a shared terminal is its location. If it is not on the user's desk the user will have to travel to it carrying whatever papers and files are relevant. It is known that travelling any distance is a major disincentive for discretionary users. Non-discretionary users may have no choice but to accept the inconvenience and they often develop a work strategy that minimises the disruption and probably their use of the terminal. Better to do a task manually at your desk than to travel elsewhere and find the terminal in use. The problem of access is directly related to system costs because extra terminals cost money. However, if the result of minimising the access points to the system is that the system becomes unacceptable to many potential users, the saving has been counterproductive.

If users are to feel confident about undertaking their work with a computer system they must feel they can rely on it. Like all tool users they must feel they can trust their tools or they will limit the degree to which they are dependent upon them. In a list of concerns about a system, *reliability* always comes high. It was the most frequently cited issue in the City firm evaluation reported by Gower and Eason (1989). Users are loath to commit information to an electronic medium if they think there is a danger of it being lost or corrupted. Committing their records to a computer is an uncertain process and difficult to control compared with the personal control one has over a filing cabinet. Any lack of confidence in the system also encourages users to retain tried and trusted methods. If they have to keep a manual record or actively make a back-up to protect against breakdown, users will feel the system is not living up to its promise of saving time and energy. Task analysis techniques will reveal the information which is most crucial and therefore where reliability is of the greatest importance. As a result user acceptability can be heavily dependent upon design decisions which ensure the system is reliable.

User acceptability of a system is often jeopardised because users fear that they cannot control access to information they regard as *confidential* to the work they are doing. If a person accepts responsibility for a range of tasks, at whatever level in an organisation, a reasonable expectation is that they will be given control of the resources necessary to fulfil that responsibility. Thus we find people being possessive and territorial about the staff, space and equipment they need to do the job. The same is true of the informational resources they need to do the job. They will need to plan activities and monitor progress, etc. and this will mean access to local information and an opportunity to manipulate it. In pre-computer work people maintain their own working papers and can, if they wish, lock them in filing cabinets when they are not in use. In this way they can maintain their own information domain and can control (to some extent) the way it is shared with seniors and colleagues.

The introduction of electronic media for the storage and manipulation of information can threaten this control of the local information domain; the user may be expected to transfer working papers to the system, together with plans and progress statements. If this information is accessible by seniors and colleagues it may significantly change the psychological experience of doing the work because the user is now executing job responsibilities in a much more public domain. It may be that this is a management objective; to make the working of the organisation more transparent and more subject to management control. The individual user, however, may see this

as a removal of personal control and may respond by trying to preserve the informational territory. This can be done in a variety of ways; by maintaining manual files
and reporting systems or even by purchasing a stand-alone personal computer which
cannot be accessed by other people. The growth in personal computers in an organisation is not just because they are relatively inexpensive; they also provide ways in
which staff can effectively preserve their independence. If users have to use the 'public'
system they can limit what they put onto it or can ensure that what it recorded is
expected and acceptable. Too much pressure on users to make their information
domain public can therefore lead to it changing so that it reflects something less than
reality. In the Hospital case described by Eason *et al.* (1989a) many doctors refused to
enter the provisional diagnosis of patients on the patient records, which could be
accessed by the administrative and nursing staff of the hospital. They did so on the
grounds that they were protecting the privacy of the patient. However, many staff
believed they were also protecting the doctors in case the diagnosis proved wrong. The
result was a system which told you everything about patients except why they were in
hospital.

In many respects the issue of information ownership parallels the debate about the
privacy of personal information. When the data is about an individual that person can
reasonably claim to have an interest in the accuracy of the information and the purposes
to which it is put, etc. In many countries, including Great Britain, there are now data
protection laws which provide citizens with protection against the invasion of privacy
as a result of data being stored on computer data bases. Whilst these laws do not
protect people who have responsibility for the work to which computer files relate,
those people have similar need to control the access and use made of the files. Therefore, if a system is to be acceptable to its users, some provision will need to be made so
that users have some control over the information domain that relates to their area of
responsibility. One possibility is to partition the data base so that it mirrors the responsibility and reporting structure of the organisation. In this way the technical
system provides a direct support for the social system.

A related issue to confidentiality is computer *monitoring*. Working with a
computer means that in theory the computer can log every move you make, i.e. how
many orders you process, how many errors you make, how long you spend on
different kinds of enquiry, etc. As a result the computer can be used as a major source of
management control information and the practice of logging the productivity of white
collar staff has become quite commonplace. It is often used, for example, to single out
staff who are performing poorly, and may be used as a basis for incentive scheme
payments. Many users experience this as a major loss of control because it introduces a
continuous form of spying into their work. Irving *et al.* (1986) report surveys of
clerical workers in the USA who are subject to this form of monitoring and who
report additional levels of stress and loss of control in their work. Bjørn-Andersen
(1985) in his Scandinavian Model of the Office of the Future suggests that computer
monitoring does not fit the democratic values of Scandinavian countries and will be
banned. The Congress of the United States Office of Technology (1985) Report on the
future of 'Offices in America' also anticipates attempts, particularly by unions, to ban
this kind of intrusion into working lives. A particular form of monitoring that has

caused widespread anxiety is undisclosed monitoring when users do not know that their work is being monitored. This practice leads to stress and suspicion between management and work-force. The non-acceptability of monitoring may therefore become a major issue in introducing a system. Even if it is introduced it can have unwanted effects as users try to cope with the new element in their work. If they are forced to achieve productivity targets, the kind of quality criteria the system cannot log may suffer. There have been reports, for example, of clerical staff cutting short complex customer enquiries because they have to process a set number of customers per day to avoid being reported to management.

Although computer monitoring can have negative consequences for users there are also many positive uses to which it can be put and it would be tragic if a blanket ban prevented beneficial uses. Monitoring, for example, is a major way, as we shall see in Chapter 10, of evaluating the adequacy of the system, i.e. which parts cause persistent difficulties. Monitoring can be used to reveal interesting new uses of the system which others might copy and it reveals which facilities are not in use which further training might lead users to exploit. Users themselves find logs very useful in helping them to set their own targets and improve their own performance. If adaptive systems are introduced they may well depend on logs of user behaviour to match system responses to user needs and expertise. If logging user behaviour is not permitted this kind of application may not be possible.

If user acceptability is to be promoted it will be necessary to establish rules for computer monitoring in each application, i.e. who is monitored, when and for what purpose, so that users are not subjected to unnecessary stress, and then to ensure that these rules can be implemented within the technical system.

Another factor which can cause loss of control is *pacing*. As we know from years of research on people working on assembly lines, human beings work best when they establish their own rhythms. They are not like machines that work at a constant pace but build up pace pace slowly, establish a rhythm, need frequent rests, etc. A constant rate determined by the technology can seem too fast or too slow. Of greatest import- ance is the fact that it does not allow the user any control over the pace of working. White collar work has typically been self-paced but the coming of information tech- nology can change this. It is possible for the computer to feed work to users at a constant rate. A common approach, for example, is to arrange for the computer to channel calls from customers to clerks as soon as they complete the previous call so that the clerk has to deal with calls without a break. Fallik (1987) gives an example of a tax collecting system in which the computer automatically calls taxpayers and, as soon as the telephone is answered, the call is channelled to a tax clerk, who has no control over this process.

It may be more effective to set overall targets, i.e. performance goals for the week or the day, than to let the system force the pace on a minute-by-minute basis. This allows users to operate at their own pace and, because they know the overall target, they frequently develop strategies that enable them to perform just as effectively.

Whether using the system leads to *health or stress* problems can depend upon many aspects of the system. The general aim must be to minimise the mental and physical load on the user of actually using the system. The dominant physical load is usually visual and the achievement of a clear, stable image (Pearce, 1985) on the screen is a vital requirement and will be a result of such properties as the flicker rate, the size of the characters and the contrast between figures and their background. Visual problems can be created by the environment in which the display is placed, so that, for example, the user is trying to read the characters in direct sunlight. Other problems may arise because the workstation keeps the user in a constrained posture for long periods. If the posture is inappropriate it will rapidly lead to backache, neckache and other signs of strain. Even if the posture is good, long periods in one position will lead to fatigue. In addition to selecting good terminals and workstations it is therefore necessary to create working practices in which people can move around, take regular rest pauses, etc. The latest advice on the creation of workstations and terminals to meet ergonomic criteria is to be found in Grandjean (1987).

A subject which is increasingly of concern to people using visual display terminals is the extent to which opportunities for *social contact* with colleagues are reduced. Social contact is an important feature of working life not only because we are social animals but because we need a good understanding of one another to work co-operatively. Information technology can interfere with social contact in two quite separate ways. It may reduce the need to contact others in the performance of the work. If there is a need for communication it may be that this is undertaken through the system and this is a more restricted communication medium than face-to-face meetings. The other problem is that even when people share an office they can feel cut off if they work all day at a visual display terminal. The terminal may obscure their line of sight so that eye contact with any of their colleagues is impossible. In planning the layout of rooms containing terminals the sense of group working can be reinforced by ensuring people can see one another whilst working.

2. Discretion and Growth

The list of control factors are negative issues — those issues which contribute to non-acceptability. We now turn to the factors which positively promote acceptability. If, as we hope, the job design procedures outlined in the previous chapter have produced work roles the users will derive satisfaction from filling, they will be looking for information technology tools which will enable them to fulfil these roles. All of the field evidence suggests that they will be looking for roles where they can be *master not servant*, i.e. that are sufficiently flexible to be used in a variety of ways as the users see fit in their pursuit of task goals. The conditions they do not want are those where they are reduced to the role of servant of the machine. This occurs when the work is simply to provide the machine with data for purposes that may be unknown, which is characteristic of some data entry jobs. Shop floor data entry devices have simply required operators to record the job they have completed and they receive no information from the system which is of use to them. Systems become acceptable to users when they are truly users, i.e they are receiving a service from the system which they need to fulfil their work roles. One of the arts of system design is therefore to create a service to the organisation at large and to every one of the individual users.

The discretion the user has over the system is an important element in its acceptability and this translates into the *level of choice* the user is given when operating the technical system. Many acceptability problems have arisen because the user finds that the system defines exactly how a task is to be undertaken so that discretion is removed once the system is switched on. This may happen quite inadvertently. A screen designer, for example, may copy a form onto a screen and arrange that the cursor automatically jumps to the next field when one is completed. This seems to be a simple case of transferring current practice to the computer but the user may experience it quite differently. The user may be used to filling in the form in any order, missing some parts which are not relevant or for which the information is not available, etc. Completing the form on the screen may force the user to start at the beginning and fill every field before going on and this may be experienced as both inflexible and inappropriate in many situations. It can be easily avoided by giving the user control over what is entered and in what order.

It is important to provide users with control over systems commensurate with the discretion they need to undertake their tasks. This is a plea to relate the flexibility in the system to the level of variability found in the task analysis. It is not a plea to give the user control over every parameter of the system since this simply adds to the complexity of the system and may render it unusable. There is usually, for example, a detailed level of operation, after a user has selected a facility, when the user is happy to follow a computer-defined procedure to execute the facility. In order to give users control but not to confront them with continuous and unnecessary choices a common practice is to provide default procedures which the user can reset at any time.

The satisfying job also provides opportunity for experiment and development which means that at times the person will want to *act informally and follow intuition*. By and large computer systems require predefined logical procedures which do not encourage informality and intuition. Henderson (1985) has suggested that systems should contain facilities to support these features of human behaviour by including, for example, a 'scrap book' area in which free text or graphics can be entered which the user can store and manipulate in some basic ways. An example would be to provide a way of annotating formal documents with the user's own informal commentary or of listing and sorting actions in some rudimentary way.

A point that Bjørn-Andersen (1985) makes with some force is that the design of the technical system should *assume knowledge* on the part of the user. Not to do so may lead to an interface that structures and teaches in inappropriate ways. It may not allow knowledgeable people to make use of their knowledge and may enforce a way of undertaking tasks which does not allow them to behave as flexibly and adaptively as their own abilities permit. The classification of the users of a system may well reveal some who must be treated as without knowledge. The one-off use of a system for a task with which the user has no familiarity is a case in point. In all other circumstances the user will bring relevant knowledge to the interaction and the system needs to enable the user to take advantage of this knowledge.

The system should go further than facilitating the use of existing knowledge by providing facilities to *support learning*. An important feature of job satisfaction is the opportunity to continue one's personal development and in the information technology context, as we saw in the earlier section on human learning, the technical system can do a great deal to help the user become progressively more knowledgeable about its facilities and how to use them. It is also important that the system should be able to widen and develop the user's own view of the tasks that are undertaken. Bjørn-Andersen *et al.* (1986) give a number of examples of managers for whom the provision of a better information base led to an enriched view of their task world, the variables that influenced the outcomes, the way variables interacted, the impact of certain kinds of decisions, etc. The more a technical system contains a valid model of reality which the user can manipulate to simulate outcomes, the more likely is the user to experience this development of task knowledge.

The final criterion relates to the fact that users rarely complete major organisational tasks on their own. The undertaking of major tasks is usually a matter of *co-operative work* in which a group of people share the workload, perhaps with different responsibilities falling upon different individuals. Hitherto design has concentrated upon the delivery of facilities to individual workstations but there is an increasing recognition (see, for example, Bjørn-Andersen and Ginnerup, 1987) that if future systems are to be acceptable they must recognise and support distribution of work between people. This may mean the ability, for example, to exchange the information freely between a defined group of users whilst preventing access by users outside the group. Within the group it should be possible to amend and develop the information base with each change identified by its initiator but there may be a set of rules which establishes who can take what actions within the system. The ways in which people work together on complex tasks are subtle and varied and the mapping of the dynamics of co-operative work onto the facilities of an information technology system is one of the major areas for development in the next few years.

A system which combines all the properties listed above could well constitute an exciting and rewarding set of tools with which to develop one's own capabilities. It could give a very positive thrust to acceptability such that people may be willing to cope with deficiencies in other criteria such as ease of use. If ever we were in the position where these properties were a commonplace experience of using systems the major problem may become one of dependence; how would we cope when deprived of this sophisticated support for our work?

Organisational Acceptability

In addition to being acceptable to individual users the technical system must also pass the test of being acceptable to the organisation as a whole. This is often a much more critical test because, whilst the consequence of non-acceptability to a specific user may be non-use or partial use, non-acceptability to the organisation may mean a discontinuation of system development or the removal of the system once implemented.

Figure 8.7 identifies two major components to this acceptability test. The first is whether the system is able to support *organisational objectives* as planned. The cost–benefit justification of the system will have identified some kind of expected benefit to the organisation which makes it worthwhile making the expenditure necessary to develop and implement the system. At all stages of development the most likely question to be asked is whether the technical system taking shape is going to meet expectations.

In Figure 8.7 the four kinds of organisational objectives for information technology systems developed in Chapter Two (and summarised in Figure 2.2) are repeated. They will form the criteria by which system expenditure will be judged. The technical system may be employed to reduce organisational costs by making *resource savings* (in staff, stock, space, equipment, etc.) or it may help to use resources more efficiently and achieve higher levels of *productivity*. It may seek to *support individual users* so that they can fulfil their tasks more effectively or it may attempt to *enhance organisational performance* directly by providing new opportunities for communication and integration between the parts of the organisation and other organisations.

It is a common finding that early expectations about what will be achieved prove groundless once the reality of the system becomes apparent. Often the process of specifying and constructing the system demonstrates that expectations are unrealistic or conflicting. There may, for example, have been unrealistic expectations about resource savings until the full complexity of the work process is revealed. Conflicts between resource saving objectives and individual support objectives may only become apparent when the allocation of system functionality to staff is determined. On the positive side, prototypes, trials and early usage often demonstrate in a more tangible form the benefits that, in planning, were intangible, and can reveal unexpected and valuable benefits. Attempting to create a technical system to meet declared organisational purposes can therefore be a much more dynamic and evolutionary process than expected. The reasons for launching the development may be revised and

Figure 8.7
Criteria for organisational acceptability

Organisational Objectives	Organisational Match
Resource Reduction	Dependency
Productivity	Flexibility
Individual Enhancement	Control and Coordination
Organisational Enhancement	Culture and Values

tightened with the consequence that parts of the technical development may be revised or discontinued. This process occurs even when a sequential development methodology has been adopted and is a planned activity in evolutionary methodologies.

As Figure 8.7 indicates the achievement of planned objectives is only part of organisational acceptability. The technical system must also achieve an acceptable 'match' with organisation custom and practice so that is does not disturb the overall ability of the organisation to function in its environment. The judgement of *organisational match* goes beyond the planned objectives of the system to examine whether the technical system being developed will have wider implications. Figure 8.6 lists four kind of implications, many of which are organisational corollaries of individual acceptability criteria. The first issue is the extent to which the organisation will become dependent upon the new systems and, if there is *dependency*, what practical steps can be taken to minimise risk. The more critical functions are performed by the technical system, the more the organisation will be vulnerable should the system break down or malfunction. The security, reliability and incorruptibility of the system become progressively more critical as the activities performed by the system become important to the organisation. Concerns of these kinds cause questions to be asked about the risks of technical failure, the availability and speed of back-up, and the protection of the system against unauthorised interference.

The social system working with the technical system can also be a source of vulnerability. There have been many cases in recent years, for example, of industrial disputes being focused upon computer operators because they have the power to inflict the greatest damage upon the performance of the organisation. Any scheme which centralises a major organisational function on a computer system run by a small team needs to be looked at carefully for vulnerability to this kind of action.

A vital organisational requirement is that it retains the *flexibility* to adapt to changes in its environment — to respond to competitors, to take advantage of new markets and to cope with changes in Government policies, for example. There have been a number of cases in recent years where organisations have been unable to go through with mergers or respond rapidly to new challenges because their computer systems would not let them, i.e. it would require man–years of effort to reprogram the systems to cope with the unexpected demand. It is unfortunately the case that the more one strives for optimal efficiency in meeting current business requirements the more one might make it difficult to adjust to new requirements. An open systems analysis of an organisation reveals the kinds of areas in which it is vulnerable to changes in its environment and it is important that flexibility is sustained in any technical system so that changes can be accommodated in these areas.

As we have described a number of times, technical systems that store, process and communicate information have implications for the *control, co-ordination*, integration and communication processes within the social system of the organisation which also depend upon information. The acceptability of the technical system within the organisation may well depend upon the degree to which there is a match between the way it handles information and the way information has hitherto been distributed between the work roles in social the system. The facilities within the system for protecting privacy, giving access, allowing co-operative working on files, authorising changes, etc. are vital if a satisfactory match on these issues is to be obtained.

Any organisation has its own, more or less explicit, *culture and values*; not what it does but the way that it does it. These properties of the organisation may cover how staff are treated, the degree to which industrial democracy is practised, the industrial relations climate, the image it projects to its customers, suppliers, the local community, etc. Increasingly the technical systems in an organisation are an important manifestation of its culture and values both to its staff and to outsiders. Since these issues are unlikely to be on the formal agenda of systems developments it is very easy for the technical system to be conveying a culture and set of values which are at variance with those the organisation is trying to promote. In staff relations, for example, management might espouse a consultative, participative philosophy in which collective decision-making is practised. The staff may experience the technical system, however, as a device for rigid, impersonal control. They are unlikely, in the climate such a system will create, to believe that the management philosophy is serious. To its customers the organisation might wish to convey a caring, helpful, flexible and courteous image. This is not helped if the technical system with which customers have to deal appears rigid, unfriendly and unhelpful. Weizenbaum (1976) gives many examples of the way technical systems can shape or distort human values rather than human values determining technical systems. Since so much of the culture of an organisation is implicit the best way of ensuring that the technical systems carry the culture is to ensure that there is user involvement at every stage of development. Since users are steeped in the culture and values of the organisation they should be able to recognise when the technical system is in danger of producing a mismatch and provide correction.

Meeting Human Requirements in Technical Development

In reviewing the four areas of human and organisational requirements in this chapter we have identified 44 criteria which could be crucial if the technical system is to be successful. Most of these criteria can be decomposed to another level of detail so that it is not hard to extend this list. The length of the list is testimony to the degree of interdependency between the technical and social systems in the organisation. The match has to be achieved at many levels; from the physical character of the human–computer interface to the mapping of organisational procedures and culture.

In the technical specification for a system it is rare for many of these requirements to be formally stated. When they are present it is usually in a global form such as 'easy to use' which is not sufficiently specific to help the design team. In order to ensure that the design process pays full attention to these issues we need to establish a procedure which can carry them through the design process. It will be obvious that they are of such diversity and affect such different levels of design that they cannot, even within a sequential approach to design, be considered in one phase of the development process. Still less can this be the case if an evolutionary, iterative approach is being adopted.

We need a procedure which charges specific individuals with responsibility for these criteria through the development process. The following are the necessary steps in the procedure:

Step 1 Appoint one or more user representatives to be the custodians of the human and organisational requirements of the technical system. The duty here is to establish the requirements during specification and to assure the quality of all proposed solutions against the criteria that are identified.

Step 2 Using the criteria identified in this chapter, develop a specific list for the project in hand. Not all of the criteria will be crucial for every development so that the first task is to identify the critical sub-set for the project. When a criterion has been identified an operational definition of the requirement has to be established. A test of whether an adequate definition has been produced is whether is would be possible to establish which of two design solutions would be best on the criterion. The likely form of most definitions would be that a specific kind of performance would be expected of a specific kind of user (manager, clerk, etc.) on a specified range of tasks under specified organisational conditions. Thus a requirement might be that the technical system includes the functionality to permit individual managers to specify the parameters of exception reports and to change them at any time. A usability requirement might be that managers can make these amendments without specific training under their normal job pressures. An acceptability requirement might be that the data base contain sections for individuals, groups and the whole user population and that procedures be established for the definition of access and for reviewing and changing definitions as the organisation changes. Note that these definitions specify the requirement but not how it is to be met; that is the task of the design process.

    It might well be that there exist some standards and guidelines to cover some of the requirements. This is most likely in the hardware and environmental aspects of human–computer interaction and to a lesser extent in the usability of software. The diversity of human requirements is such, however, that it is likely that the standard or guideline will need tightening and tailoring to the specific requirements of the project. There are many sources of standards and guidance for these purposes including Cakir *et al.* (1981), Damodaran *et al.* (1980), Smith and Mosier (1984), Shneiderman (1986) and the Human Factors Naval Engineering Standard, Gardner (1988).

Step 3 Identify when and where in the development process decisions relating to the criteria will be made. Many of the user and organisational acceptability issues, for example, are addressed in outline at the conceptual specification stage and again in specific form during implementation. In between it is a question of maintaining flexibility so that tailoring to specific requirements can be achieved during implementation. The functionality and usability issues may well be addressed in purchasing decisions about equipment and software. In bespoke systems development it may be a question of ensuring that individual programmers are aware of the usability goals towards which they are working.

Step 4 When a stage has been identified which has implications for human and organisational requirements, support that stage of design with contextual information about the requirements. This may mean providing more information about users and their tasks to clarify the requirement, facilitating access to relevant users, organising prototype tests, etc. It may also mean identifying sources of human factors and organisational guidance which will help in specifying solutions. The references given in this chapter should provide a starting point for such a search.

Step 5 Whenever a proposed solution is offered in the design process devise and undertake an evaluation procedure to examine whether it meets the requirements of the relevant criteria. Chapter 10 is devoted to a consideration of the different kinds of evaluation that can be undertaken on human and organisational issues. The essential points to note here are that the evaluation should be undertaken sufficiently early for remedial action to be taken if technical solutions do not meet requirements. This may mean redesign. In the case of criteria that cannot be met or conflicts between criteria (which are bound to occur) it may mean a review of the criteria to redefine them or prioritise those that are in conflict.

Conclusions

In Chapter 6 we explored many levels of system specification and in Chapter 7 the issues in designing the social system. This chapter has explored the requirements for the technical system. It will be apparent that many levels and stages of contact between the social and technical design are necessary if a socio-technical system is to be created which will meet the specification. The tradition of systems development has been entirely counter to this process; at best the technical and social aspects of design are separate developments. There are so many pressures that encourage this separation that it requires a deliberate policy throughout the development process to keep the two sides of design together. The policy advanced here is to establish design teams in which technical specialists and user representatives work together on all aspects of design. In keeping with the concept of a customer–contractor relationship the user representatives are charged with developing a formal description of the human and organisational requirements, of facilitating the search for solutions to meet these requirements and of evaluating the degree to which the solutions are adequate. This process causes the user organisation to work for a progressive articulation of its requirements and the technical specialists to be continually aware of the variety of criteria that have to be met. The multiple criteria framework provides the link which holds the technical and social development together.

Chapter 9
Implementation and Support

The Critical Phase

Many a carefully designed system has crumbled when implemented. Many times has the enthusiasm of those engaged in the design been washed away in the fear and resistance of those who were to use the system. Implementation is the acid test in many ways. It can end in disaster without a working system. More often the implementation process becomes greatly extended as issues that should have been dealt with earlier now become unavoidable. Often the result is that the system is only partially implemented or, even if fully implemented, is only partially used.

If we want to avoid these difficulties we have to plan the implementation process carefully. Too often this does not happen; design is exciting and glamorous but implementation requires hard, detailed work and does not attract the same devotion from designers. Often the same process has to be repeated many times for different groups of users and it requires the same time and attention every time. It is the time when the system suddenly explodes from being the intellectual territory of the small number of people concerned with its design to being the practical property of the larger population that is trying to use it. Whatever other considerations arise the sheer increase in numbers of people affected by the system can make the process more difficult to manage effectively.

If the process is effective it will end with a technical system able to support the work to be done, a social system that has adjusted to exploit the technical system and a population of users able and willing to use the technical system. This suggests that there are some goals to be achieved in parallel during implementation. They may be listed as follows:

1. *Loading, Testing and Validating the Technical System*. This is the stage when the system is loaded with real data to be used for real tasks. It can be a time-consuming and laborious process to build up reliable and accurate data bases which users will feel able to trust.
2. *Local Design*. Within the overall design there will be many design decisions that can be taken at the time of implementation; tailoring the software to meet individual needs, organising workstations and room layouts, etc.
3. *Organisational Change*. If the technical system is to be accompanied by major changes then there will be many issues to consider; task allocation, rosters, reporting arrangements, demarcation agreements, pay and grading and other conditions of service — many with industrial relations ramifications. Even when no

major organisational change is planned there will be organisational issues to consider; who has access to which parts of the system, who may up-date data bases, who has responsibility for start up and maintenance of the system, etc.

4. *Acceptance of Change.* If people are to use the system effectively they need a positive attitude towards it. Even if participative practices have been followed in design phases there are likely to be many potential users who are encountering the system for the first time at implementation. Unless this process is effectively managed they could treat the system as a major threat requiring passive or active resistance.

5. *Training and Support.* The technical system and any new social structures require people to use them who understand them, have the skills to operate them and feel confident in the use of these skills. The provision of training and other ways of helping people adjust to change is a major part of implementation. It is also a process that must continue after implementation to maintain and develop the skill level of the user population.

6. *Maintaining the Integrity of Throughput.* The changes listed above are daunting in themselves but in many organisations the implementation is made much more difficult because it must be accomplished whilst staff go about their normal business serving customers, making products, etc. This is one respect where the implementation of information technology systems is often different from the implementation of other technical systems (for example, the opening of a shop, the launching of a ship or the commissioning of a factory). In these cases the system builds up to normal operation from nothing. Most information technology systems are introduced into on-going operations which must maintain the level and quality of the throughput thoughout the transition.

With this array of goals to accomplish simultaneously it is small wonder that implementation is often problematic. Emphasis tends to be given to the technical requirements, with some effort devoted to local design and training. Other problems tend to be faced when they are encountered rather than systematically planned and the whole process is played out against the constraints of having to 'keep the shop open'.

In this chapter we will examine strategies for managing all of these processes in a systematic manner. The process will be guided by the primary requirement to introduce change in a way and at a rate which people feel able to cope with and which they are largely controlling. Once people feel threatened by a headlong rush into an uncertain and uncontrolled future we can expect resistance at all levels. User participation and control over the implementation procedures are therefore of paramount importance.

The structure of this chapter first examines the overall strategies that might be employed in implementation and their respective advantages and disadvantages. Thereafter techniques for each of the human and organisational issues are examined. Finally the requirements for post-implementation support and development are considered.

Implementation Strategies

There are various ways in which implementation can be approached and these are listed in Figure 9.1. The strategies can be cast on a dimension ranging from the most revolutionary — where users stop using the old system one day and switch to a fully working new system the next — to the most evolutionary — where users progressively make the changeover in a period of months or years. There is no universal right solution, only appropriate solutions for different situations. The five broad strategies listed in Figure 9.1 are not mutually exclusive. We will identify the main principles of each strategy and evaluate them against the goals that have to be achieved for successful implementation.

Figure 9.1
Implementation strategies

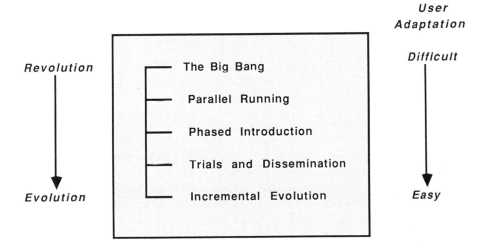

1. The Big Bang

As its name implies this is the strategy of the instant changeover, when everybody associated with the new system moves to the fully functioning new system on a given date. The most celebrated example in recent years was the overnight switch of the London Stock Market to electronic trading in 1986. Obviously the operation of this strategy requires very careful planning because everything has to be ready to work simultaneously. All the different components of the system must be tested, loaded with data and validated, all the organisational changes must have been determined and agreed and all of the users must be trained and ready for the great day. For a large system this requires meticulous planning. It must inevitably constitute a considerable risk to normal business because the chances of everything functioning smoothly from the first day are not high.

There is a regular pattern to the process of organisational change, known in the literature as the 'initial dip phenomenon' and depicted in Figure 9.2.

Figure 9.2
Adaptation to change

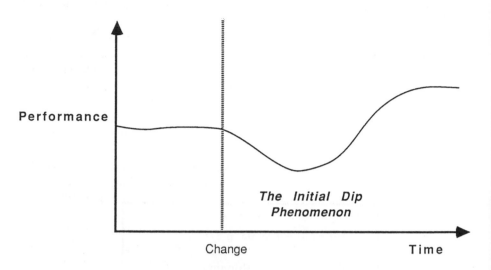

At the point when a change is introduced organisational performance usually falls. This may be due to equipment problems but is also because people are struggling to master the new equipment and the new ways in which they need to relate to others. After a period of weeks or months, if the new system is of value, performance may return to normal and even achieve new heights. This phenomenon has two implications. Firstly, management must expect it and be prepared for a difficult period. Secondly, steps can be taken to minimise the period of disruption.

The chances of catastrophic failure can be minimised by holding off-line trials before launch which not only test the system but also allow staff to rehearse new operating procedures. However, scaling up the operation to full, live working will inevitably throw greater strain on both equipment and staff and some provision must be made for back-up in the event of failure.

Before the change and for the settling period after the change there will be a considerable need for extra resources. This will be a recurrent theme in presenting these strategies; normal business requires resources and introducing change also requires resources. As a result, even if the ultimate aim is to reduce resources, the period when the change is introduced will actually require more. This is usually accepted when the resources are specialist staff whose business is change; technical staff, trainers, etc. What is not so readily accepted is the need to supplement user resources. Users need time to plan for major changes, to train in the use of new equipment and to practise new operating procedures. If this is crammed into short periods or people are spared one at a time so that normal work is not jeopardised, the preparation for change will be inadequate. In a 'big bang' approach this can be very dangerous because underprepared staff will almost certainly take longer and make more mistakes. A strategy used in a number of large organisations where change is recognised as a norm rather than an exception is the maintenance of a buffer of experienced staff who can go into any office and take over the duties on a temporary basis so that the staff can plan the change, undergo training, etc. Some form of this strategy is vital if the 'big bang' is to be successful.

Given the problem of trying to bring the many-faceted aspects of a complex change process into focus in a single implementation phase, there would need to be a strong reason for adopting this approach. It inevitably places regular staff and change staff in stressful conditions. The reasons usually given are that the 'big bang' strategy provides an integrated centrally managed way of insuring the implementation takes place. By making both the technical and organisational changes simultaneously there can also be no confusion about the work system being operated, which can occur if the changes are made piecemeal over time.

It is also the only way in which some kinds of application can be introduced. If, for example, a system gives little benefit until a 'critical mass' of functionality or users has been achieved, it is important to achieve this level as quickly as possible. An electronic mail system, for example, becomes progressively more useful the more people you can reach through it. An airline reservation system is effective to the extent that the different locations at which reservations can be made around the world all have real-time access to the data base. Since nothing can be worse for user motivation than labouring for months with a system that is giving little or no return because it has not achieved a suitable scale, the 'critical mass argument' is probably the most compelling reason for adopting the 'big bang' strategy.

2. Parallel Running

One solution to the risks of the 'big bang' instant changeover is to run the old system alongside the new one until the new system has been shown to be reliable and everybody is familiar with its operation. Some degree and duration of parallel running is common in many installations where avoidance of risk to current business is a major priority.

This form of implementation strategy provides an insurance policy against failure but is not without its costs. Running two ways of working simultaneously inevitably involves extra work. The same data, for example, will be put on the new system as is being processed manually. If the extra work falls upon existing staff with no additional resources they are likely to experience strain which may develop into negative reactions to the new system. Extra resources are essential if this strategy is adopted. If staff are putting data into the new system for no apparent reason whilst using the old system for real tasks, they may experience the new system as a futile waste of time. If it keeps failing or producing rubbish they may not develop confidence in it and may seek to prolong the use of existing procedures. Conversely, if the operation of the new system saves much time and energy or confers other benefits, it can be very frustrating to continue using the old system. Running two systems together invites staff to make comparisons and can build up motivational problems. It is essential under these circumstances to plan the implementation programme with the staff affected so that they understand the rationale for parallel running, can see the progress being made as tests are carried out, and can participate in the decisions concerning when and how the switch to the new system is to be completed.

Another problem with parallel running is how and when to make organisational changes. Whilst it may be possible for staff in their traditional roles to operate both technical systems simultaneously it is very difficult for them to operate two organisational structures and procedures at the same time. There is therefore a tendency to retain the existing social system through the period of parallel running which may produce its own tensions and may inhibit the search for and implementation of more advantageous organisational structures. Parallel running can therefore inhibit organisational change.

3. Phased Introduction (by Function or User Group)

A very common implementation strategy is to introduce the new system slowly over a period of time. This may be done by introducing some of the functionality of the system before the rest or by introducing some users to the system before others. The advantage of this process to the technical staff is that they can concentrate upon part of the system or some of the users and can therefore spread their resources more evenly. There is also less need to provide massive extra resources to support users although some support will be needed. For the users, this strategy often enables them to cope with the change a little at a time which makes it more manageable.

The process of providing functionality in phases is very common when it is a bespoke development since the first part of the system can be introduced whilst later parts are still being programmed. If this strategy is adopted the sequence in which the system is delivered becomes critical and what makes technical sense may be at variance with what makes sense to users. Technically, for example, it may be sensible to get all the procedures for capturing data in place before creating the program for manipulating data and providing outputs. This sequence could lead to users providing data with little or no service by way of return. For many users the first experiences of a system tend to be 'front end' effort for no reward and, for busy people, this can be a frustrating experience and can sow the seeds for subsequent rejection of the system. A good rule when planning the phased introduction of a system is that each group of users should get a service they value early in the implementation to provide a positive experience of the system upon which to build.

The phased introduction of a system to different groups of users is best accomplished when users in different departments or branches are to use the same system but can use it relatively independently of one another. It is common to create an implementation team which moves from department to department, installing equipment, tailoring the system to local needs and training users. Such a team may also contain people who can take over user roles on a temporary basis so that they can familiarise themselves with the new system. By moving from place to place the implementation team should develop expertise in understanding and meeting user needs. There is the danger, however, that the familiarity of the process to the implementation team will blind them to its unfamiliarity to each new set of users. It is easy to believe that, if the first implementation took, for example, four weeks, the tenth implementation should be a lot faster. If the limiting factor is the rate at which users can learn and adjust to the new situation, there will be no difference between the first and last implementation.

4. Trials and Dissemination

Given that there are many problems in implementation to overcome, a trial can be a very good way of initiating the process. A trial is usually a small-scale implementation with one department or section, ideally using the system for live working. The aim is to test the system which it is planned to implement on a wider basis. This form of trial should not be confused with prototyping (see Chapter 6) which is normally undertaken in order to test and develop a system specification. A trial is undertaken later in the design process when a system has been developed or selected and is ready for implementation.

The purpose of a trial is usually to test the technical system; will it do the job required by the work organisation? It is normally perceived as a test of a single solution but in fact it can be used to test a number of detailed options both technical and organisational (for example, the allocation of duties in running the system, the level of access to be provided to different types of staff, the specific outputs to be provided for specific staff, etc.). These may seem small issues within the totality of the system but they are of great importance to the staff directly affected and it is important to provide an opportunity to identify the problems that users will have in adjusting to the system, the kind of training that will be required and many other practicalities that only become apparent when the technical and social system have to work together to meet work objectives. The role of trials in serving human and organisational objectives will be considered in more detail later in this chapter.

The (often implicit) assumption behind a trial is that, once it has identified and resolved most of the problems, the system can be disseminated without too much difficulty throughout the user population. The major weakness of the trial approach is that this cannot be presumed. The lessons from a trial cannot easily be transferred to other users. There are two problems. The first is that aspects of the solutions may not be appropriate to other groups because they have different task needs or local customs. The second problem has been known since the 1930s as the 'Hawthorne Effect', following the series of experiments conducted at the Hawthorne Factory in Chicago under the supervision of Elton Mayo (Rothlisberger and Dickson, 1939). In one of these experiments a group of workers were provided with progressively better working conditions (better lighting conditions, better rest breaks, etc.), and productivity progressively improved. Then the conditions were gradually returned to their original levels and, to the surprise of the investigators, productivity continued to improve. They concluded that the explanation was the positive attitude of the operators because of their involvement in the project, being specially selected, studied and considered in ways they had not experienced in their normal factory life. A trial system can put staff 'in the spotlight' in the same way and a positive response can be the result. The danger is that subsequent groups will not feel specially treated, will not feel they are participating in deciding their future because this was done earlier, and may be quite negative about the introduction of the system. As a result of these two issues, the move from trial to dissemination has to be handled carefully with participating opportunities for each new group of users.

5. Infrastructure and Incremental Application

The final implementation strategy is a mixture of strategies whose common themes are evolution and local, user-led design. The objectives are to create applications that are tailor-made to the needs of the individuals or groups of users which can develop in sophistication as the users learn to exploit the technology and understand better how it might serve them. It is a strategy used for professional or managerial groups of users where a failure to match needs exactly leads to system rejection. It is also a strategy which mixes design and implementation to such a degree as to make a phase model of the design process almost irrelevant.

One form of this strategy is the *ad hoc*, 'end-user development' approach in which each user group acquires generic applications, usually based upon microcomputers. This approach tends, across the organisation, to produce an unplanned evolution of applications which, as we saw in Chapter 3, can lead to dead ends, technical incompatibilities and users who cannot trade information with one another. The advantage of end-user control is also gained at the expense of users themselves having to expend a great deal of time and effort if a working system is to be implemented. Wroe (1986) describes a number of user-led applications by small builders in which a common finding was that the loading and validating of data bases by non-technical staff proved a much more time-consuming process than any of the users envisaged. Unless the user organisation had spare resources available, the result was that implementation became a long-drawn-out, part-time activity to be undertaken when time permitted. The promise of the working system tended to be always 'just around the corner'.

If evolutionary design is to be effective end users need support and central organisational planning is vital. Evolution should not be equated with lack of planning. The aim has to be to provide a policy infrastructure within which end-user tailored applications can thrive. Three elements to this infrastructure are necessary. Firstly, technical support is necessary in order that appropriate equipment is acquired both for the user's purposes and for the maintenance of compatibility and enhancement capability within the organisation. Secondly, implementation support is required to provide technical help in setting up applications and the extra resources needed to facilitate the work necessary to implement the application. Thirdly, organisational policies are required which stipulate the type of application that is acceptable without limiting the freedom of user groups to develop systems appropriate to their own needs. The key to most of these policies is the balance betweeen user freedom and organisational control. If all three elements are not present applications are likely to falter or to become dysfunctional to corporate policy. Maskery (1986), for example, describes an attempt to allow users to develop a planned, micro-computer-based range of applications within a

Bank. Technical and organisational policies and some forms of technical support were provided centrally but no extra user resources were available which meant that the rate and form of application was heavily dependent upon who had the time available and who had the strongest motivation to put in extra time. These factors tend to distort evolution so that it may not be the most desirable to the organisation. Corporate strategies for the support of projects of this kind is one of the themes of Chapter 11.

Choosing an Implementation Strategy

As with most other issues in the application of information technology, the selection of an appropriate implementation strategy is dependent upon the goals to be achieved and the type of application. Although five discrete strategies have been presented they can be used in combination and there are variations within each of them. A technique for choosing an implementation strategy, following the general form of techniques in this volume, is to prioritise the goals to be achieved and evaluate each strategy against them. To summarise, the significant goals are likely to be:

1. Setting up and validating a technical system which will give a worthwhile service to the user population. If the system will need a large 'critical mass' before a service can be achieved, some form of 'big bang' or general 'parallel running' will be necessary.
2. Minimising the risk to normal business during the transition. If the risk is a major consideration some form of trial is important and 'parallel running' or phased introduction thereafter will ease the problem.
3. Facilitating the move to other organisational forms. This is best achieved when technical issues do not dominate the implementation timetable. Adequate preparation of both technical and organisational changes through trials and clear-cut change points for the whole socio-technical system are necessary as in the 'big bang' or phased introduction strategies.
4. Moving at the rate users are able and willing to learn and change. Too rapid a rate of implementation can lead to fear, overload and rejection. Too rapid a rate does not give users time to understand and therefore to be able to participate effectively in decision-making. Where user rejection or inability to cope is a major consideration some form of phased or evolutionary development, possibly including trials, is appropriate. However, too slow or dissipated development will lose its identity and become a victim of organisational inertia.
5. Providing maximum opportunities for local design. If it is important for users to tailor systems to their own needs, the strategy needs to provide users with time and opportunity to learn and develop. Trials and evolutionary design techniques are the logical way to proceed.

It is, of course, quite likely that several of these goals will be deemed very important and several strategies will have conflicting attractions. In this situation it is worth remembering that no implementation can be successful without the ability and willingness of staff to co-operate in it.

Human and Organisational Aspects of Implementation

Whatever strategy is adopted there are a number of human and organisational aspects to implementation which will have to be considered. They reflect the culmination of the different strands of design discussed in earlier chapters; we need a temporary organisational structure to conduct the implementation, we need detailed technical design to tailor the system to individual needs, we need workstation and environmental design to tailor the physical characteristics of the technical system to the circumstances in which users will employ it, and we need organisational design to implement the detail of any organisational change policy. In this section we will deal with each of these topics and consider their implications in respect of different implementation strategies. We will treat user trials as a separate topic since it is a way of dealing with many of these issues. Similarly, we will treat the issue of training and user support as a separate topic at the end of the chapter both because of its importance and because it is a topic which pervades implementation and post-implementation.

Organisational Structures for Implementation

It is likely that the design team which developed the system will have to be supplemented during implementation. There will be many more people to deal with, users to train, etc., and different skills may be required, for example, training and workstation design experts. It may also be necessary to implement the systems at different locations which will demand the involvement of different groups of staff.

The general principles advanced in Chapter 5 which determine who is involved and in what capacity remain applicable in this phase but there are variations. Most of the major technical issues should have been resolved and the major issues now concern the integration of the technical system into the organisational fabric.

There is a powerful argument that this stage should be controlled by user management with technical support provided to commission the system. Within the customer–contractor model this could be the stage when the contractor hands over the system to the customer. It is often the case that a senior manager needs to be seconded to take charge of implementation to ensure that every facet of the process is considered. If implementation is left to technical staff it should be no surprise when technical issues dominate the process and the problems of introducing organisational change (for example, changes in duty rosters, grading, industrial relations issues etc.) come as a surprise to everyone. A senior user manager will have the authority and the knowledge to mobilise the normal organisational procedures (for example, consultative processes with trade unions) to deal with these issues. A user 'champion' is particularly vital in those strategies where the impetus for change can be lost because of ordinary work pressures. Evolutionary development, for example, can stagnate and trials can become permanent with no dissemination to the rest of the organisation. It is important that someone senior within the user organisation has overall responsibility for ensuring that progress continues and can act as a focus for maintaining the impetus.

The role of people who have earlier acted as user representatives in design is particularly important during implementation. By this time they should be knowledgeable about the technical system and its organisational and human implications. If they have consulted and informed their colleagues throughout the design process, they should already have built up a constructive relationship with them about the impending change. They should now be able to capitalise on their knowledge and role by acting as local co-ordinators as the system is implemented in their location. Under the direction of the senior user manager with overall responsibility and with the technical support of the technologists, they can help their colleagues through the change process. They can, for example, organise, run and evaluate trials, personalise systems, help plan changes in office accommodation and equipment installation, plan the development of suitable training regimes and facilitate the organisational changes that must be necessary. Whilst many of these activities can be planned centrally they must be administered locally and will need to be adapted to local conditions. The local user representative is in an ideal position to undertake these tasks.

Personalising the System

If technical systems are to be more usable and acceptable to their users they need to be closely tailored to the task needs and the characteristics of the users. Where a system serves a variety of users, the tailoring should mean that the system will need to show many different faces. Increasingly, information technology systems have the capacity for personalisation, and in the implementation phase this capability has to be harnessed. The range of system components that can be personalised is tremendous and growing with every new generation of products. It is not easy to classify them but one important dimension is the ease or difficulty a naïve user might have in harnessing the adaptability without technical support. An illustrative classification based on this dimmension is given in Figure 9.3.

Probably the simplest forms of personalisation are letting the system know the code names and numbers by which one will gain access, the address one wishes to adopt, etc. At a more complex level there may be a need to give names, sizes, etc. to personal files, to create personal lists of names, addresses, telephone numbers, etc. These may seem trivial issues but they represent effort the user must make before any benefits accrue. If the system is not easy for the naïve user to use in 'setting up' mode, this 'front end' effort can be daunting and can be a barrier to these facilities being used.

Many systems are for multi-user usage and some of the setting-up may involve issues of levels of access to information and to facilities, how monitoring and recording facilities are to be used, etc. As we noted in Chapters 7 and 8 these are very sensitive issues and need to complement the job design and work organisation objectives of the user organisation.

The opportunities within systems to select and structure outputs represent important ways in which users can personalise the service of a system to serve their specific task needs. They may, for example, be able to select the data parameters they want displayed in a table, the grain of detail they require, whether the output should be tabular or graphical and many other parameters. They may also be able to vary processing parameters, for example, giving the system decision rules for 'management-by-exception' reporting. In theory all these choices could be made each time the system is used but in practice most users settle into a routine, and organising the way

Figure 9.3
Personalising systems

Easy

Assigning security codes, addresses, labels etc.

Creating personal files, lists, abbreviations etc.

Organising group structures, procedures, access etc

Selecting and developing personal reports, setting personal decision rules and defaults etc.

Organising personal data bases, loading and validating data.

Using packages to create special applications

Programming new applications

Difficult

they will use the facilities of the system when it is first implemented is an important task if they are to avoid using the system inappropriately. Eason *et al.* (1974), for example, gave several examples of user groups complaining of a poor 'task fit', when in fact the systems they were using were capable of meeting their needs. After months or years of usage, they had forgotten the facilities existed to match the system more closely to their needs or had forgotten how to use these facilities.

Users may also find that it is possible, within the software packages to which they have access, to structure their own personal data bases and, in effect, create their own applications. Whilst the customisation of these packages does not involve programming, the rules that have to be followed, and the rigour required to obtain a viable service, can seem to users to be as complex as programming. Finally, if the system contains a general purpose programming language, there is no technical reason why users should not program unique applications of their own.

Not all users will be offered this range of choice but even in the most routine of applications there is likely to be value in offering different groups of users some degree of latitude to customise the system to their needs. If the system is for discretionary, occasional users, each with their own professional or managerial responsibilities, the need for personalised services will be vital if usage is to develop. The problem is that it is necessary but not sufficient to offer the choice. The full array is baffling and daunting to new users and, left to their own devices, they will make little use of the opportunities. Users will need support in the 'setting up' phase to make the best use of personalisation opportunities. A combination of user representatives and technical staff is possibly the best team to support users in this 'fine tuning' process. The effort required to get this right should not be underestimated. The process requires an individual or group analysis of task needs and user characteristics and probably trial usage of selected options to test whether they meet the needs. A local, participative, process which uses many of the design concepts discussed elsewhere in this volume is necessary if the technical capability for personalisation is to be harnessed to good effect.

Work Station and Physical Environment Design

In recent years considerable effort has been devoted to getting the physical ergonomics of displays and controls to a higher standard. It is therefore amazing that much of this is wasted when a visual display unit is simply placed on a desk in a position which makes it very difficult to operate. A terminal placed with its screen in direct sunlight will, for example, be stressful to read whatever the quality of the display. It is important during implementation that the ergonomics of the workstation and the physical environment are carefully considered not only because what could be easy to use can be made difficult to use if they are not but also because this can be a major cause of the health and stress disorders which have been associated with the use of visual display units (backache, visual fatigue, neckache, etc.). Many studies, for example, Hünting *et al.* (1980), have shown that these symptoms are more common among full-time users who are fixed in poor postural conditions by inappropriate workstation positions.

When a visual display unit is implemented in an office or factory environment there are a variety of physical ergonomic issues to consider:

1. *Furniture for the Workstation.* The visual display unit will probably be placed on a desk. It may have associated equipment such as a disc drive and printer. If the user is working from documents a document holder may be necessary. Desk space will probably be required alongside the terminal and a suitable chair for working at the terminal and away from it will be required. It will be clear that it is necessary to select more than a terminal and that all of these pieces of equipment and furniture should be compatible so they can form an integrated work station. Pearce (1989) provides an example of the design of a workstation for a bank cashier.

   Where a terminal is to be portable the workstation problem is different. In practice, this means the terminal has to be much more robust so that it can be used in many different circumstances. Davies (1989) gives an example of a portable billing machine to be used by electricity meter readers. This device had to be used wherever household meters were located and therefore had to be read in conditions ranging from direct sunlight to semi-darkness. The keyboard also had to be capable of use in normal temperatures and, outdoors in winter, by a person wearing gloves.

2. *Adjusting the Workstation.* Terminals now have detachable keyboards and often the screen has tilt and swivel. Similarly, desks, chairs and other furniture, sold for use

with visual display terminals, may also be adjustable for height, angle, etc. These adjustments are important if the workstation is to be appropriately set up so that users are, for example, reading the screen at the proper distance and operating the keyboard at the correct height. It is not sufficient to provide the equipment and let the user make the adjustments. In the same way that the customisation capability of software may not be used by users, the adjustments on furniture may be ignored. Even when they are used, the user may not have the knowledge to set them correctly. During implementation it is necessary to have a specialist such as an ergonomist set up the workstation, to promulgate standards or to provide users with training to do it for themselves.

3. *Room Layout.* Information technology equipment has usually to be accommodated with existing office or factory equipment. Not only do individual workstations have to be designed but entire room layouts may need rethinking to match the flow of work from one person to another. Some job design criteria may be heavily influenced by room layout decisions. A work-group, if it is to function well, needs a clearly defined territory within which to work. The orientation of workstations to one another should provide the opportunity for eye contact between individuals working together and the location of shared equipment can help to avoid the problem of social isolation that comes with heavy usage of a visual display terminal. Where full-time usage is common the provision of rest rooms will also be a necessity. The layout will also need to conform to safety and health legislation for circulation space and the space provided for each person.

Whilst room layout can be undertaken by specialists, it is another area where user participation can be practised to good effect. In the City firm example presented by Gower and Eason (1989), secretaries worked with an ergonomist on room layout, the ergonomist providing technical inputs on space standards etc., and the secretaries providing information about task flows and preferences about location of equipment, orientation of workstations, etc. People who will have to work in work spaces have strong views about workstations and room layouts and value the opportunity to contribute at this level of planning. It is a level where everybody can contribute to the systems design process.

4. *Physical Environment.* The use of information technology equipment is sensitive to a number of environmental dimensions. Lighting conditions are most critical because users are often making simultaneous use of paper, which is visible because of reflected light, and screens which emit their own light. Getting a room appropriately lit for both of these conditions and for variable external sources of light from windows, is quite a difficult problem. Noise may be a problem if printers are located close to workstations and can be expected to be more of a problem when speech input and speech output devices are more widely used. Visual display terminals emit heat so that there can also be heating and ventilation considerations. When a room is to contain many terminals the physical environment may need careful design if users are not to be subjected to discomfort and stress.

Guidance about the design of workstations and physical environment is available from a number of sources (for example, Cakir *et al.* 1980, Damodaran *et al.* 1980 and Grandjean 1987). There are several ways in which this knowledge might be applied during system implementation. One way is for an ergonomics practitioner to provide specialist technical advice, although this input should always be provided as part of a dialogue with users, and to permit the exercise of user preference within the domain of satisfactory technical solutions. Another approach is to train one or more of the implementation team (for example, a user representative, safety officer or building services specialist) in these topics and encourage them to work with users to find acceptable solutions. Finally, the solution adopted in some organisations is to develop internal standards on these issues (usually a sub-set of published standards) and to circulate the standards whenever implementation is taking place. A number of trade unions have also published guidance documents to assist their officials and members in assessing these issues during implementation. This approach certainly ensures a wider awareness of the importance of these issues but there is a danger that blind adherence to guidelines can produce unsatisfactory results. Preference should always be given to having specialist knowledge available to ensure formalised guidance has been appropriately interpreted for local conditions.

Implementing Organisational Change

The design process may have identified the need for organisational change, and decisions about new forms of work organisation may have been taken, but there is still much to do during implementation to bring these organisational changes to fruition. It is useful to divide the required activities into two categories:

1. amending personnel policies in the organisation to meet the new requirements; and
2. helping the individuals concerned to make the changes.

In most organisations there is a more or less formalised body of policy which constitutes the 'contract' between employer and employee. In various ways this body of policy may define aspects of working conditions which may be affected by the implementation of an information technology system. Examples may be task allocation procedures, demarcation procedures, working hours and work–rest pause regimes, grading and salary levels, reporting procedures and career developments. It is also likely that the organisation will have procedures whereby these policies are reviewed and changed and that they will, to some extent, be negotiated by management and representatives of the work-force.

If the effective introduction of a new socio-technical system requires changes in these policies, and the more radical the development the more likely this becomes, then the changes will need discussion and perhaps negotiation by the agreed organisational procedures. This process has a tendency to take the debate away from the specific location of implementation into a wider organisational arena. It may also become enmeshed in other ongoing debates which have nothing directly to do with the system being implemented (for example, there may be a group of employees with a long-standing grievance about grading who see this as an opportunity to restate their case). Faced with these possibilities there is a tendency for user managers and technical staff responsible for implementation to avoid taking the case for organisational change to these procedures or to leave it as late as possible. This may mean technical systems are introduced without the necessary organisational changes. Quite often it means the system is implemented in one location where users were willing to go beyond the agreed procedures but it cannot be disseminated more widely because that would require organisation-wide negotiation. Failure to deal fully and formally with these issues is often the reason why organisations do not exploit the advantages of the technology.

To avoid this obstacle the requirements for change need early identification and early presentation to the relevant bodies to ensure there is time for informed debate. One mechanism that has proved useful in facilitating change is the New Technology Agreement, an agreement between the organisation and the representatives of the work-force about the way issues will be handled whenever information technology systems are implemented. Such an agreement should prepare the way for any implementation and avoid the need to create *ad hoc* and probably anomalous procedures for each separate implementation. Ideally the New Technology Agreement specifies the procedures to be followed for each issue, i.e. who is to be consulted and within what policy framework. Sometimes within the Agreement attempts are made to specify acceptable outcomes (for example, that no user will work on a visual display unit for more than two hours without being permitted a break). Such specificity can prove very inflexible later to the disadvantage of everybody. An expression of the spirit of the agreement, together with the parties to be involved in the decision-making and the body of knowledge they should consult, sustains flexibility and encourages local democracy.

The actual implementation of changes in a specific location involves local decisions about who does what, how they relate to one another, etc. This should be within the normal purview of line management — possibly with the help of people (for example, user representatives), who have been directly involved in planning the development and have a deep understanding of the changes to be made. For the staff concerned this process is not only about change decisions but also about learning to adapt to change; to understand new responsibilities, new ways of working with other people in different roles, etc. Involving people in planning the change is, once again, the best way of ensuring that they understand and are committed to it. One technique for accomplishing this process when people are going to work together in new ways is team building. In this technique the people who will need to work together are brought together away from their normal working environment. They are then given the opportunity to plan how they will work together under the new conditions, to share perceptions of the problems that will have to be overcome, and appreciate how each person intends to interpret their new role. It may also be appropriate for the team to work out how to move from the current to the future situation. This off-line discussion can avert a lot of problems later because it builds up a team understanding that allows people, under the stress of normal work, to interpret correctly how others will behave under new conditions.

The Conduct of User Trials

It has become common to precede the main period of implementation with user trials. Given the many issues that may become apparent and will need to be resolved once implementation begins, a trial period is a sensible precaution. A trial can provide a test of whether the technical system can cope with normal operational pressures and whether its functionality is suited to user purposes. It can also show the extent to which the system is usable and acceptable and test the organisational changes that go with the technical implementation. Whilst a trial is a test of the system that is intended for implementation (unlike the prototype tests described in Chapter 6) there will probably be opportunities to try alternatives at a number of levels (for example, altern-ative interfaces, training procedures, implementation strategies, forms of work organi-sation, etc.).

Given the frequency of trials it is surprising how little is learnt and how many problems still arise when full implementation takes place. The problem is that if the trial is not well planned, the lessons from it are not learned and used in later imple-mentation. In many cases it seems to be sufficient to put in the technical system, and if it survives and is used, the trial is deemed to have been successful. This is very wasteful of what could be learned and may not be a good predictor of subsequent implement-ation.

In this section we will first consider different types of trials, then identify the major principles that need to underpin the conduct of trials and, finally, the process of dissemination to wider implementation.

There are many types of trials or pilots but probably the main distinction to make is between off-line and live trials. An off-line trial is a simulation or an experimental use of the technical system using dummy data and simulated tasks. It has the advantage that, because it is not live, it does not matter if the system fails or mistakes are made and more alternatives may be tried. When a large system is being planned, especially a large military system, an off-line simulation is frequently created as a test bed for the system and can also serve as a training environment for future users.

A trial that is one-step removed from a live trial is the implementation of the system for parallel running alongside the existing system. The output from the new system may not be used but it can be used with real tasks by real users and its perform-ance compared with existing methods. As we discussed earlier in this chapter, the main disadvantage is the increase in workload the operation of two systems entails.

A live trial actually asks users to make real use of the technical system for their work and they may have to make organisational changes as part of the process. This is a trial in the sense that it is likely to be closely monitored and, if there are serious problems that cannot be overcome, it may be withdrawn. It is unlikely, under oper-ational conditions, that major experiments will be undertaken to try different alter-natives although sometimes different trials can be undertaken in comparable locations to test alternatives.

The strength of the 'off-line' trial is that it is a safe forum in which to try alter-natives. The weakness is that it may lack important elements of reality and, in particular, it is not embedded in organisational structure and practice in the way that is inevitable in the live trial. In practice, although not in theory, the off-line trial is used to test issues of functionality and usability whereas the live trial will reveal problems of acceptability and organisational consequences. A fuller presentation of alternatives and their strengths and weaknesses is given by Tapscott (1982) who bases his user-driven method of introducing office automation on the evolutionary use of pilot studies.

Whatever the type of trial there are a number of principles to the good conduct of trials if they are to be effective guides for full implementation:

1. *Realism and Representation.* The aim of the trial is to test the system in a small-scale situation as a guide to what will happen in full-scale implementation. It follows that it will only be a good guide to the extent that the small-scale version faithfully mirrors the conditions of the full-scale reality. This affects many aspects of how trials are undertaken. The tasks that are undertaken in the trial should show the diversity and frequency to be found in the full-scale reality. The users should have knowledge, skill, motives and characteristics similar to other users. The conditions under which people work in trials should be similar to those found outside. The technical system should operate as it will when it is serving the full user population, no better and no worse. If these requirements cannot be met, note must be taken of the deficiencies and attempts made to assess the way in which these might influence or bias the results of the trial.

   These factors affect the off-line and live trials in slightly different ways. The problem in the off-line trial is to simulate reality in an artificial setting which is especially difficult with respect to user motivation — which will be different because it is not real but is observed. The live trial is inevitably realistic but the choice of location may not be representative of the range of locations. There is a tendency to choose a location because it is isolated or local to the design team or has a sympathetic manager or may be easier to handle than other sites. These are all pragmatic reasons but they suggest the location will not be characteristic of other locations. The prime criterion should be that the location is representative on as many dimensions as possible.

2. *The Purpose of the Trial.* A trial can serve many purposes but, without clarity of purpose, the lessons for one purpose can become confused with the others. It is a primary principle of experimental design that different variables should be controlled in such a way that it is possible to associate cause unambiguously with effect. It is not the purpose of a trial to undertake formal, controlled experiments but the lessons are just as valid. There is no point, for example, trying to use a trial to assess the merits of two forms of training procedure when the trial changes the skills needed for the group of users using one form of training but not the other. There is a tendency to drift into a trial just to see whether the system works which can lead to a situation where no one is certain what has been gained from the trial. It is important to establish the purposes of a trial and to define what criteria will be used to judge whether the trial has been successful. The structure of the trial should then become evident because it will have to have a shape which serves these purposes. Tapscott (1982) gives examples of different structures for trials for different purposes. This may sound as though everything about the trial has to be fixed before it is started. This will be true in circumstances where a comparison between major alternatives is planned because changing one in mid-trial may invalidate the comparison. However, another kind of trial is an iterative process in which progress

is regularly assessed and changes are made to overcome difficulties and improve performance. This is a different kind of trial but an equally valid process.

3. *Subjects as Participants in Design.* Once a trial is under way there is a tendency to think of the users as subjects in an experiment whose reactions are under study. In the spirit of user-centred design they should be treated as participants in a design process in which the trial is informing them of the consequences of design decisions and means they are very well prepared to discuss options and preferences. It may be argued that this encourages the Hawthorne Effect; ensuring that the special involvement people feel with the process creates commitment to the system and its implementation. If the trial was a formal experiment in which this effect was unwanted this might be a problem. In this situation it is a force to be sought and utilised. The only counter-argument is that the trial may be positive because of the Hawthorne Effect and this may be misleading with respect to later implementation when the special participation effects will not be present. As we shall see below, the best answer to this is to try to sustain the special participation effects throughout implementation.

4. *Measurement and Evaluation.* A trial implies some kind of evaluation of success which implies ways of measuring success. In many cases trials are set up with no clear evaluation procedures or measures which can lead to subsequent arguments about the meaning of the trial. In the next chapter we will look at evaluation methods in general and discuss what can be measured and how it can be measured. An important issue is who does the evaluating. Because technical designers and users may have a vested interest in the outcome it can be very useful to give responsibility for the evaluation to an independent agent.

5. *Learning the Lessons and Disseminating the Findings.* The results of the trial should influence what is subsequently implemented and how it is implemented. Too often most of the lessons learned by those involved in the trial are not passed on to others. There are two reasons why this occurs. One is that no formal assessment is made and, even when it is, no one is charged with receiving and acting on the findings. The organisation setting up the trial has to ensure it has set up a process of receiving, debating and using the findings. The second problem is time-scale. It takes time to run a trial and logically the evaluation should come towards the end when some degree of steady-state working has been achieved. An evaluation report would then need to be prepared and discussed. The timetable for widespread implementation may not be able to wait for this process, however. Implementation might be under way even as the trial is revealing the faults in what is being implemented. If full implementation cannot wait it is important to plan successive evaluations of the trial so that early lessons can be disseminated in time for them to be of value.

The other problem of dissemination Tapscott (1982) expresses in this second law of office systems: 'The ease of a pilot implementation is inversely related to the complexity of its operational extension' (p. 199). There are many reasons why it gets difficult just when everybody in the design team thinks the work has been done. One reason is that the technical problems of supporting a full-scale, operational system alongside the existing operational systems are often much greater than supporting an isolated and temporary trial system. Another is that, since the work has now been done, there may be a scaling down of effort and time so that resources are not available when they are needed. The resources that were needed for development are almost certainly now needed to support implementation. The third reason can be summarised as the 'not invented here' syndrome which is the adverse of the Hawthorne Effect. Where people enthusiastically embrace that which they have helped to develop they may resist that which was developed by others. This may be because the system does not fit their needs as well as it does those who were involved in design or it may simply be that they were not involved and see the system as an imposition and a threat. A representative form of user participation employed in the early phase of design will mitigate against this reaction but there will still be many users who have been relatively uninvolved. It is here that the principle of minimum critical design can be used to good effect because, if it has been applied, there should be opportunities for each new group of users to plan for themselves how the system can best serve them and how they are going to use it. As a result of the trial, the implementation team should be in a good position to help the users see the opportunities and make best use of them to make the system their own.

Training and User Support

The most obvious human requirement of implementation is the training necessary to ensure all users can cope adequately with the new situation. This has been deliberately left to the end of the chapter because it is a complex subject deserving special treatment.

There is a set of assumptions about training new users of information technology systems which guides many design teams which we must first make explicit. It is assumed that what users need to know is how to operate the new equipment; they need, for example, 'keyboard skills'. At the time of implementation there will, therefore, be a training programme which will build up these skills in the user population to a criteria level which will allow them to operate effectively when the system is implemented.

This procedure is an inadequate way of coping with user learning needs in two major respects:

1. People who are going to be regular or full-time users of a system may be willing and able to attend a full training course. An increasing proportion of the user population are, however, going to be occasional users who will not see the value of attending a full course. Even if they did attend such a course, subsequent, intermittent usage would mean they would have forgotten the detail before they got round to using it.
2. Training people in the operational use of new equipment is only part of the adaptation people need to make to take advantage of information technology. They may have to make emotional changes before they can make cognitive gains; they may feel threatened by the technology and fear they will not be able to cope. A full skills

training course they are expected to pass in a given period of time may only heighten their fear. It is said that this is one of the major obstacles for the older worker. They will also have to learn many other things besides how to operate equipment; they may need to view their jobs differently, the tasks may be different, they may need to be able to decide which facilities on the system are to be used for which task purposes, they may find they have to learn different ways of relating to colleagues, customers, etc. A new socio-technical system involves much more adaptation to change than operating a keyboard and training has to reflect this.

The differences between the way the full-time and the occasional users can be treated warrant different treatment in the implementation process.

Training for Regular or Full-time Users

Training design for regular users can to some extent follow the guidelines offered for training course design. Before implementation an assessment is required for training needs. This should be based on the user and task analyses described in Chapter 6 because these will show the knowledge that will be required and the existing skills, capabilities and characteristics within the user population. The definition of the skills and knowledge required must represent the range of socio-technical changes users must confront to operate in the new situation and should not be restricted to becoming 'computer literate'.

The design mechanisms for helping people adapt from their current skills and capabilities to those they will need may include a training course sitting at a terminal but may involve many other ways of developing learning as well. The creation of manuals for use when the system is in operation is one important medium. Involvement in design and planning exercises and trials is both a way of participating and a way of learning. Overcoming fear of new technology may require a different kind of training before formal training can begin. What is needed is an introduction to the technology in a risk-free environment, i.e. an opportunity to play with the technology without fear of making mistakes or of 'breaking it' and without performance being monitored. It may be appropriate to set up a free access 'play room' where people can come to terms with equipment in their own way and where they can meet people of their own kind who have been through the same process.

When a formal training course is to be established there are several points to remember. Firstly, the course should be task-centred — not system-centred. It is very easy to slip into a course structure which explains everything the system can do when users may need to know a lot about some parts of the system and little about the rest. Examples users work through should be based on their own work and not on some imaginary 'generic' tasks. People should be encouraged to proceed at their own rate rather than be expected, as a whole class, to achieve specific levels at specified points. Finally, no attempt should be made to cram all of the necessary learning into one training course. As one user said in the survey conducted by Gower and Eason (1989):

> At the end of the training course I was like a learner driver who had just passed the driving test; I knew the basics but I was naive and nervous 'on the road'. Yet

the course had tried to make me into a Grand Prix driver straight away, teaching me all the clever tricks and unusual facilities in the system. After several months establishing my basic skills in operating the system I was ready for a refresher course to teach me the advance facilities but I could not take them in when they were given in the first course.

The question of who can provide this training is problematic. If the definition of what is required is computer skills then computer specialists tend to do the training. When the system is made up of generic products, the supplier of the products often offers the training. The main difficulties with this approach are that the training is not specific to the tasks of the user and it tends to neglect the non-technical skills users also need to acquire. An alternative approach that is gaining popularity is for user representatives to devise and deliver the training and to write user manuals. They have the advantage of knowing their user colleagues and being able to tailor the training materials to their needs. The weakness of both of these schemes is that neither technical specialists nor user representatives are training experts and they may have the right material packaged into very poor instructional forms. The process also needs an input from specialists in training to get the best from technical experts and user representatives.

Training for Occasional Users

As we noted earlier one of the recurrent findings about occasional users is that they tend to under-utilise the facilities at their disposal; they rely on a few facilities with which they are familiar and ignore the rest. This phenomenon seems to occur because of the following factors:

1. *Limited Training.* The fact of intermittent use means that on a 'cost–benefit' basis it is rarely worth the user undergoing comprehensive training before using a system. Training is usually limited to a short 'familiarisation' session. As a result the intermittent user rarely begins system use with an organised understanding of what it contains, what benefits it can provide and how to use it.
2. *Initial Exploration.* In the first stages of usage there is a 'honeymoon' period in which the user is prepared to devote time to trial and error and getting to know the system. A number of researchers (for example, Gambino *et al.*, 1983, Englebart 1982) have noted that this phase comes to an end and is replaced by a phase in which task performance dominates the user's thinking. In this phase 'costs' in terms of time and effort to use the system become much more critical.
3. *The Domination of Known Facilities.* When a user is primarily concerned with task completion there is a tendency to favour known ways of achieving task goals rather than explore unknown alternatives. Exploration of unknowns involves extra effort with no guarantee of success which puts up the 'costs' side of the equation.
4. *Implicit Judgements.* It would be wrong to infer that users spend their time making conscious selection decisions. A better model in many circumstances is the habitual execution of familiar procedures until they do not work, in which case there may be a forced exploration of alternatives.

5. *Unknown Benefits*. The minimising of effort and time 'costs' appears to be the dominant factor but there is a consequence on the 'benefit' side of the equation. Since there is no formal training and limited exploration of capability there is a tendency for users not to appreciate the benefits they could get from the system.

The effect of these factors on the knowledge state of the user is depicted in Figure 9.4. The full-time user (4) can, in theory, be taught the use of many system facilities in the training phase and, whilst there will be some fall back in operation, a good training course will provide a good basis for use. The most frequent progression in the knowledge of the intermittent user is that identified as (1). Although this is described as a learning curve it might be more correct to call it a non-learning curve. The user tends to learn some features of the system to an operational level in the early exploratory phase and this becomes the core knowledge for the stable phase of usage that follows. Alternatively (2) there may be a decline as some of the facilities initially learned may in practice prove to be of little value. Another alternative (3) is seen under some circumstances, where knowledge continues to increase during the period of operational usage. There appear to be three conditions under which this occurs:

1. *The Enthusiast*. Although it may not be central to the work tasks, there are nearly always a few users who become excited by the technology and who spend much more time on it than their colleagues (sometimes to the annoyance of their colleagues who want them to get on with the 'real work instead of playing').

Figure 9.4
The learning curve of full time and intermittent users

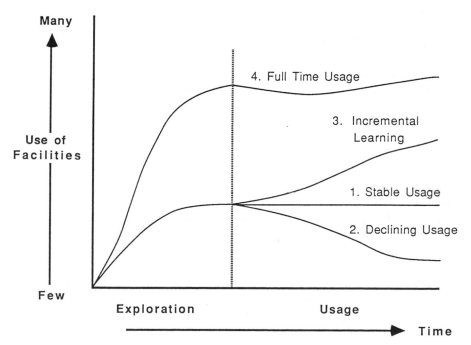

2. *Spare Resources*. In a study of regional banking, Maskery (1986) found that some offices detailed people who were temporarily spare resources, for example management trainees, to learn about the system and support others in its use. This process formally took the pressure off the 'cost–benefit' assessments and allowed exploration to continue for a longer period.

3. *Enhancement of Benefits*. Under some conditions users found they had tasks which meant that exploring unknown facilities was worthwhile because there was no existing way of achieving required benefits. One specific way in which this could happen was when superiors or colleagues adopted practices which required the user to make use of a particular facility. An example might be when the rest of the work group is using electronic mail for communications and you become isolated if you do not use this facility.

Although these situations can work to continue the learning process after the normal exploration period the dominant patterns of behaviour appear to be (1) and (2).

Current Techniques for Promoting Learning in Occasional Users

Before turning to ways in which we might promote learning we should look at the ways currently in use when these products are delivered to users.

1. *Familiarisation Sessions*. Although full training is rarely possible short sessions of perhaps an hour's duration are often acceptable to occasional users and are used by trainers to convey the rudiments of the system. These sessions usually involve a demonstration of the range of facilities on offer, concentrating on the ones that will be used most frequently, perhaps with some limited 'hands on' opportunity. Users tend to be left with a hazy idea of the range of facilities, operational knowledge of one or two things and a deteriorating memory of how to do anything else.

2. *Manuals*. All new products come with some kind of documentation which in theory enables the user to make use of any of the facilities. Many of them are badly designed and offer users very few clues as to where they will find the single pieces of information they need in order to proceed. Even if a manual is well designed, with indexes using the task need terms from which users start their searches, manuals are often under-utilised. The practice of most users, intent on achieving their task purpose, seems to be, as one user described it 'to blast my way through the problem by a trial and error procedure and to use the manual only as a last resort'. In our user studies we have found a remarkably low level of search behaviour among intermittent users, seemingly because they are usually working under an immediate task deadline. For example, in the branch banking study (Eason, 1989) many users justified their lack of use of the manual by saying that 'when you have a customer standing at the counter waiting for you, there is no time to look in a manual'.

3. *'On-line Help'*. As discussed in Chapter 8 most systems now include in their software some kind of on-line support for users (for example, help buttons that give more information about current options, informative error messages when the user is behaving inappropriately, 'pull down' menus which, at any time will list the facilities available and demonstration routines and examples to show how facilities

could be used). Undoubtedly these facilities could provide a rich and easily accessible learning environment for users but often they are the Cinderella of the system design process, left until last, neglected and starved of resources. As a result when they do exist they are often not very good.

4. *'Hotline' Support.* Intermittent users often find themselves in a similar position to the average motorist; they have very little technical knowledge to fall back upon if they run into difficulties. They need the equivalent of roadside rescue services. This is often provided in the form of a telephone 'hotline'; a permanently manned service whereby any user can discuss problems with a technical expert. These services are often provided within an organisation by the in-house technical specialists but they are increasingly offered by suppliers as part of their support services. In theory these services should provide a very flexible form of support but in many of our surveys the answer to our question 'To whom do you turn for help?' is not the official support staff but a member of the user's immediate work group. We have christened this person the 'local expert' (Damodaran, 1986). It is usually a person who is an enthusiast about the system or who has been given the time and responsibility to learn about it. As a result the local experts have the advantages to their colleagues of being knowledgeable, accessible and they know the task environment. The only danger is that their knowledge may not be very reliable and could lead their colleagues into bad habits and false beliefs. Another problem is that often these people do not have an official responsibility to support their colleagues and they and their superiors might consider it a nuisance which impedes the performance of assigned tasks.

Towards an Enriched Learning Environment

The current forms of support for intermittent users are not sufficient to promote the kind of learning which will enable users to exploit the potential of the tools at their disposal. The main problem is that we cannot rely on effort being provided for learning purposes except for a short initial period. Thereafter learning has to be a secondary activity associated with completing the task; 'learning by doing' is the order of the day. As a result 'point of need support' — providing the specific knowledge to answer a particular need at the time of the need — becomes the main priority, and reducing the effort needed to locate this information is a crucial corollary. If we can achieve these objectives, knowledge can grow in an evolutionary manner as tasks occur for which features of the system may be beneficial.

It will be apparent from the earlier discussion that there are a number of different kinds of learning necessary if a user is to exploit a system, from learning what benefits it can bring to which key to press. We can now look at each kind of learning and ask how it can be supported given the requirement of 'learning by doing'. Although the requirement for 'point of need support' is most clear for occasional users it is also necessary to sustain and develop the learning of regular users. The ways of delivering learning presented in Figure 9.5 are therefore applicable to both kinds of user. In Figure 9.5 the range of ways of delivering learning is presented in a matrix which allows each to be evaluated against the different kinds of learning required.

The types of learning that are required range from those that are specifically related to the technology to those that are about the application of the technology to the user's tasks. In order to use the information technology the user will have to have some basic idea of the nature of the technology, concepts of inputting information, holding it in a temporary or permanent store, being able to manipulate it electronically and output it in various forms. There is very little need for the average user to understand the technical basis of these operations or to be able to program. Early texts which purported to be guides for managers went far too far in this direction, even to the extent of teaching the manager binary arithmetic, and this simply created another hurdle the user had to jump before he could begin to use the technology. The analogy with the car owner is again useful; as the industry matured it realised the car owner did not have to be a mechanic and driver education concentrated on driving skills and road craft.

If the user has the basic idea of the technology, the next stage is to convey the

Figure 9.5
Learning needs and modes of promoting learning

| Delivery Mode | Learning Needs | | | | | |
| | System Centred ← → Application Centred | | | | | |
	I.T. Basics	System Model	Command Learning	Skills	Task-System Match	Application Build
General Education	✓✓					
Familiarisation	✓✓	✓✓	✓		✓	
Main Interfaces		✓✓	✓✓	✓✓	✓	✓
On-Line Help			✓✓	✓		
Manuals and Prompts			✓✓		✓	
Expert Support						✓✓
Local Experts			✓		✓✓	✓

specifics of a particular system. The obvious things to teach are what and how; what it can do and how you get it to do it. Most training concentrates on the command structures, for example the command words, menu items, etc., which are needed to operate the system and the physical skills necessary to evoke them — keyboard skills for example. Early attempts to train occasional users, such as managers and professionals, were particularly concerned about their lack of keyboard skills but, as we shall see later, this may not be as big an obstacle as it appears.

If command knowledge and operating skills are acquired in a piecemeal fashion as is likely with intermittent use, there is a danger that the user will not obtain a coherent or accurate view of the total system. Each facility of the system may be learnt separately by a rote procedure, details will be forgotten from one occasion to the next and there will be no generalisable knowledge that can be applied to unknown facilities in the system. It would be much easier for the user to learn the system if it operated consistently on a small number of general principles which could be easily grasped by the non-technical user. The user could then operate from first principles when trying a new facility or returning to a facility not used for some time. The learning procedure should therefore attempt to convey a system model, i.e. some general principles which will help in understanding and operating the system.

The above forms of learning may teach the user about a system but it is of no value until it can be related to work tasks and benefits can be clearly perceived. Another learning need therefore is to look outwards from the system at the work tasks and to seek task needs which system provisions can beneficially serve. It is likely that no two users will have quite the same profile of task needs and therefore this kind of learning need tends to be unique to the individual. If a beneficial use of a system is identified it may just be a case of applying the relevant commands and completing the task (for example, operating the code on the telephone so that it monitors a busy line until it is free). However, there are many other beneficial facilities which require a lot of preparatory work. Maskery (1986), for example, notes that, of a range of facilities on a personal computer, users had to spend a lot of time learning how to build a useful application with the spreadsheet and data-base packages. Applications that have to be built locally involve quite a lot of learning and operating effort before there is any benefit, a major problem for the busy executive. Packages are increasingly offered that are flexible and adaptive so that users can tailor them to their own specific requirements, but, if this requires an unacceptable amount of learning effort, it is not likely to be a successful strategy.

There are other forms of learning that might be considered which relate to the consequences of computer use for relations with colleagues, organisational implications, etc., but we will assume these are being resolved by team building exercises described earlier.

Figure 9.5 identifies seven main ways in which required learning can be delivered and indicates the major kinds of learning each could service, together with some secondary roles it might play. We can examine these possibilities in four groups:

1. *Pre-use learning.* If users are intermittent comprehensive training is not a viable option. We therefore rely on general education about information technology and short familiarisation sessions that can be held before implementation. There is an

oft-quoted belief that the problems we have at the moment will only apply to this generation of occasional users, such as managers and professionals, because with children becoming familiar with the technology at school and at home, they will be well prepared when they enter employment. Whilst this must be true to some extent it is important not to expect too much. Children and people who use other systems may usefully learn the underlying principles of the technology, develop realistic views of what it can and cannot do and appreciate that they are able to cope with it. All these lessons are important. Many new users make extreme and unrealistic assumptions about the technology and are very nervous about their ability to cope with it. If they come to a new system with realistic expectations and confidence about their own ability they have made a good start. On the negative side, however, such is the lack of standardisation in the information technology industry and such is the rate of change that almost nothing of the specific learning associated with any earlier system they have mastered can be transferred to the new system. Indeed there are many cases of negative transfer, where, for example, the RETURN key on the previous system is the DELETE key on the new one. It will be necessary to rely on specific rather than general education to cope with these forms of learning.

The familiarisation sessions before implementation, although short, can be extremely valuable. They run into difficulties if trainers treat them as a limited time period into which to cram all that they would put into a full training session. The result of this can be very confused users. It may be that these sessions should not attempt too much operational detail. Instead, there are two areas they can usefully contribute. If the users have not developed a general familiarisation with the technology and are wary of it, they may need an opportunity to explore and 'play' with it outside formal sessions.

The other kind of familiarisation relates to the specific system to be implemented. This is an ideal opportunity, and may be the only one, to give users a coherent overview of the system; what facilities it contains, what value they may be in the user's task world and, above all, a simple model of the system, i.e. the general rules by which it operates. Ideally these need to be presented in their general form and demonstrated on specific facilities. Given that users will subsequently have to learn most of the system whilst working, it is also useful to convey general principles about how best to learn about the system (for example, the use of search strategies, the use of on-line help facilities, the structure of manuals, etc.). The aim has to be to set people up for learning, and not just to assume this is the only learning session.

2. *Main Interface Features of the System*. If users are not going to engage in extensive learning or exploration before attempting serious use of a system, the main interfaces of the system, the means by which the user accomplishes tasks, must support the user directly. There are two ways this can be accomplished. The interface can be made self-explanatory so that it carries all the learning that is necessary. Or it can be designed to minimise the necessary learning. The former case means, for example, that all options open to the user should be explained on each screen along with the actions required of the user. In practice, this means the

system structures the interaction for the user. This is usually welcomed by beginners but becomes tiresome and limiting once some experience has been gained. As described in Chapter 8 some systems as a result have adaptable interfaces, offering the same facilities via a structured, self-explanatory procedure for the beginner and a fast flexible command-driven procedure for the experienced user. In the latter case the user has to know the commands to use the system; in the former this is unnecessary. In the ideal system the beginner screens not only get the job done but teach the commands so that after some experience you can move on to the command-based dialogues.

A more radical approach is to try to minimise the learning necessary by changing the nature of the interface. One way of doing this is to create a system that obeys a simple set of rules at all times; when users have acquired this model of the system, they have complete control over it. A linked idea is to base the system model upon a set of rules or stereotypes which already exist in the user's environment. An example is the 'desk-top' model where the interface treats documents in the same way as a user might treat documents on the desk (for example, forming piles, taking some from in-trays, putting others in out-trays, others in the waste bin etc.). The principle behind these approaches is to render the operation of the system natural or transparent so that the user can concentrate upon the task in hand and not upon the mechanics of operating the system. Many of the usability dimensions discussed in Chapter 8 are directed to this end.

If they are successful, interface designers who follow these principles will succeed in rendering obsolete much of the operational knowledge currently necessary to use a system. In Figure 9.5, therefore, the main interface is described as the principle route by which a system model is acquired, commands are learned and the necessary skills developed. This is because the self-explanatory mode will support learning and the natural interface relies on existing knowledge and skills which makes new learning unnecessary.

3. *Formalised Point of Need Support.* In this category we can include the on-line help provided within the system (help facilities, informative error messages, demonstration routines, back-up menus, etc.) and the manuals and other forms of documentation provided with the system. Intermittent users tend not to explore by reference to these sources and will rely more on the main interfaces to support them. This does not mean that other types of user (for example, specialists, full-time users, etc.), who will use faster, less explanatory main interfaces, will not make great use of these forms of support. Where these facilities are likely to be useful to the intermittent user is where they want to try new routines or are having difficulty and they are prepared to spend the time seeking a fuller explanation.

4. *Human Support.* The other main kind of learning the users need is to find ways of beneficially harnessing system potential to the specific tasks they wish to undertake. Since the task needs are, at a detailed level, going to be defined locally, perhaps at the time of using the system, it is difficult to see formal pre-prepared learning support as a complete solution. The system and the documentation can explain themselves but they cannot explain the user's own task world or relate the two. In practice, users seem to rely on others (the technical support staff and local experts)

for this kind of support because they are able to explain their problem or need and ask the other person to relate it to the way the system operates. One of the main reasons for under-utilisation at the moment is that no one has responsibility for helping users establish useful task–tool connections, i.e. what is worth using for what purposes, with the result that many users limit themselves to the few obviously useful connections. The person who can most easily help at this level is the local expert who understands the person's work and has sufficient knowledge of the technical system to be able to link the two. Unfortunately, this role is often unofficial and until it is formally recognised, it is unlikely to give users this kind of support. An alternative is to use the technical support staff but they are often distant and not very knowledgeable about the user's tasks. One possibility is to devolve the support structure so that each group of users has easy access to their own technical support officer. Another important role for the technical support staff is to help the user build an application when a suitable opportunity is found. Many users, having found something worth doing, then lose their momentum when they find it is going to take a lot of time and effort to get it established.

There are three important conclusions to be drawn from this examination of user learning requirements. The first is that the different requirements need different kinds of servicing and no implementation process can depend on only one method. The second is that the changing nature of the technology should change the nature of the learning that is required; there should be less need for training in specialised equipment operation and more need to learn how to relate complex facilities to the tasks in hand. Finally, whilst there is a need for specific training during implementation, there is a continuing need after implementation to supply 'point of need' support to help users develop their mastery of the technical facilities at their disposal.

Conclusions

Although the development phases are important, from a human and organisational perspective, the implementation phase is the time which is most critical. It is the phase when there are many different but equally critical objectives to be achieved. Not only has the new socio-technical system to be tried and tested but a process of organisational change has to be undertaken usually at the same time as normal operations are being continued. It is a phase when user participation is crucial and the array of technical help that is required includes training and physical ergonomics expertise as well as information technology expertise.

Chapter 10
User Evaluation

Evaluation, Feedback and Evolution

Systems are implemented to achieve specific purposes and it is important to the development of any organisation that new systems are evaluated to check what has been achieved. Evaluations of systems in operation can serve a number of objectives. Firstly, they can demonstrate whether the intended increases in productivity, decreases in resources, etc. have been achieved. It is quite common for organisations to devote a lot of time and resources to cost justifying a system development, so it would seem natural to check whether the assumptions were justified. Secondly, evaluations can show the barriers and difficulties that prevent the full exploitation of the system by its users and can lead to action to remove these barriers. Thirdly, evaluations can provide the evidence upon which future development plans can be built. Users with experience of an existing system are in a much better position to be realistic about their requirements for the next generation of system. Fourthly, evaluations can reveal unexpected side-effects of systems which may be positive and provide new avenues for development or deleterious and require remedial action. In short, evaluation is vital if an organisation is to learn from the change process it has undertaken.

Evaluation is not only important when the system is in operational use. It is also important during the process of development. System proposals need evaluating, prototype systems need evaluating and trial implementations need evaluating if the design process is to be kept user-centred. The design process needs a succession of feedback loops and the opportunity to redesign in accordance with the feedback provided. If feedback within the design process and feedback following the design process can be achieved as a normal part of information technology innovation, the evolution of systems within the organisation can, over time, be kept user- and business-centred. Without these feedback loops from the user community there will be a drift back to technology-driven evolution as the main impetus for change becomes the latest range of information technology products on the market.

Evaluation is therefore a vital ingredient at all stages of a system's life if the broader purposes of the organisation are to be reflected in its development. In most system developments evaluation is at least part of the development methodology but it is rarely undertaken as thoroughly as is required. In the design process, evaluation is often the stage that is omitted when development is running late. If it is undertaken, the results may be so late that the design team can pay little attention to them. Once a system is operational, evaluation is often reduced to technical criteria (for example,

187

broad usage statistics etc.). It is comparatively rare for organisations to institute an evaluation of how well a system has achieved the objectives for which it was introduced. There may be a number of reasons for this omission. It may be that it is quite difficult to tease out the effect of the system since other factors will no doubt also have changed in the organisation. It may be argued that the money has been spent and there is little point in checking whether it has been well spent. It may also be, of course, that people close to the system would rather that such an evaluation was not carried out.

Whatever the reasons for the relative lack of attention to evaluation, this state of affairs makes it less likely that the organisation as a whole learns from its information technology experiences and improves its policies and practices in future developments. This chapter is therefore devoted to the nature and conduct of evaluation studies and their place in the system development process. Following the system development process it might be logical to consider first the kinds of evaluation that can be conducted on early versions of systems and to end by considering the evaluation of operational systems. However, all evaluations during design are attempts to predict what might happen once the system is implemented. We will therefore gain a fuller picture of evaluation issues by considering first how this can be undertaken when the system is operational. We can then review what limited sub-set of these issues can be treated for predictive purposes during the design process.

User Evaluation of Operational Systems

There are many types of evaluation that can be conducted on an operational system. In this section we will first consider the different types and the purposes they might serve before examining some of the methodological considerations in undertaking evaluations.

Figure 10.1 identifies four different levels at which evaluations can be conducted. The narrowest type of evaluation examines how the technical system is performing on criteria such as number of enquiries, system response statistics, file space, downtime, recovery time after crashes, etc. This type of evalution can be of value in assessing technical performance against specification and for establishing requirements for upgrading. It does not, however, give any direct evidence of whether the system is serving the purpose for which it was created. Since most technical systems serve user and organisational purposes it is evaluations at these levels which will show the value of the technical system. The next level therefore is an evaluation by individual users of the quality of the service they obtain from the technical system; does it, for example, provide the information that is required, allow data to be manipulated as necessary, etc? This level of analysis can be very instructive of the functionality and usability of the system but may still not show whether the organisation is benefiting from the development. Much of the benefit may be shown in the changes of performance of individual users. Are they, for example, answering more queries, processing more orders, producing better designs, making better decisions, etc? The third level of evaluation therefore looks at the impact on individual users both in terms of their job performance and in terms of ramifications affecting job satisfaction etc. In most cases it

Figure 10.1
Levels of evaluation

Technical

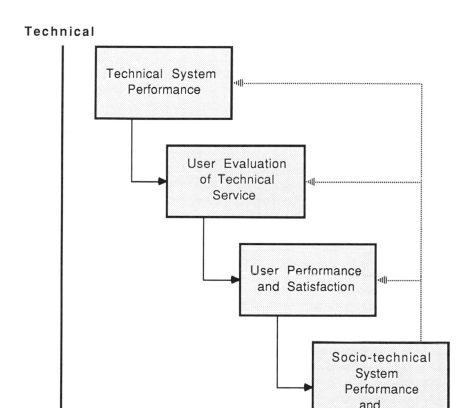

Organisational

is a new socio-technical system that has been introduced so that the final and broadest form of evaluation is an organisational evaluation to establish whether the new work system, with both its social and technical sub-systems, is performing effectively and efficiently. This is the level at which questions can be answered about whether the system has achieved its objectives and is cost beneficial.

Since we are concerned here with user and organisational issues, we will omit considerations of purely technical evaluations and concentrate upon the different types of user evaluation.

User Evaluations of Technical Service

The obvious way in which the technical system can be evaluated is to check the degree to which it is being used by the user population, and to explore what is being used and why. This kind of analysis is particularly relevant when users are discretionary since the amount and type of use is an indication of the degree of user acceptance. Even when users are non-discretionary there is much that can be learned from the pattern of usage because it is often the case that some facilities are much more heavily used than others.

The first requirement therefore is some kind of usage log. Many systems are capable of logging system usage in great detail and potentially this is a very valuable source of information. There are, however, three problems. The first is the problem of confidentiality. If users are unaware of the monitoring or are anxious about its purposes, the log may become a contentious issue which will itself affect usage. The second is that many systems aggregate the usage data in such a way that it is impossible to extract data about particular users. This may protect the individual but it makes it very difficult to understand user behaviour with the system. The third problem is that such a lot of statistics may be obtained and they may accrue at such a rate that it may become a monumental task to reduce the data to a usable volume. We have found in practice (see, for example, Eason, 1989, Sutcliffe and Old, 1987, and Pullinger, 1987) that a logging procedure that concentrates upon the frequency of use of the different facilities on the system and the errors that are made is usually a sufficiently detailed log for most purposes. Ideally, the purpose and nature of the log should be agreed with users before implementation with the stress on the evaluation of the system and not the performance of users. If it is not possible to obtain a system log another possibility is to ask users to maintain a usage diary, perhaps on a sample basis. If this procedure is to be a success the diary will have to be kept very simple and the results fed back to the users regularly to sustain the motivation to keep filling it in. Another alternative is to interview users about their pattern of usage. This is likely to yield reasonably reliable evidence about the facilities the user makes use of, but may produce unreliable evidence of frequency of use. It should be regarded as a crude representation of the use of the system.

A log of usage provides a description of what is occurring and may show interesting patterns, for example, some facilities in widespread use whilst others are ignored, heavy usage by some users and marginal use by others, steadily increasing use of some facilities whilst the use of other facilities is in decline and clusters of errors associated with certain operations of the system. To explain why these patterns are occurring may require closer investigation of user behaviour. One way of achieving this is to observe people using the system. This is a common procedure for evaluating a prototype or pilot system as we shall consider later in this chapter. An operational system may have a lot of users spread over a large geographical area, however, and we may want to study them using the system in the course of their normal work for specific tasks. If they are intermittent users this may be impractical to organise and observational exercises are usually undertaken with groups of full-time users.

The alternative is to seek the users' own explanation of the pattern of usage by asking them to evaluate the service provided. This process has in practice proved a simple and direct way of explaining user behaviour. Methods for undertaking evaluations of this kind are described in Damodaran (1984) and examples of them in use are provided by Stewart (1986).

The principle upon which these evaluations are based is that users can evaluate a technical service by comparing what they get with what they require to do their job. This is 'match' or 'fit' evaluation where functionality is matched against task requirements and usability is matched against user characteristics. The simplest procedure is to ask users to make a series of ratings with responses on a 'fit' scale from 'very good' to 'very poor'. A 'poor' response suggests there are problems which can be explored in an unstructured way to reveal the particular causes. The evaluation would therefore give data at two levels, a set of standardised ratings which allow comparisons to be made and an unstructured commentary which shows the key problems users encounter with the system.

There are many dimensions of a technical service which can be examined in this way. Following the analysis of the technical service presented in Chapter 8, the structure which has informed most of our evaluations is based on four categories which correspond to the dimensions of functionality and usability and these are summarised in Figure 10.2.

A. *Task Match*. The functionality of the system can be evaluated by asking users how well the service matches their task requirements. The specific dimensions that are used for rating need to reflect the functionality of the system. In evaluating the service provided to managers by information systems based on large data bases, Stewart (1986) used nine dimensions which are common properties of such an information service: availability, timeliness, precision, relevance, comprehen-

Figure 10.2
The evaluation of system service

Task Match	The ability of system functionality to serve user task needs, eg. relevance, timeliness etc.
Ease of Use	The usability of system operating procedures, eg. navigation, data input etc.
Ease of learning	The adequacy of the user support methods provided for user learning, eg. in-system aids, manuals etc.
Environmental Stressors	The degree to which environmental factors permit ease of operation, eg. seating, noise etc.

siveness, validity, reliability, privacy and safety. In contrast, Gower and Eason (1989), in evaluating a text processing service, used dimensions such as turnaround time, editing capability and print quality. Although these dimensions can be applied to the whole system for all user tasks, a more refined evaluation can be gained by obtaining ratings for each facility within its appropriate task domain. An analysis at this level can be undertaken alongside the usage record. For example, the rating scales can indicate why certain facilities are used for certain tasks. Conversely, the user can also indicate that some facilities cannot be used because they are irrelevant, invalid, etc. for the tasks that have to be undertaken.

B. *Ease of Use*. Usability aspects that are associated with the ease of use of the system can be evaluated by asking users to rate the operational characteristics of the system. The ratings can be of those system features that are more or less common across the range of facilities (for example, the keyboard, log on procedures, navigation aids, etc.). However, usability problems are usually associated with attempts to use specific facilities to achieve particular task purposes and the general rating may mask this. It may therefore be more appropriate to obtain a rating for each facility on the system (for example, in the case of text processing, for text creation, editing and printing, etc.). There are two main issues which can lead to an evaluation showing a system to be easier to use than it is. Regular users will inevitably have overcome most of the difficulties they experienced when first using the system and will tend to rate the system easy to use. It is therefore important to include users with the full range of system experience (from a little to a great deal) or to ask regular users to evaluate ease of use as they first experienced the system. The other factor is that users will tend to assess the system in terms of the facilities they use and ignore the rest. Unfortunately the ones they do not know tend to be the more complex. Indeed it may be they do not use them because they expect them to be difficult to use. It is important therefore to know the basis upon which users make their assessments and to ensure some responses are obtained from people who have made use of the full array of facilities.

C. *Ease of Learning*. The ease with which a system can be learnt is a combination of the ease of use of its operating procedures and the adequacy of the user support facilities which are there to facilitate learning. It is therefore possible to seek ratings of the various forms of user support available (for example, in system support such as help facilities and error messages, manuals and other forms of documentation, training courses, liaison staff and local experts). The evaluation can be extended to explore which facilities are used for which purposes, an analysis which can be helpful in developing improved support facilities. The evaluation of user support facilities is affected by the same problems as ease of use; it may be that the user makes little or no use of some forms of help, typically the manual, because it looks difficult to use. The user may therefore be able to offer an evaluation of some facilities based on real experience but not all of them. The danger is that the ones that they know little about are the ones that need most attention.

D. *Environmental Stressors*. The workstation and the physical environment contribute in an indirect way to the technical service. They are not in a direct sense 'easy to use' because using a system does not involve using, for example, the noise of a printer. However, if these environmental factors cause the user stress, they can make use of the system more difficult. There are two ways in which an evaluation of these factors might be undertaken; by asking users to rate each potential stressor or by asking about the incidence of stress responses. In the former category, for example, users could be asked how they rate the workstation, i.e. seating, desk height, etc., and the physical environment, i.e. lighting, noise and heating. In the second category, users could be asked to report the frequency of stress reactions such as visual fatigue, headaches, backache, etc. Hünting *et al.* (1980) provide an example of an evaluation conducted on this basis.

Evaluations of this kind can serve a number of purposes. Conducted regularly they provide evidence of the degree to which the system is improving or, alternatively, is drifting out of touch with the changing needs of users. Each evaluation tends to highlight the specific problem areas to which system enhancement should be addressed. It can also be a way of highlighting groups of users who may not be as well served as their colleagues. The evaluation of a Hospital system reported by Eason *et al.* (1989) identified, for example, a groups of users who received a very poor task service from a system although the general evaluation of the system was good.

User Performance and Satisfaction

Many technical systems are designed to improve the task performance of their users. As discussed in Chapter 2, the benefits may be more orders processed by the clerk, more letters typed by the secretary, better designs produced by the designer or better decisions made by the manager, etc. Evaluating the success of a system should therefore look at the impact upon user performance. We may, for example, find that a splendid technical system, meeting all its technical performance specification, has in no way improved user performance in the ways intended.

It is natural to think that the best evidence of user performance would be objective and quantitative. We could, perhaps, count the number of keystrokes achieved per hour by an operator before and after the introduction of a new system. Since computers are good at making such counts this would seem a desirable route to take; an automated way of following in the traditions of time and method study. There are two main problems with this approach, however. First, it is easy to slip into a strategy whereby these statistics are used to assess individual performance — to distinguish between good and bad operators. If this is the case, or if operators think it might be the case, they may change their behaviour accordingly. If, for example, the system monitors keystrokes but cannot judge the quality of the work completed, it is an invitation to sacrifice quality for quantity. The second and related problem is that measures of operator performance on the terminal may have little relation to improved task performance. A record of a manager's productivity on a keyboard, for example, will not tell us whether his decision-making has improved. Even the relation between keyboard performance and task performance in clerical jobs can be problematic. It might be thought, for example, that the best index of performance of a word processor operator would be the number of words processed. In a narrow sense this is true and most organisations find word processors mean many more words can be processed. But they are often left wondering whether this is a benefit. A common finding is that when authors discover they can get words processed faster, they go through many more drafts and end up with the same number of documents. The issue then is whether the quality of the document is an improvement in content and in presentation. This is a different kind of evaluation requiring a different set of criteria.

The attraction of simple, quantified metrics associated with technical system operation can then obscure the question of whether there is an improvement in task performance. A more useful way of approaching the problem of evaluation is to ask what criteria should be used to judge overall task performance and to gear the evaluation to these criteria. If a doctor introduces a system to help clear his waiting list then the evaluation should examine whether after a period of time the waiting list has fallen. If the stock controller is trying to keep stocks to a minimum whilst being able to fulfil all the orders placed, this provides the basis for an evaluation of whether a system is helping him in this task. The success of this kind of evaluation turns on two factors. It is necessary to be able to express overall job performance criteria. This is often problematic because the job holder has to balance a number of potentially conflicting objectives and some of them may be difficult to give quantitative expression. The other requirement is that there should be measures of these criteria before the new system is introduced in order that benefits or losses can be determined. Whereas the user evaluation of the technical system can be based on a 'fit' between provisions and requirements, a user performance measure depends upon a before-and-after assessment. Evaluation is not therefore a topic one can begin to address after the system has been introduced; it has to be planned from the conception of the system.

The problems of obtaining a meaningful, quantitative assessment of user performance can be insurmountable and there is a simpler way of obtaining interesting and valuable data. Indeed, when the system is designed to enhance the way people work and identify new ways of operating, this can be a superior technique. This method is to seek the perception of users of the changes that have taken place in the way they work and their assessment of whether these changes have been beneficial or detrimental. Bjørn-Andersen *et al.* (1986), in their survey of the impact of information systems upon managers, used such a measure to assess the impact upon changes in tasks. They examined three aspects of the task; the intrinsic character of the task (the degree of complexity, the feedback obtained, etc.), structural factors (the degree to which it became standardised etc.) and load factors (workload, workplace, etc.). Of the 85 managers studied over half were aware of changes in all these aspects of the task. Ratings of the degree of change and explanations of specific kinds of change demonstrated the way in which the availability of more and better information was changing the way these managers were able to approach their work. One common finding, for example was that more information led to an enriched perception of the task; that it was in fact more complex than hitherto understood and better performance would depend upon a more subtle treatment of the variables than had previously been possible. Another common finding was that tasks had become more standardised because of the formal language and structure necessary to use a computer system. Perhaps surprisingly, greater standardisation and greater insight often went together;

the clarity of structure helped the task performer to see more clearly. This kind of evaluation can help the users to articulate the experience they have been through and can help identify new directions for system evolution which can build on the learning and discoveries the users have made.

An important part of this evaluation is the assessment by the user of whether the changes are to be regarded as positive or negative. The summation of these ratings gives a very good view of the motivational state of the user; whether the changes are perceived as giving good value for the effort they entailed. The specific evaluations can also indicate aspects of the system that need to be addressed. Where the change has led not only to a new technical system being introduced but also to changes in work organisation, an evaluation of changes in job satisfaction may also be useful. There are many standard ways of assessing job satisfaction, for example, the Job Diagnostic Survey (Hackman and Oldham, 1975). These methods can be useful for checking whether the overall effect has been to improve or decrease job satisfaction and specific answers can be used to pinpoint problem areas which may be addressed by changes in the technical system or in the organisation of work.

Socio-Technical System Performance and Ramifications

Introducing a new information technology system and making organisational changes leads to a new socio-technical system which is hopefully a more effective way of the enterprise pursuing its corporate aims. To check whether this is indeed the case there is a need for a macro-level evaluation which is pitched at the effectiveness of the division or department which is the socio-technical system which has undergone change.

As in the previous forms of evaluation there is a choice of evaluation methods between objective and quantified performance measures and the subjective evaluations of those who work within the system. Both techniques have their value and their problems.

Objective measures are the most widely accepted as evidence of the value of the changes that were made; ideally financial values can be placed on any gains and can be compared with the costs incurred in making the changes. There is a tendency in making this kind of evaluation to take before and after measures of the variable which was the main target for the change. If the aim was to reduce the volume of work in progress or to reduce the number of staff required for a given level of output, then these will be the variables that are measured and success will be reduction to the planned levels. The problem with this approach is that the effectiveness of the socio-technical system may depend upon a range of factors and measuring one or two may obscure the fact that there have also been changes on other important dimensions. There may, for example, have been a reduction in staff levels but quality may be suffering as efforts are made to sustain quantity, or long-term flexibility may have been lost in favour of short-term reductions in cost. An objective evaluation of a major change should take measures of all indices that are important to the short- and long-term health of the organisation since changes in one index almost invariable have impacts on others.

Evaluations at this level have considerable value in assessing the overall effectiveness of the work system but they are often difficult to relate to the adequacy of the information technology system that was introduced. This is because the new system is but one element in the success of the enterprise. Success or failure is also related to the changes in the organisational structure and the ability of the staff to cope with the new situation. There may also have been other major factors influencing performance (for example, changes in the market, other company policies, etc.) and these make it difficult to identify cause and effect. Another problem is that it takes time for a major change to settle down and give clear indications of whether it has had the desired effects upon performance.

When it is difficult to interpret the meaning of objective measures, the most useful source of evidence is the views of the staff who have lived through the change and who can give evidence about the way in which overall effects have come about. This is one role that subjective evaluation exercises can play at this level. Another advantage is that the views of people are statements of the acceptability of the changes and these will be direct evidence of whether there is a positive will to make the new socio-technical system work or whether there are major obstacles to overcome. A related issue is that subjective evaluations can be used to gather together the new learning about the way the organisation might function as a result of the strides that have been made. It is not uncommon, for example, to find people saying that the new information resource could be used to plan the further evolution of the work organisation. The final value of subjective evaluations is that they can pinpoint the negative ramifications of the changes that have been made, often deleterious effects which were never intended. If these can be identified it may be possible to ameliorate the negative effects.

The simplest way of conducting an evaluation of this kind is to list the dimensions that are important to the performance of the enterprise (for example, output, staff morale, flexibility, competitiveness, resource utilisation etc.), and to ask staff to judge whether there has been a change in each dimension, what form the change has taken, when it occurred and whether they regard it as positive or negative. Questions about what further could be done reveal the difference between what has been achieved and what could be achieved. The main problem with this approach is that it depends upon individuals having thought through the impact of the change process and this is a rarity. It is quite common for the people to say there have been no significant changes but when prompted by enquiries about particular issues to conclude that, when they think about it, there have been significant changes. One way of overcoming this problem is to ask a sample of people representative of the different functions and levels in the organisation to evaluate the effects upon their functions and responsibilities. People are much more able to pinpoint changes they themselves have to deal with. Summating the responses of the sample can then give a view of the overall impact. Another technique is to use the measuring instruments that have been developed for research purposes to assess the impact of technological changes in organisations. There are now a wide variety of such techniques in the research literature. In their multi-level evaluation of eight cases, for example, Bjørn-Andersen *et al.* (1986) employed measures of changes in manager–subordinate relations, communications patterns, changes in discretion, power and influence, changes in management style — from personal to impersonal — and shifts between decentralised and centralised forms of organisation, etc.

The Conduct of Evaluation Studies

Whatever the level at which evaluation studies are undertaken there are some important considerations which will determine the extent to which findings will be valid and useful. These considerations are common to most forms of social science investigation within an organisation and Klein and Eason (1989) provide a fuller discussion.

Figure 10.3 summarises the main factors to be considered. The sample of users from whom data is gathered is of course crucial to the validity of the findings. Getting the views of the manager of the user department may not adequately reflect the impact of the system. Neither is it relevant to collect the views of the most avid users; it may be of greater value to interview non-users who were intended users (although it can be problematic to frame questions about 'usage' in such circumstances). For a scientific study it would be necessary to obtain numbers for the sample to be representative of all levels and types of users. An evaluation for practical rather than scientific purposes may not need to be rigorous about numbers but it should include the full range of users.

Figure 10.3
The conduct of evaluation studies

Topics	Issues
Sample Conduct Time	Representative Impartial Agents After Initial Dip
Measures Objective Subjective	Confidentiality Non-Intrusive Structured/Unstructured
Feedback	Designers and Users General and Specific Data and Recommendations

If the data is to be valid the people who undertake the study may be an important consideration. Users may well be influenced in how they perform or what they say by the person collecting the data. This is obviously the case if the person is their line manager but it can also apply if the person has been closely associated with the design and implementation of the system. It may be necessary to place the conduct of an evaluation study in the hands of an outside agent who can be impartial and, more importantly, can be perceived to be independent.

The timing of an evaluation study is also crucial. If it is conducted shortly after implementation the results may be heavily coloured by the problems of transition and adjustment when there may, for example, be an 'initial dip' in performance. These results may be of interest but are not the same as results obtained during steady-state usage. If the evaluation is left until a long time after implementation the impetus to act upon the results may have long been lost. Ideally, a series of evaluations is needed which track the changing usage patterns and attitudes of users. However, if this is not possible, the art is to choose a time when the new system is just beginning to seem the normal way of working to the users.

The nature of the measures used in the evaluation is very important and has been discussed at length above. A few general points bear repeating. If users are to give valid data they need to be assured the data will not be used against them personally. The best way of ensuring this is to render the data untraceable to a particular individual which is another reason for using independent agents. This is particularly important if objective data about usage and performance are being collected which could be used to assess both the system and the person. If it is untraceable it cannot be used for the latter. If the user has confidence in these measures there will be no attempt to hide or adjust the data. If the data is to be valid the collection of information should be as unobtrusive as possible so that the study does not of itself produce artificial data. It has been known, for example, for studies to require users to engage in tasks they do not normally undertake in order to generate data. Unobtrusiveness should not be equated with secrecy, however; it is vital that users know when data is being collected about them.

A user who has confidence in the confidentiality of a study will also be more inclined to give straightforward subjective responses. Another issue in any subjective evaluation is whether to use structured or unstructured questions. Structured questions have the virtue of easy analysis and direct comparability. Their weakness is that they pre-define the answers it is possible to give and may not therefore permit the user to report the most important issues. We have always found it useful to use a structured approach to reveal issues and, once an issue is located, to use an unstructured method to explore the nature of the issue.

There is no point undertaking an evaluation study if no use is made of the results. The nature and target of the feedback from the study is therefore vital. A golden rule for evaluation studies should be that there is a person or a group charged with receiving and acting upon the results. Otherwise the study may not be worth undertaking. Ideally, the target should be both designers and users because there will almost certainly be something from which both can learn. Whilst a general report may be made available, feeding back specific and confidential results to individuals may be an important factor in their own development. The latter process can be a useful way of confirming that an accurate account of the users' position has been obtained.

The form of feedback is important if the results are to be well used. Each target, i.e. design team, user management, representatives of users, etc. may need a different kind of feedback which reflects their particular concerns about the system. In most circumstances it is important to report general conclusions but to support them with specific examples. There is usually an expectation that any report will contain recommendations for action but often this is perceived as threatening or inappropriate by those who receive the findings who wish to appraise the results to draw their own conclusions. It is important to agree the form of feedback before the evaluation is undertaken to avoid any misunderstandings about the nature of the output.

Evaluation Studies During System Development

A recurrent theme in this volume is the importance of evaluation studies conducted at all stages of the development of a system. Early assessment of the degree to which a system meets the needs of users and the organisation provides an opportunity to change the design and improve the probability of the final system being successful. One way of looking at early evaluations is to see them as attempts to predict what would happen if the system were to be implemented. An early evaluation is therefore an attempt to create a test environment similar to that which will pertain when it is implemented. Most of the difficulties about early evaluations are that it is not easy to establish realistic test conditions at early stages of development.

Earlier chapters have presented evaluation procedures tailored to the specific issues of stages in the development process. Rather than repeat these descriptions the purpose here is to offer an integrated view of the range of evaluations that can and should be undertaken during development and to review the issues which affect the validity of these evaluations. Figure 10.4 provides a summary of evaluation methods associated with different stages of development.

Figure 10.4 identifies four major stages in systems development when evaluations can be conducted and the kinds of evaluation appropriate at each stage. It will be noted that a number of different forms of evaluation are listed and that these change in character as the system is developed. Initially the system exists only as an outline, abstract description and evaluation consists of mapping it onto an abstraction of the user/task/organisational world it is to serve. This 'abstraction' may be in the head of a user or an expert on these issues. Another approach is to formalise the abstraction into user models or organisational models and to test the system plans against these models. Once a concrete version of the technical system has been constructed, as for example in a prototype, real users can use it and their reactions can be evaluated. Once it becomes possible to put a working system into an organisation, it becomes possible to make direct performance evaluations. The evaluations that are made with 'real' users in 'real' settings are likely to have high predictive value with respect to operational use of the system. The early evaluations are more distant from this reality and may have lower predictive value. However, the early evaluations are more likely to influence significant design decisions because they occur at a time when design is still flexible. Two conclusions follow from this. It is important to test the accuracy of early forms of evaluation against subsequent field evaluations, i.e. was the expert right? It is also

Figure 10.4
Evaluation procedures during system development

Design Stage	Evaluation Aim	Form of Evaluation
Outline Functional Specification	Test for Organisational Value and Match and for User Acceptability	User and Organisation Cost-Benefit Assessment
Detailed Physical Specification and Prototype	User Test for Functionality, Usability and Acceptability	Prototype Evaluations and Simulations
Working Technical System	User Test of Technical System in Organisational Context	Field Trials with Organisational Changes
Implemented Operational System	Performance of Socio-Technical System Against Objectives	Evaluation Studies of Operational System

important to build rapid prototypes as early as possible to that 'real' users can experience what is intended before design decisions are frozen.

The first milestone for system development is to have an *outline functional specification* which embodies both the technical system, the social system and the allocation of function between them. With such a statement it becomes possible to evaluate the proposal for its value to the organisation, i.e. what benefit would it bestow in respect of organisational objectives, and for organisational match, i.e. what changes would be required in the existing structure? It is also possible to review such proposals for their implications for particular kinds of users and thereby to assess user acceptability. The conventional way of undertaking this kind of evaluation is to describe the proposal and ask experts or users for their reactions. One of the problem areas of systems development, as described in Chapter 5, is that people asked to react in this way may not understand the proposal and may not be able to see the organisational implications. Some kind of formal evaluation procedure is necessary which presents the proposal in a systematic way and thus makes explicit the way in which the technical and social systems would relate, and which provides a structured means of examining each potential area of change. A formal structure of this kind gives respondents the best opportunity to make an informed judgement of the implications of the proposal. The User and Organisational Cost–Benefit Assessment Technique in Chapter 6 and detailed in the Appendix is an evaluation technique of this type.

Further into the systems development process the *physical specification* for the product will have been detailed in part and then in total. With fourth-generation languages rapid prototypes of the technical system (or parts of it) can be produced during this phase. In this phase the functionality to be offered the user will be defined and the means by which the technical system will deliver it will be established. It is therefore possible to make evaluations of the functionality, usability and user accept-ability of the technical system. Again, the conventional procedure for evaluation at this stage is to make expert or user assessments. Indeed it may be that the designer or other members of the design team will make these evaluations. There is often no more a formal procedure than 'walking through' the proposed system in a meeting and asking people to comment about features of the system.

Currently under development are a variety of formal techniques which may make it easier and more systematic to conduct these evaluations. Many of them are directed at the evaluation of the interface proposals for acceptability. One theme is evaluation against user standards which may be national or in-house. Another theme is the development of expert systems derived from the kind of interface design rules described in Chapter 8. Using these rules the expert system could evaluate proposed interface solutions in much the same way as a human factors expert. A slightly different approach is the development of tools which check the consistency and complexity of specifications since these features have important implications for usability. Yet another approach is to develop formal models of user characteristics for example their ability to receive, process and store information, and to evaluate system specifications against these models. Most of these approaches are currently research instruments but they could, in time, be integrated into the advanced design environ-ments used by future design teams so that systems developed in the environment could be evaluated by models held within them.

Even if these formal methods are a major success it is likely that they will enable evaluation of only some of the features of a specification which are of concern to the user population. An important part of the evaluation process will therefore remain user trials in which representatives of the users can try the system and make judgements of functionality, usability and acceptability. Rapid prototyping provides the opportunity to present users with a concrete representation of the intended specification. Early evidence of the use of rapid prototyping suggests it can be a very useful medium in which users and designers can discuss the adequacy of the specification. The danger, as discussed in Chapter 6, is that the prototype will be demonstrated to the users and they will be asked their views. To be able to fully assess the system the users need to be able to work with the prototype, to undertake realistic tasks using it and to follow a structured methodology in assessing its strengths and its implications. The methods of conducting user trials with prototypes described in Chapter 6 provide this support for users.

When a significant part of the working technical system is available it is possible to conduct evaluations which will predict the kind of user–task performance to be expected when the system is in use. User trials can now be sufficiently realistic to permit measures of quality and quantity of performance to be taken as well as subjective ratings of functionality and acceptability. It is at this stage that products are typically tested in usability laboratories and analyses offered of the kinds of problems users encounter, the errors they make, etc. The validity of such tests depends not only on the quality of the technical system but also upon the degree to which the subjects, tasks and settings are representative of the circumstances in which the system will be used. If these are not reasonably realistic, generalisation of results may not be appropriate. Ideally, if the technical system is to be tested in the laboratory, attempts should be made to create a simulated version of the real setting. It is common for usability studies to be undertaken on individual subjects working though a range of system-orientated tasks, for example, moving a paragraph in a text processing system. Systems are often designed to support people working in teams and to assess such a system needs multi-user trials in which subjects work through the organisational tasks they share with one another, for example, preparing a complete document from origination to distribution. Simulations that permit multi-user trials have long been a feature of the development of major military systems and, as Hannigan and Kerswell (1986) demonstrated in their study of advanced telephone systems, this approach can equally be used in the development of systems for the commercial world.

When the technical system is complete a field trial is often undertaken before widespread implementation takes place (see Chapter 9). These are often perceived as technical proving trials but they can of course be major opportunities to explore all the user issues that relate to the system. If the trials permit real users to use the system (for simulated or real tasks) then data about usability, acceptability and user–task performance can be obtained. In addition the process of establishing the trial and the kinds of organisational problems encountered can be very useful evidence about the organisational change processes that will have to be managed when the system is fully implemented. The main problems with this kind of evaluation, as discussed in Chapter 9, are that the field trial will have elements of being a special simulation, probably engendering a 'Hawthorne Effect' among users, and the generalisation of results to full implementation has to be undertaken with care.

Once the system has been implemented and some degree of 'steady state' has been achieved an evaluation of the system can be performed which examines all the issues covered in the studies within the design cycle. If appropriate performance measures have been taken, a before-and-after comparison of the performance of the socio-technical system is possible. The process of undertaking evaluations of systems in use has been described earlier in this chapter. In addition to providing evidence of the success of the system, these evaluations also provide a way of validating the evaluations undertaken during design, i.e. was it as usable as the laboratory studies suggested?

Conclusions

Most people involved in systems development agree that evaluations of the kind described in this chapter are vital to the success of systems. It can be very expensive to try to implement a system that proves itself unable to meet organisational needs — not to mention the drain on user resources as they try to make it work rather than concentrating on their primary tasks within the organisation. Early evaluation can avoid these dangers. And yet in many cases evaluations are not undertaken, take too long so they have little impact on design decisions or are undertaken badly so that they do not reveal the important issues that need design attention. In part this is because costs and time pressures tend to create a design imperative in which evaluation is often seen as a source of additional cost and delay. In many cases this leads to evaluations conducted on a 'least effort' basis, i.e. get the person nearest to you to try it and take the measures that are easiest to take. As this chapter has repeatedly indicated this can be dangerous and misleading. To be useful all evaluations of user issues have to be designed so that they properly evaluate the emerging system against the reality of the user's world. There are ways of doing this for each level of evaluation that needs to be undertaken. If these forms of evaluation are built into the design process and protected when there are pressures to take short cuts, the organisation may truly be said to be user oriented in its design work and to be learning the lessons of its own experience of developing information technology systems.

Chapter 11
Information Technology Strategies

Policies for Information Technology

The potential of information technology in organisations is immense. We may already be in the early stages of an 'information revolution' which will transform society to the same dramatic degree as the Industrial Revolution. Already information technology is one of the major forces shaping the way organisations are changing. We might then expect information technology applications to be a major item on the agenda of Company Boards and for senior management resources to be devoted to the study of the potential of the technology. Whilst there are a growing number of organisations where this is the case there are a great many more where the subject is left to the technical specialists on the principle that it is a technical matter of no concern to general management. There are a number of reasons why this is a dangerous policy:

1. *Organisational Objectives.* The time when information technology applications should be cost justified on the basis of straightforward resource reductions or productivity gains has gone. The strategic application of information technology depends on conceiving of ways in which the technology can be harnessed to serve major organisational objectives and senior management must be involved in setting these objectives and judging ways of meeting them.
2. *Organisational Impact and Change.* The implementation of information technology goes hand-in-hand with major organisational change. The establishment of future forms of organisation structure and the management of the change process are the normal business of senior management. Unless this process is carefully managed the implementation of the technology can lead to unwitting organisational impact which may have deleterious effects on the effectiveness of the organisation and may limit the opportunities senior managers have to manage the enterprise.
3. *Sectional Interests.* The application of information technology can be used to strengthen the power of some sections of the organisation against others. It tends to produce 'winners' in some departments and 'losers' in others. Shifts of power can also occur between end-user departments and technical departments. If senior management are not involved in deciding what is in the interests of the organisation as a whole, the application of information technology may be determined by the most ambitious rather than the common good.
4. *Control of an Integrating Technology.* Most definitions of information technology draw attention to its convergent nature — it brings together data processing, text

processing and telecommunications. In a large organisation there may be three different departments responsible for these activities. Who is to control the integrated whole? Whilst *information technology* may be the responsibility of technologists who act as suppliers inside the organisation, *information* is the lifeblood of the organisation and is of major concern to all. Who therefore should control the information resources of the organisation? No one can answer these questions but the senior management of the organisation.

It is imperative that information technology applications are planned at the highest level in an organisation and this chapter is devoted to an exposition of the kinds of policies that are appropriate and necessary for this purpose. It is based upon the kinds of information technology strategies that are being developed by the user organisations that are at the leading edge in the application of the technology. In the first part of the chapter we will examine the structure necessary to manage information technology applications and the specific policies that may be needed to manage individual information technology projects. Since this has been the subject matter of much of this book, this will provide an opportunity to summarise the major points about the project organisation. Finally, we will return to the theme of the kind of organisation towards which information technology may be carrying us. In this case, rather than define the Utopia that is the ultimate hope or hell, the aim is to define an organisation that is capable of managing the process of continual change.

General Structures and Policies for Information Technology

To maintain a perspective on behalf of the whole organisation, the structure responsible for information technology applications has to have a senior management presence and bring together the needs of end-user departments and the services of information technology suppliers. A structure of this kind is depicted in Figure 11.1.

Given its significance as a force shaping the future of the organisation, the body controlling information technology applications, which we will call the Information Technology Strategy Committee, needs to report directly to the Board of the Company. Since the technology is ultimately at the service of the operating divisions of the organisation, the Chairman of the Committee should be one of the general managers on the Board. If the main duty of the Board is to set company objectives and monitor progress towards their achievement, the remit of the IT Strategy Committee should be to pursue applications which serve the Company's objectives. This will ensure that application objectives relate to the goals of the organisation and are not driven by new technical possibilities, or by the particular concerns of a user department. Sometimes this puts pressure on the Board to clarify the objectives of the organisation. Shackel *et al.* (1989) describe a strategic systems development which raised questions about the degree of centralisation or decentralisation planned for the future which the Board had to debate before the computer plan could be finalised.

The membership of this Committee must include a cross-section of the interested parties in the organisation which will include representatives of end-user departments and the senior staff of the information technology providers within the organisation.

Figure 11.1
Controlling information technology

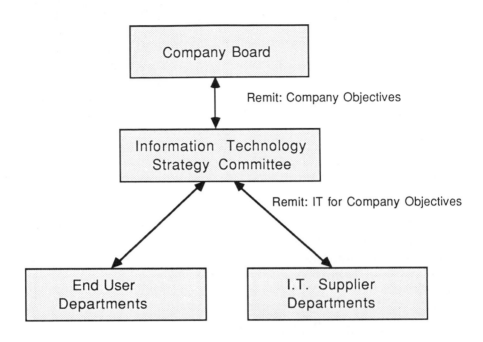

Since information technology applications are as much about organisational change as technical innovation, the membership should also include the relevant human and organisational specialists in the Company, for example, the Personnel Director.

One of the main activities of this Committee is to review and approve plans for specific projects. It is a common experience in companies that are beyond the first stages of computerisation that there are many demands for the upgrading of systems and the implementation of new ones. The Committee will need to establish criteria for assessing plans for development and for assigning priorities. It is easy under conditions of demand from end-user departments and technical departments for the Committee to simply become reactive, responding to requests as they are made. This can lead to an uncoordinated array of applications. If this is to be avoided, the major proposals have to be created by the Board and the Committee in order to serve the Company objectives. The Company objectives should also be used to frame the criteria by which priorities for individual projects suggested by specific departments are assigned.

Within this general framework there are a number of major topics which are likely to be on the agenda in any sizeable organisation. The remainder of this chapter is presented as a set of topics to be addressed by an Information Technology Strategy Committee.

Centralisation or Decentralisation of Systems Development

One of the issues which is likely to exercise the Committee is the extent to which system developments are undertaken by a central team or are the results of 'end-user developments' as described in Chapter 3; applications created for a specific user department by members of that department. A few years ago the majority of applications were bespoke developments run on a mainframe under the control of an in-house Data Processing Department. Two forces are acting to change this pattern. User departments, as a result of working with computer systems for a number of years, are becoming progressively more sophisticated about their requirements and the way they can be met. Simultaneously the introduction of mini- and microcomputers means that it is easy for user departments to purchase computer equipment from within their own budgets. The resultant computer anarchy is causing concern in many organisations. An audit of the computer equipment in some large companies would reveal nearly every make of computer and a large number of software products performing identical functions.

In many organisations these forces are leading to a major debate. Should end-user applications be banned or should they be encouraged? The argument for banning end-user developments is usually made by senior management and Data Processing Departments. This points to the difficulty of managing and co-ordinating an organisation in which each department keeps its data on machines that are incompatible with other machines so that the free exchange of information in the organisation is no longer possible. Many early applications, especially integrated management informa-

Figure 11.2
The centralisation of system development

For	Against
Compatibility	Meeting Local Needs
Maintenance	Over Dependence on Mainframes
Control	In-house Developments Unnecessary
The D.P. Power Base	Decentralise Technical Support

tion systems, were specifically developed to provide a means of tighter central control over the activities of departments. They provided senior managers with regular reports from all parts of the organisation and, by introducing standardised terms and procedures, they ensured that different departments were able to operate within a common framework. The proliferation of local systems threatens this harmonisation and control.

The technical staff of the organisation are usually particularly concerned that they cannot maintain the large array of computer equipment that may be purchased and that they could not train users in the use of the many kinds of software.

There is another very significant reason why technical staff in Data Processing Departments should be suspicious of decentralised systems developments. When all computer developments were based on mainframe installation, computer power was by definition centralised and all developments could be planned from a central Data Processing Department. As a result, in many organisations,the DP Department has grown large and powerful as the organisation has come to rely more and more on large, mainframe-based applications. The proliferation of computing throughout the organisation threatens this power base and raises questions about the role of central teams of technical staff in the organisation. Not unnaturally the staff of these central teams may seek to maintain their power base by ensuring that all developments remain centralised.

There may then be reasons why senior management and central technical staff will favour centralised control of systems development. The alternative view is usually put by end-user departments. Central developments which put emphasis upon standardisation are often perceived as not paying sufficient attention to important and legimate local needs and variations. Similarly, if the emphasis is placed upon central control through the information reported to senior management, end-user departments may experience the system as an unnecessary threat to their autonomy. The possibility of developing local systems therefore provides the chance of develop a system which will serve local needs and will not be part of some larger control system.

Technical reasons can also be advanced for local developments. Many end-user departments feel that central DP staff automatically look to the mainframe as the technical base of any system. They are perceived as doing this because it is the technology with which they are most familiar and it is a way of maintaining central control. End users may argue, however, that mini, micro and network solutions offer much better solutions.

Another development is about feasibility. A few years ago central development was necessary because technical programming expertise was required for the construction of bespoke systems and these skills did not exist in end-user departments. Now there are powerful generic products on the market which can be tailored to local needs without sophisticated programming expertise. In addition, by virtue of their experience with earlier systems, there are often within the user departments members of staff who have acquired considerable knowledge of systems development, certainly with respect to requirements specification and system evaluation. These people, with the new products available, can now develop complex systems without central help. Where specialist help is required, it may be possible to obtain it from the suppliers or from outside consultants and, if it is appropriate to use internal technical staff, why should they not be decentralised to serve the end-user departments? The argument for this is that large central teams are no longer necessary for systems development and technical staff need to play more of a support role for end-user departments. If this is the case they can do it from within the end-user departments rather than from a central location.

This debate is to be heard in most large organisations with any history of information technology. Unfortunately, because it involves power and influence and affects individual careers, it can be a very destructive debate and may not lead to a sober consideration of what information technology policy is best for the organisation as a whole. It also tends to polarise so that, for example, all developments have to be centralised, and independent end-users' developments are banned. We have encountered personal computers that have to be hidden when there are visitors from head office because they are illegal.

It is important that any Information Technology Strategy Committee address this issue not as one of centralisation or decentralisation but as a question of the degree and type of centralisation that is needed for the well-being of the Company. To this end three concepts may be of service:

- information resource management and information technology management
- functional integration in the organisation and the need for integrated information systems
- the devolution of responsibilities in the organisation and devolution of information resources.

The control of information technology may well be considered the responsibility of specialists that understand the technology but the information resources of the organisation are the property of everybody. It is important to separate the policies that relate to the information resources from those that relate to the technology that handles much of the information. The policies that relate to the information resources should be established by general management and need to cover issues such as who has access to which classes of information, who has the right to update, change and delete information, etc. The technologists can then recommend the best means of implementing these policies. In the following sections the policies relating to information resource management are examined before we examine the policies that relate to information technology.

Information Resource Management

The degree to which an organisation standardises its information flows and uses integrated information systems as a control mechanism is an issue to be determined by management rather than technologists because it is in part a matter of management philosophy. However, it also relates to the degree to which there has to be functional integration within the organisation for it to be successful. There are, for example, some kinds of organisation which have to be tightly integrated because what happens in one part directly affects other parts. Managing a fleet of aircraft, an oil refinery or a manufacturing facility, for example, needs careful integration. By contrast there are organisations where the parts are in loose affiliation, for example, the departments of a university, where a greater degree of autonomy at a local level can be acceptable. An analysis of the relationship between functional interdependency and organisational structures is to be found in Thompson (1967).

An analysis of this kind is likely to show that there are some information flows which the organisation needs to standardise because they are shared by everybody and provide important control information for senior management. There are also likely to be local information needs which have few links with the rest of the organisation. Returning to the university example, it may be important to co-ordinate the inform-ation resources that relate to the registration of students but the data collected in an experiment by an individual researcher are of little concern to the organisation at large. It may be possible to identify some 'data highways' which everybody will share and which need standardised treatment and a lot of 'byways' which could be developed much more independently. It may still be necessary to be able to transfer aggregated data from the 'byway' to the 'highway' but the growing ability of systems to handle 'open system interconnections' should make this a progressively less significant technical issue. With an understanding of the structure of the organisation it should then be possible to construct a policy covering the degree to which decentralised systems can be developed without damaging the need for overall co-ordination of the organisation.

Another organisational variable that can be used to guide the development of a policy for information technology development is the way in which the organisational structure assigns responsibilities to managers and their staff. Within these policies it is likely that individual managers will be charged with the attainment of specified objectives and provided with a range of resources, i.e. manpower, finance, equipment, etc. to enable them to tackle these objectives. Within broad organisational policies they may accept considerable autonomy in the way they use these resources. We may usefully treat information as a resource with similar characteristics. Thus, if inform-ation originates within a specific department as part of the work of a specific individual, that person is in an important sense the owner of that information and has certain rights and obligations with respect to it. Within a specific application it is important that managers should know the degree to which they have control of the information resources arising from the work of the department. They will need to know, for example, the rules by which data bases pertaining to the department are available to their superiors, the rules by which data can be transferred, the time-scales involved, etc. An important objective is to ensure that the rules and regulations relating to information systems are compatible with and support the organisational structures in the organisation.

Developing an information resource management policy is then a matter for general management which needs to be closely related to other management policies within the organisation. The policy should be able to specify rights and obligations for the control of information in the organisation and, by the same token, it should indicate the degree to which systems are centrally developed or end-user departments have freedom when they develop systems for their own use.

Information Technology Management

Having specified information resource management policies, the Information Technology Strategy Committee would then have to establish policies governing the technical means of serving these goals. Since this is a technical issue a full review of these policies will not be provided here. We will examine, however, those issues which affect the relationship between the technical staff and user departments especially as it relates to the debate about centralisation and decentralisation.

In order to create a compatible and manageable information technology architecture across the organisation most central Data Processing teams charged with this responsibility would like to control the purchasing policy so that equipment and software is obtained which is compatible with the overall system. They usually prefer to deal with a small number of suppliers — both to ensure compatibility and to limit the range of hardware and software their staff are expected to explain and maintain. End-user departments may take a different view. They may seek the equipment which best seems to serve their particular requirements and with the wide availability of cheap microcomputers and even cheaper software packages it is very easy for an organisation, for example, to find itself with several dozen varieties of word processor package.

One solution to this problem is for the Information Technology Strategy Committee to agree a range of equipment and software the technical staff are able and willing to support. In practice, it is likely that such a list would have to be supplemented in a number of ways. It may be necessary to distinguish between when it is mandatory to conform to the list and when there is discretion. If, for example, the equipment or software is to be connected to the main applications of the organisation the choice may be limited. Where it is a stand-alone application for a very specific purpose it may be necessary to go outside the list to satisfy the requirement. Where a department goes outside it may be necessary to stipulate that educational and technical support cannot be provided within the organisation and outside arrangements must be made. Given that both user departments and technical staff have vested interests in this debate it may be important to establish a mechanism whereby these issues can be considered by the overall committee or a sub-committee with a representative composition.

Information Centres and Support Centres

Another feature of the decentralisation debate is that user departments may need technical advice in order to decide what to purchase, support in installing it, training in its use and continuing support after implementation. This is often the starting point for the creation of Information Centres (Bird and Firnbeg, 1984) which are now common in large user organisations. Although the role of these Centres varies they are most frequently established as a place in which user departments can explore the possibilities of using microcomputers and their associated software. They are usually not directly concerned with mainframe applications although the links between mainframe and micro may well be an issue. The Centre is usually staffed with technical people able to discuss the requirements with users and able to suggest a variety of ways they might be met. It should then be possible for the user to try some of the alternatives physically in the Centre and to evaluate them with the technical staff. Subsequently the user may purchase one of the systems and the Centre staff would assist with training, installation and support. The Information Centre concept has been described as an 'Information Shop' in which the wares of the information technology industry are on display and can be explained by experts. There is a cynical view that central technical teams have established Information Centres as a way of protecting their power base inside the organisation, i.e. instead of the user visiting the Computer Shop in the High Street where they might be sold anything, they go to the Information Centre where they are only offered goods from the approved range. If there is an overly restricted range dictated by technical considerations alone, no doubt the High Street will soon be attracting end users again. There have been examples of Information Centres attached to the main Data Processing Department restricting their role to helping users select from the approved list, providing help with technical installation and then leaving users to their own devices. Not surprisingly users then have difficulty exploiting the equipment they have obtained and may seek help elsewhere.

To be successful Information Centres need to gain the confidence of users that their requirements are being seriously considered and the best solutions sought. If the Information Technology Strategy Committee were to consider how best to organise Information Centres to gain the confidence of user departments it might consider the arrangement illustrated in Figure 11.3.

Figure 11.3
The organisation of information centres

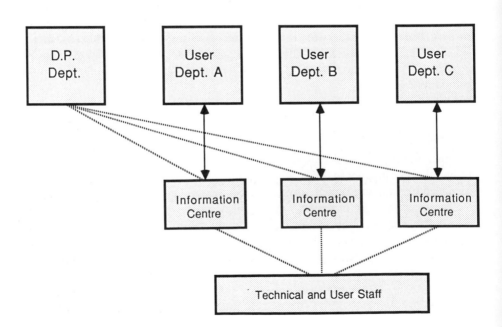

If the major role of Information Centres is to support decentralised developments in User Departments perhaps they should be decentralised themselves so that each department of a reasonable size can be given its own centre. If the User Department is to feel that it is obtaining a customised service from its Information Centre perhaps the manager of the Centre should report to the User Department Manager with a technical (dotted line) responsibility to the Data Processing Department. The development history of other staff functions in organisations has followed this pattern. For example, in many organisations each department has a Personnel Manager who reports to the Head of Department but refers on personnel policy matters to a central Personnel Department. It may be that the evolution of information technology management in organisations will show a similar pattern.

The role of the Information Centre should not be perceived as dominantly technical. If it is to service the needs of the members of the Department it should take on many of the support functions identified in Chapter 9. From requirements analysis, through installation and training to operational use there is a continuous need for support if systems are to fit their purpose and staff are to be helped to use them. It may be, for example, that a local Information Centre would be well equipped to take on the duties of customising systems for local use, for ensuring workstation and room layouts do not lead to user stress and for developing user manuals tailored to local needs so that users do not have to cope with general purpose manuals. In some organisations departments use the title Support Centres rather than Information Centres which may be a better representation of the function to be fulfilled.

Any local Centre of this kind needs to contain expertise about the technology and expertise about the special characteristics of the user department. As Figure 11.3 illustrates the staff of the Centre should then be drawn from technical and user backgrounds. Given the array of human issues to be addressed in implementing systems and supporting staff, there is also a requirement for staff from human science backgrounds such as ergonomics. The role of staff with user-department backgrounds raises a broader issue. In many departments there are people who have developed considerable expertise in information technology because, for example, they have been the user representative in a number of system developments. We have noted in many organisations that staff seconded into this role for the period of development rarely go back into their original user role. After implementation they are the Department's expert on the system and they act as the support staff for their colleagues. When future developments are mooted they may again become the user representatives. In many organisations there is now a group of staff who occupy a somewhat ill-defined role somewhere between being a technical specialist and being a user. Good people in these roles are probably the difference between success and failure in many applications. There is, however, very little of a recognised career path for such people and their role is frequently undervalued. It could be that the development of local Information or Support Centres would provide an appropriate organisational niche for these staff who would then see their role as a permanent task of supporting existing information technology applications and working for the development of future user-centred applications. If the Centre does report to the User Department, the staff of the Centre would be the natural group to support user management in negotiations about major applications in the organisation and could take responsibility for the many activities needed in system development and implementation that have been identified in this book as being in the user domain.

The combination of Figures 11.1 and 11.3 provide a view of a possible permanent structure of information technology responsibilities, centrally and locally, within a large user organisation. It is an attempt to specify appropriate roles for technical specialists and users and to manage the centralisation versus decentralisation debate. Very few organisations display structures of this kind at the moment although many contain elements of it. Often the Data Processing Department is the permanent structure and all other structures are temporary creations to serve specific developments. As the management of information technology comes to be seen as a permanent and major activity for both technologists and users we may see more of these features as a normal part of the organisational structure.

Policies for Individual Projects

We have reviewed the major policy matters concerning structure and process which the Information Technology Strategy Committee will have to address. We now turn to policies which will be required to control a particular development project within the organisation. If the Committee is charged with the responsibility for authorising and managing individual projects, what policies should it adopt? In many respects this book has been concerned with individual projects and this provides an opportunity to summarise some of the main points.

1. Ensure user management is responsible for the specification and evaluation of user requirements, for the field testing of technical systems, and for the planning and management of change. Technical specialists are responsible for technical specifications and for the delivery of technical systems to meet these specifications. Where more than one user department is involved in the development the overall project direction should come from the level at which all the relevant user departments report. This is necessary to ensure sectional interests do not dictate the development.

2. In judging the cost–benefit of a development make a rigorous assessment of the business case but do not rely on objective measures of savings against costs. Examine how the development will serve and enhance the business objectives of the organisation and try to value the expected improvement in the performance of the relevant socio-technical system as opposed to the technical system. Expect indirect consequences beyond the target user departments and plan positively for their design and management.

3. When users are involved in the development of applications within their departments ensure there is end-user representation as well as management representation.

4. When users are involved in developments ensure they have the training and the time to execute their responsibilities properly.

5. Since information technology systems have ramifications beyond their immediate business objectives, develop mechanisms for early consultation with the stakeholders whether they be staff representatives, customers, or suppliers.
6. When technical systems are being specified and designed provide users with maximum opportunity to make their contribution by using prototypes, trials, evaluations and evolution to give them opportunities and time to assess ramifications. Do not permit technical deadlines to reduce the opportunities for necessary evaluations and ensure there are opportunities for redesign when evaluations show it is necessary.
7. Remember that information technology developments will lead to organisational change and ensure that they are treated as opportunities for planned and positive job design.
8. Recognise that the implementation of change puts strain on any organisation that has to maintain normal business and provide additional temporary resources and select implementation strategies to minimise the additional load.
9. Since technical systems are only as good as the ability of staff to exploit them, make sure that users are well prepared for the change and that ongoing, point-of-need support is provided after implementation.
10. When a system has been implemented commission an evaluation of how well it is meeting its socio-technical objectives — both to assess the system and to ensure the organisation learns better how to undertake information technology developments.

These points do not cover all of the issues that project management will need to address but are deliberately chosen to express the requirements that are often overlooked or which tend to be lost when questions of time and cost take priority. When this happens the result is often a difficult implementation and an under-utilised system.

An Organisation in the Information Age

In Chapter 1 a number of visions of the future with information technology were presented. It is important that the Information Technology Strategy Committee should possess a vision of what kind of overall organisation it is striving for with information technology as a vehicle for change. This is one way of ensuring there is some organisational coherence to the many developments taking place. Such a vision should go beyond immediate business objectives to questions of philosophy and culture; what kind of management style will it adopt, what kind of people will it employ, etc? There will, for example, be an increasing need to formulate policies on such questions as telework; whether, for example, many staff will become 'tele-commuters'; sub-contractors working from home (Kinsman, 1987) or the organisation will become geographically decentralised and operate from a number of small locations linked by powerful communications systems.

Each organisation will have to work out its future for itself. Information Technology permits many futures; it is a very flexible technology which renders obsolete many of the reasons why organisations are as they are. It is then a question of how organisations conceive of and debate these new possibilities. Given that there are many choices it is not possible to present one Utopian view of the organisation in the information age. However, it is possible to present some features that would follow from the principles presented in this book. The one feature of the future about which we can be reasonably certain is that rapid change will always be with us. The successful organisation will therefore have to be an adaptive organisation.

What features must an organisation possess to be capable of surviving in an information-rich age and of coping with continuous change? One feature is the ability to exploit the information technology it possesses and another is the ability to keep present forms of organisation under constant review. Ensuring the organisation exploits its information technology needs three kinds of role; the line role where end users are responsible for its application to work, the technical role where IT specialists maintain the technical systems and the in-between role which is emerging, for example, in Information Centres, which is a mixture of user support and local technical delivery. An examination of each of these roles will help to demonstrate some of the practical requirements of the information-rich, adaptive organisation.

The Line Role

In an organisation with this capability it is likely that the majority of work roles which have line functions, i.e. contribute directly to the products and services provided by the organisation, would have the three components identified in Figure 11.4.

The first component is the familiar one of *operational tasks*, the achievement of the day-to-day work, whether it is making the product or serving the customer. Traditionally this is the largest component of the work role but ever since the Industrial Revolution, technical innovation has had the effect of reducing it. The technology engages directly with the work materials so that the human being takes a more distant role, contact with the raw material of the work being mediated by the technology. From hacking coal with a pick and shovelling it into tubs, the coal miner, for example, operates coal cutting machines that do much of the physical work on the coal. The same process is occurring with information technology; from typing a letter, physically correcting mistakes, stamping and addressing envelopes, posting the mail, filing copies in a filing cabinet, etc. the secretary may be able to create an electronic file and command the system to do the rest. The result is that less time is spent on operational tasks and more time on the management of the technical resources which undertake or support operational duties. We think of some roles (for example, the process controller) as being one of managing complex technology from control consoles but increasingly it is true of many work roles. To return to the secretary, for example, this role may now have access to word processing, electronic storage and retrieval, telephone and other communication facilities, copying equipment, etc. The ability to choose correctly which facility to use and operate it successfully is increasingly a major feature of the job. Similarly the engineering designer will have to manage a

Figure 11.4
Human roles in an information age

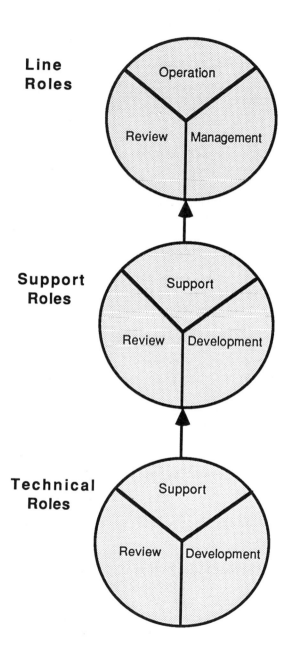

Computer Aided Design system and the teacher an array of technology to support the teaching process. In Figure 11.4 therefore all line roles will have a significant *technology management* component to the work.

The second feature of the organisation of the future is that it should be capable of self-review and development. One way of achieving these conditions would be to have an operational wing of the organisation that made heavy use of the technology and another wing, a 'think tank', which was responsible for the review function and initiating new developments. Such a division may be natural but would reinforce the split between designers and users which has led to many current problems in planning and introducing change. The concepts of user participation and user department control over developments are based on the idea that change needs to be planned by those who must live with the consequences.

The concept of user-centred design carries with it the idea that most people who will become users will play some role in the planning and implementation of new systems. The third component of the typical line role in Figure 11.4 is a *review function*; it is the opportunity to stand back from the day-to-day work and consider the future. It is common for managers and professionals to find themselves in these review activities but we tend not to think of machine operatives, clerks, secretaries, etc. having similar responsibilities. However, it is increasingly common for this to occur. As staff representatives on various committees (for example, health and welfare), they step outside their operational duties. If the organisation institutes Quality Circles (see, for example, Ouchi, 1981) all the employees may find themselves in regular group meetings to consider what can be done locally to improve work performance. If major change of any kind is being planned, they may find themselves assigned to task forces to contribute their expertise. Rather than seeing these activities as abnormal, *ad hoc*, and infrequent interruptions to normal work, any organisation which sets itself the target of being responsive to change at all levels needs to build activities into all work roles. They not only have the effect of bringing all the relevant expertise of the organisation to bear on its future thinking but they create a culture where everyone expects change to occur.

In respect of information technology the review aspect of the work role encompasses a number of activities. It must include the learning activities necessary to understand and use the potential of the technology, it should include participation in evaluation studies to assess whether the systems are adequately supporting the work tasks and it could include a wide variety of activities relating to the development of new systems (requirement specification, system selection, engagement with prototype evaluations, trials, job design, work place design, implementation planning and so on).

An analysis of this kind demonstrates one of the reasons why forecasts of the job losses caused by information technology are usually gross overestimates. They tend to be based on the idea that if human labour can be substituted by technology for large amounts of the operational work, large numbers of people will be displaced. What seems to happen is that the operational sector is reduced but it is often greater than expected because more of the work is non-routine than was anticipated and therefore continues to need direct human intervention. The management of the technology is a new element to the human work that takes time and, if change is to continue, more people become involved in the review and change process. We are seeing a widespread change in the role played in the work process and, if we handle it well, it could lead to more adaptive organisations and more satisfying occupations. There are requirements that all staff will be educated to a level which will enable them to fulfil the three components of the work role which has implications for general education and the specific training given in-house.

Support Roles

If line staff are to be able to use information technology effectively they need local support both during system development and when the system is in use. We have explored the need for these support roles elsewhere and have noted the way organisations are creating these roles in *ad hoc* ways to meet emerging needs. As a result of this unplanned development there is no clear pattern to the nature of these roles or the kind of people needed to fulfil them. At one extreme is the decentralisation of technical staff to Information Centres to provide user support. At the other extreme is the local expert; the user who continues with the normal line role but acquires, perhaps without formal recognition, the role of supporting his immediate colleagues in their dealings with the technology. On a more official level, but still treated as a temporary assingment, is the secondment of a user to be a user representative in systems development. Then we can add others who bring specialist skills to the support role (for example, the training specialist and the ergonomist).

Whatever the route into this role we can analyse its components (as in Figure 11.4) in the same way as the line role. The main operational task is to give the relevant user population *support* as they try to realise the potential of the technology. Some of the support may be pre-planned as training sessions or user-specific manuals but most of it will be devoted to providing 'point-of-need support'. A second major component to the role is a contribution to the *development of new systems*. The primary characteristic of this role is that it is a facilitative rather than a design activity; the person is essentially a go-between helping users to work effectively with technical specialists rather than making all the user decisions. It may therefore involve helping users express their requirements, organising trials and evaluations, providing training and planning implementation procedures. It may increasingly involve the customisation of computer facilities to user needs, the configuration of systems to match organisational structures and the setting up of work stations and environments to satisfy human characteristics. There must also be a *review* element in this role. It is particularly important to establish an ongoing process of review for roles which are still unclear. By regularly checking the requirement for support the organisation can avoid creating structures that survive beyond their useful life and ensure, for example, that the support services change to match the growing sophistication of the end-user population. It is also an important element in defining what skills and knowledge are necessary to fulfil the role.

The qualifications needed to fulfil this role are an interesting open question. Where a formal requirement for a local support role is recognised the main requirement is seen to be training in information technology because this is what is being delivered. This is certainly the case but a person who specialises in programming new systems would be out of place in this role. The need is for someone with a broad knowledge of the technology who can administer its application on a broad front from explaining how to set up a data base to plugging a terminal into a network. Where support staff emerge rather than being selected they are usually from the user population and an important element in the support role is the ability to understand the user's tasks and to empathise with the user's problems. There is therefore a case for in-house training of support staff from the user population. Finally, many of the skills needed come from human and social science training – for example, planning offices and workstations to avoid user stress, designing manuals and training, customising services to suit specific user needs, managing change processes and, above all, acting as a catalyst so that everybody can be involved in an appropriate manner.

This specification does not fit neatly the average syllabus for technical training courses or in-house courses for the development of line staff. It may well be that the support function needs people from several backgrounds until such time as training and career structures start to produce people with the breadth of skill and expertise to meet these requirements.

Technical Roles

Developments in information technology threaten the nature of end-user jobs but it is not so widely recognised that they pose even greater threats to the jobs of in-house data processing staff. A few years ago a large user organisation needed large teams of programming staff because systems development required man–years of special purpose programming.

The majority of the technical staff were systems analysts and programmers working on bespoke system developments to run on mainframe computers. The requirement for technical specialists is rapidly changing. The developments in the technology mean that there is less need for bespoke programming and systems are not necessarily mounted on mainframes. The existence in some organisations of several generations of computer systems and the growing sophistication of user departments means that more time must be spent supporting existing installations and supporting the needs of end users for technical help, training, etc.

Figure 11.4 identifies three components of the role of the technical specialist. Previously the dominant role was the development of new systems, but in many organisations, it has already been replaced by the *support role* and this trend looks set to continue. A complex infrastructure delivering an array of vital information services across the organisation will need substantial support even if local user needs are met by a decentralised network of support centres. There will continue to be a role in *new system development* but in a number of organisations programming staff have expressed anxiety about their own futures because the need for bespoke programming is declining. This appears to be another case of changing job content rather than job loss. Whilst coding may not be in such demand there will remain a great need to investigate and understand user requirements, translate them into technical specifications and help build and install systems to meet these requirements. It seems likely that the technical job will be less solution creation by the individual development of lines of code which will meet the specification. Instead it will be joint system specification with the systems analysts working alongside users, followed by system selection, configuration and evaluation with users via prototypes and trials. This is a demanding change of orientation for which the training of most programmers will not have prepared them. It is often the case, for example, that the technical staff of an organisation who have deep experience of data processing techniques cannot readily see the value of rapid prototyping and find it difficult to incorporate fourth-generation languages in their development work. Similarly they may not be prepared for the demands created by the changing nature of the relation with the user population. There is a need for retraining of technical specialists so that they can recognise and meet the new requirements being placed upon them.

As with other roles the final component is *review*. In a world where the technology in which you are a specialist changes dramatically every few years, reviewing your own role is essential. There will be obvious requirements to keep abreast of technical developments and renew technical knowledge and skills. There are also the less obvious requirements to review the role within the organisation as changes occur in user attitudes and requirements and in the way these requirements can be met by the technology.

Conclusions: Socio-Technical Infrastructure

Some organisations have the equivalent of an Information Technology Strategy Committee but the agenda is usually dominated by technical considerations. The review in this chapter has sought to demonstrate that there are many strategic organisational issues which should also be on the agenda because there is unlikely to be another forum which will consider these issues as part of its remit. The goal should be to develop an organisation mature in its application of information technology and mature in the ability of its staff to exploit the technical capability at their disposal. The final section highlights the fact that there are two requirements if these goals are to be met. Firstly, the staff who deal directly with the business of the enterprise must feel that the technology is a tool that provides information services to help meet business objectives. Secondly, in order to ensure that the users get the systems they need and that they can use them effectively a local and central support structure needs to be created that both maintains and develops the technology and provides a continuous source of support so that the users can gradually extend their own abilities with respect to it. This is another level of socio-technical design; to create not just a technical infrastructure for the organisation but a socio-technical structure which not only delivers technical systems but also the human support necessary to develop and maintain the systems.

Towards User-centred Design

The thesis of this book has been that we are on the threshold of an information revolution of considerable potential for business objectives and for the pursuit of individual goals. This revolution, like others before it, is being driven by technical imperatives. The goals are technical, the leading designers are technical specialists and the tools they use focus on technical issues. The consequences, however, are human and organisational and the revolution is proceeding slower, with more failures and distortions than might be expected. Until we learn to design socio-technical systems rather than technical systems this pattern is likely to recur. Throughout this book we have looked for ways of promoting this outcome and the central theme is user-centred design; bringing the people who will use the system within the organisation into the development process. We have examined the roles users can play in development and the tools they need if their contribution is to be effective. Finally, we have examined the policies that need to be pursued at senior levels within an organisation if a user-centred philosophy is to be sustained.

Many accept this general thesis but find that in practice the technical and economic arguments and methods of those in dominant positions to influence systems wash away the efforts to look at consequential human and organisational issues. Without denying the importance of these perspectives, the structures, arguments and techniques presented in this book are offered in the hope that they can ensure a systematic user-centred approach at all levels to the application of information technology in organisations.

Appendix
Cost–Benefit Assessment of the Organisational Impact of a Technical System Proposal

Introduction

Of the many tasks that have to be undertaken if information technology is to be successfully implemented one of the most crucial is the early assessment of the organisational impact of a proposed technical system. Typically the wider implications of technical system implementation are not appreciated until development work is well advanced and it may be difficult to change direction. The earlier this assessment can be made the more influence can be exerted upon technical system design and the methodology for its implementation. The problem, however, is how to make an assessment when the proposal is only an outline 'on the drawing board' and there is nothing concrete for users to evaluate.

The procedure presented here is designed to meet this need. The rationale and general structure is presented in Chapter 6 and the check-lists that follow provide the working documentation for the assessment. The circumstances under which this procedure is most relevant and has been most tested are as follows. As a result of a feasibility study an outline conceptual specification for a technical system has been proposed for a specific organisational setting. A group, perhaps comprising user management, technical staff and user representatives are charged with assessing this proposal for organisational and user acceptability.

The procedure takes a group of this kind through the following stages:

1. *Systems specification*. Stating the technical proposal in a form which facilitates the assessment of organisational impact.
2. *Organisational specification*. Outlining that part of the organisation which will be affected by the system and describing the actual or planned work roles that will be occupied by users of the system.
3. *User Cost–Benefit Assessment*. An assessment of the impact of the system upon the major work roles of potential users.
4. *Organisational Match Assessment*. An assessment of the overall impact upon the organisation.
5. *Socio–technical Design*. A series of check-lists to support the development of a strategy for the development of an acceptable socio-technical system.

In addition to its value in assessing specific technical proposals it has also proved useful as a training aid, helping people appreciate the way in which technical systems influence organisational issues and thereby developing their ability to play a constructive role in technical developments within their own organisations. In this instance case studies need to be developed with technical and organisational specifications similar to the organisational contexts with which the trainees are familiar.

Stage 1: The Technical System Specification

The following information needs to be extracted from the outline conceptual proposal.

1. Purpose and Overall Configuration
   - What is the overall rationale for the system?
   - What scale is envisaged (how much of the organisation will be affected)?
   - What kind of system is envisaged (an integrated, mainframe-based system, a net work, stand-alone micros, etc.)?
   - How does the system relate to existing technical systems, i.e. does it replace them, extend them, have to be compatible with them, etc?
2. Planned Benefits
   - What benefits are used to justify the planned expenditure?
     - resource reduction?
     - resource effectiveness?
     - individual enhancement?
     - organisational enhancement?
   - What priorities are placed upon the achievement of these benefits?
3. System Functionality
   - What, in global terms, are the main categories of service to be offered to users?
     - reports/enquiry facilities available?
     - communication facilities?
     - text processing services?
     - data processing and calculation services?
     - control facilities, e.g. for monitoring and directing equipment, and processes? etc.
   - What requirements, in global terms, will this place upon users?
     - requirements for data input to the system?
     - requirements for standardisation procedures across the organisation?
     - requirements for timing, security, etc?
4. Management Development, Management Control
   - From what location will the completed system be managed both on a routine and a developmental basis?
   - From what location will the system be developed and what plans exist for the management of the project?

– What kind of development and implementation strategy is envisaged (e.g. proto-types and trials, phased implementation, 'big bang', etc.)?

It should be noted that very little information about the physical characteristics of the system is sought at this stage; indeed such information should not be available because decisions of this kind should follow a detailed examination of the concepts being advanced. This means that the assessment of impact can cover functionality and accept-ability but not usability since this depends upon the specific form of system delivered. However, the analysis of users to be undertaken can lead to the statement of usability criteria to be used as the system is developed.

Stage 2: Organisational Description

A statement of the characteristics of the organisational setting into which it is planned the technical system will be implemented.

1. Organisational structure and work roles
   – What is the reporting structure in the part of the organisation to be affected by the system?
   – What are the main categories of work role to be affected by the systems?
     – primary users?
     – secondary users (occasional or indirect users)?
     – tertiary users (those affected but without direct access)?
     – non-users but affected by implications, e.g. job displaced by the system?
   – What changes are envisaged in the work roles or reporting structure by the time the system is implemented (either as a result of the system or because of other organisational changes)?
2. Overall allocation of relevant tasks to work roles
   A top level task description of the way in which the activities of the organisation that the technical system is designed to support are currently handled in the organ-isation. It should show:
   – How the overall tasks are subdivided and allocated to existing work roles (how are responsibilities allocated?)
   – The existing contribution of technology to the tasks undertaken within each work role.
   – The task interdependencies between the work roles. It may be that these can be shown as a time-related task-flow, as a complex process is worked through. However, care must be taken not to assume a too simplistic or well structured set of relationships. An analysis of the relationships between responsibilities may provide a more abstract and powerful expression of the interdependencies.
3. An Allocation of Functionality Table
   The development of a table expressing the planned allocation of the functionality of the technical system to the work roles in the organisation. This brings together the system specification and the organisational specification and provides the basis for the cost–benefit assessment.

System Functionality	User Work Roles						

- Take each major work role and list the system functionality which will be available to the role.
- Annotate the list with the allocation of responsibilities for data inputs and any other requirements which will be laid upon the work role.

Stage 3: User Cost–Benefit Assessment

The following check-lists can now be completed on behalf of each of the user work roles identified in the allocation of functionality table. The aim is to express the changes that the planned system would bring to each user role and to assess how the users would be likely to evaluate these changes.

In making the evaluation the underlying rationale is that users will be concerned with two aspects of the change:

Benefits: which may be in terms of the ability to perform tasks more effectively, desirable changes in the nature of the job, improved salaries, greater power and influence or enhanced career prospects, etc.

Costs: which may be financial but include the effort it takes to use a system, loss of job security, effort to learn and adapt, risk of failure, loss of job satisfaction and loss of privacy, etc.

The check-lists cover the major changes that research has shown often result from the introduction of information technology. The list is divided into five kinds of impact that range from the most direct to the most indirect. In practice, it is easier to predict the effects at the top of the list than at the bottom. The first issue is job security because when there are issues of this kind affecting a user group they will tend to dominate the entire evaluation process. Supposing a job remains to be done, the next section reviews the changes in information service that result from the functionality in the system which will be provided for the user group. The main categories of service need to be entered in this section. It is important to consider both the categories the access to and those that are provided because access by others to facilities debarred from the user group may have important consequences for them.

The third section reviews the major dimensions of a job that may be changed and this is followed by a section examining the organisational procedures that may change and influence the user. Finally, the indirect effects upon personnel policies which affect the user are reviewed.

In completing the questionnaire the significant changes that may affect the user are first listed. It is most unlikely that any specific user group will experience changes on all of these dimensions so this is a question of trying to identify major areas of change. Where there are changes an assessment can be made of the likely evaluation of users. Separate columns are provided for benefits and costs because some changes have elements of both, for example, job changes can lead to the loss of valued skills but the development of new ones that will be valuable in the future.

It may be sufficient to give a qualitative expression to this evaluation, simply identifying all benefits as positive outcomes and all costs as negative outcomes. In practice, however, we have found that teams engaged in this exercise like to give quantitative expression to the evaluation. If this is done an overall score can be given for each user group and, across the user population, the winners and the losers can be clearly seen. We give below the scoring system that has evolved for this purpose but we would caution against too literal a use of the figures; the ability to predict changes and human responses to them is not such as to support fine discriminations between the totals that result.

To score the check-list put a total between + 1 and + 5 in the benefit column for each change that would be regarded as a benefit. A high score represents a change the user would be eagerly awaiting, a low score is a marginal benefit that would excite little interest. Similarly where a change may have a negative element to the user enter a score in the costs column of between − 1 and − 5 where − 5 is a striking issue and − 1 is a minor anxiety that may soon be forgotten. Averages can be calculated for each subsection, treating costs and benefits separately. Dimensions where no changes are anticipated should be ignored. Totalling the scores for each subsection gives an overall score for the user group where the total possible is 25. Although the totals must be treated with caution a high benefit, low cost conclusion is indicative of a good response. A low benefit, high cost outcome will probably lead to user resistance and it may be useful to explore what form this might take (for example, non-use, partial use, opposition to implementation, negotiation for protection or other benefits, etc.). Quite often a high benefit, high costs outcome is obtained which suggests the reception of the system could be good if only some of the costs could be removed. In practice, it is common to find all of these outcomes for the same system because different user groups are affected in different ways.

The first check-list is an assessment of the *probable* outcomes of the planned system. It is quite likely that in completing the check-list respondents think of ways in which the outcomes for the users could be improved by changing the nature of the technical system, the way it is implemented or the social system of which the user is a part. A second check-list is provided for these *desirable* outcomes. It includes the same dimensions and can be scored in the same way. In this case, wherever a more desirable

Check-list 1

USER COST–BENEFIT ANALYSIS

Probable Outcome

User Group:...

Issues	Change	Benefits	Costs
1. *Job Security*			
2. *Information Facilities in System* (System Functionality) (a) .... (b) .... (c) .... (d) .... (e)			
Average			
3. *Job Content* (a) Task Variety (b) Effort Required (c) New Skills/Old Skills Lost (d) Work Pace/Deadlines (e) Workload (f) Satisfaction			
Average			
4. *Organisational Procedures* (a) Discretion/Autonomy (b) Standardisation/Formality (c) Power and Influence (d) Privacy (e) Communications (f) Status			
Average			
5. *Personnel Policies* (a) Basic Pay (b) Other Rewards (c) Career Prospects (d) Industrial Relations			
Average			
TOTALS			

Check-list 2

COST–BENEFIT ANALYSIS

Desired Outcome

User Group:...

Issues	Change	Benefits	Costs	Conditions
1. *Job Security*				If...
2. *Information Facilities in System* (System Functionality) (a) .... (b) .... (c) .... (d) .... (e)				If...
Average				
3. *Job Content* (a) Task Variety (b) Effort Required (c) New Skills/Old Skills Lost (d) Work Pace/Deadlines (e) Workload (f) Satisfaction				If...
Average				
4. *Organisational Procedures* (a) Discretion/Autonomy (b) Standardisation/Formality (c) Power and Influence (d) Privacy (e) Communications (f) Status				If...
Average				
5. *Personnel Policies* (a) Basic Pay (b) Other Rewards (c) Career Prospects (d) Industrial Relations				If...
Average				
TOTALS				

outcome is identified an 'If. . .' statement could be inserted to specify the conditions under which this desirable end would be obtained. A complete list of 'If. . . . .' statements constitutes a useful specification of the requirements of the user groups, and can be used in replanning or detailing the system. There is of course no guarantee that the requirements of the different user groups will be compatible with one another.

If the end product of this evaluation is a number of user groups who have very negative scores it is unlikely that the system can be effectively implemented except by management coercion. It may be, however, that the analysis has identified a number of more productive routes and an effective strategy can be to reformulate the technical plans and repeat the evaluation to check whether a better prognosis can be obtained. When the outcome is reasonably positive, i.e. all user groups show some positive outcomes even if there are considerable costs, stage 4 of the evaluation can be addressed.

Stage 4: The Assessment of Organisational Cost–Benefit

Check-list 3 provides a basis for making an assessment of the cost–benefit of the system from an organisational viewpoint. It is likely that a formal cost–benefit assessment will be made in terms of the value of tangible benefits set against the costs of system development and purchase. The aim here is to express the cost–benefit to the organisation across a wide range of organisational impacts.

The check-list has the same construction as the check-lists for user groups. It provides a number of dimensions for which the cost–benefit can be assessed by identifying the change and evaluating this for positive and negative implications.

The first section lists the major forms of planned benefits which were discussed in Chapter 2. It would be expected that the main positive effects would arise from this section. However, the achievement of one type of benefit may well inhibit the achievement of other benefits which may be regarded as a negative outcome.

The second section lists the direct organisational implications of using information technology systems which are discussed in Chapter 8. They range from issues of data security and reliability to the degree to which new systems are compatible with existing systems.

Broader organisational issues are considered in section three. A technical system may, for example, help or hinder the organisation's ability to respond flexibly to external demands, to adapt over time and to adopt values, control mechanisms, etc. of its choosing.

The final section summarises the likely reactions of the major user groups. The results of the earlier analysis can be summarised for all the user groups on a $+5$, -5 scale as a way of reviewing the ease of difficulty of implementing the system as planned.

Completing this check-list provides a basis for assessing whether the planned system as outlined is likely to be beneficial and acceptable to the organisation as a whole. If it is, we can proceed to stage 5 which presents procedures for detailing and developing the system. If there are significant difficulties it may be appropriate to review the technical system outline, the organisational structure or the development plan to seek a better match with organisational needs. A new concept derived in this way may be evaluated by conducting stages 3 and 4 once again.

Check-list 3

ORGANISATIONAL COST–BENEFIT ANALYSIS

	Change	Benefits	Costs
1. *Planned Benefits* (a) Resource Reduction (b) Resource Optimisation (c) Individual Enhancement (d) Organisational Enhancement			
	Average		
2. *System Operation* (a) Reliability (b) Security (c) Compatibility (d) Vulnerability to Stoppages			
	Average		
3. *Organisational Match* (a) Control Mechanisms (b) Flexibility (c) Adaptibility (d) Culture and Values			
	Average		
4. *User Group Responses* (a) .... (b) .... (c) .... (d) .... (e) .... (f)			
	Average		

Stage 5: Developing a Strategy for Design and Change

The outline, conceptual plan which has been assessed as acceptable can now be detailed. It is likely that the analysis will have revealed a range of problems and a series of desirable outcomes. In developing the plans for the system and the way it is designed, these 'costs' and 'benefits' need to be carried forward to ensure the benefits are realised and the costs are eliminated or managed. The strategy that is developed should set this as a target for the organisation as a whole and for each of the major user groups.

The strategy has three components reflected in the three check-lists that follow.

The first step is to review the social system (and therefore the organisational change) that is appropriate to achieve the business goals of the enterprise. The second step is to construct an outline technical system which will support the social system. Finally, a project design process is required to construct and deliver the planned socio-technical system.

The check-list for the social system is based upon Chapter 7 and part of Chapter 9. It attempts to identify the overall enterprise goals and to structure the social system to serve these goals. This section may be about a major or a minimal change and should use the ideas generated in the analysis phase. It should be remembered that the assumptions of no change in the social system if a new technical system is implemented are not tenable. Therefore, even if no change is intended, this section should be reviewed because enforced changes may have to be managed. The second part of the check-list identifies the dimensions of the organisational changes that will take the enterprise from its current to its future state.

Check-list 5 is a specification of those aspects of the technical system which most directly support the social system, i.e. support the role allocations between users. These issues are discussed in the user acceptability section of Chapter 8. The check-list does not provide for a complete technical specification but concentrates upon the articulation of system services and requirements to match the articulation in the social system.

The final check-list seeks to establish the composition of the team who will develop the system and the procedures by which they will work. It is the design of the temporary vehicle which will manage the innovation. It is based upon Chapter 5 and concentrates upon the roles of users and technical staff in the development of the system.

The outcome of completing these check-lists should be a broadly-based specification of a socio-technical system which should serve significant enterprise goals and should be functional, usable and acceptable to the user groups within the organisation. Furthermore, the composition of the design process should assign responsibilities for this specification to users so that the system can be developed in detail without losing sight of the user and organisational variables that have been identified as significant.

Check-list 4

SOCIAL SYSTEM DESIGN

Organisational Objectives
1. *Enterprise Goals*: state as operational aims in specified time-scales.
2. *Organisational Structure*: overall section/department/group structure to take responsibilities for enterprise goals.
3. *Job Design Philosophy*: policies with respect to the allocation of duties to individual employees.
4. *Control and Co-ordination*: policies to govern the way in which activities are co-ordinated in pursuit of goals.
5. *Values and Customs*: policies to govern the ways in which goals will be pursued.

Organisational Changes

For each of the following assess the degree of change and the appropriate mechanisms for making the transition.

1. Structural Changes in the Organisation.
2. Jobs to Phase Out.
3. New and Different Jobs to Introduce.
4. Skill Changes.
5. Implications for training, grading, team building, etc.
6. Industrial Relations Implications.

Check-list 5

TECHNICAL SYSTEM SPECIFICATION

Within the specification derived from check-list 4 develop a technical system specification which supports the social system which addresses the following topics for each user group.

1. *Facilities*
   – who needs what services from the system? (How is system functionality to be allocated?)
2. *Access*
   – who should have what degree of access to data bases?
   – how should access be controlled?
3. *Data Input*
   – by what means will data be entered, verified, etc.?
   – who has the authority/responsibility for updating or amending which data?
4. *Interface Specification*
   – what special requirements will users have of the man–computer interface (ease of use, ease of learning, etc.), i.e. what will define usability for each user group?
5. *Customisation*
   – what requirements will there be for customisation of services to specific user groups?
6. *Adaptation*
   – what requirements will there be for adapting or evolving the system to meet developing user needs?
7. *Implementation Strategy*
   – what strategy will be used for implementation? e.g. prototypes, trials, phased introduction of facilities, etc?

Check-list 6

PROJECT DESIGN PROCESS

Considering the needs of (a) the management commissioning the system, (b) the technical staff and (c) each of the user groups, construct a process of designing the system by establishing the following:

1. *Steering Committee*
   - what is the customer–contractor relationship?
   - who makes policy decisions?
2. *Main Design Group*
   - should there be user representatives?
   - what is the role of user representatives?
   - should users be trained for systems design?
   - should it be full- or part-time secondment?
3. *Working Parties*
   - should there be working parties on specific issues?
   - if so, which issues and what composition?
4. *Consultation, Training and Support*
   - who should consult and train each group of users?
   - what strategies should be used?
   - what point of need support strategy should be employed after implementation?
5. *Information Dissemination*
   - by what means will everybody be kept informed of design progress?
6. *Other Organisational Management Procedures*
   - What need is there to report to/consult existing management structures in the organisation?
   - Board of Directors
   - Information Technology Strategy Committee
   - Industrial Relations Bodies
   - etc.

Bear in mind that user participation has to be accomplished whilst the pressures to get the work done remain as normal.

References

Ackoff, R. L. (1967), Management misinformation systems. *Management Science*, **14**, (4),

Allen, R. B. (1982), Cognitive factors in human interaction with computers. *Behaviour and Information Technology*, **1** (3), 257–278.

APEX (1979), Office technology: a trade union response. Association of Professional, Executive, Clerical and Computer Staff Report, March.

Barron, I. and Curnow, R. (1979), *The future with microelectronics* (London: Francis Pinter).

Bass, B. M. and Barrett, G. V. (1981), *People, Work and Organisations*, 2nd Edition (London: Allyn and Bacon).

Bennett, J. (1979), The commercial impact of usability in interactive systems, In Shackel, B. (ed.), *'Man–Computer Communication'* (Maidenhead: Infotech State of the Art Report), vol. 2.

Bird, E. and Firnberg, D. (eds) (1984), The Information Centre (Maidenhead: Pergamon Infotech State of the Art Report), **12**, (2).

Bjørn-Andersen, N. (1985), Are human factors human? In Bevan, N. and Murray, D. (eds), *Man–machine Integration* (Maidenhead: Pergamon Infotech State of the Art Report), **13**, (1).

Bjørn-Andersen, N. and Eason, K. D. (1985), Myths and realities of information systems contributing to organisational rationality. In Mowshowitz, A. (ed.), *Human Choice and Computers 2*, (Amsterdam: North-Holland).

Bjørn-Andersen, N., Eason, K. D. and Robey, D. (1986), *Managing Computer Impact* (Norwood, NJ: Ablex).

Bjørn-Andersen, N. and Ginnerup, L. (1987), The support of cognitive capacity in future organisations: Towards enhanced communicative competence and cooperative problem structuring capability. Invited paper for the FAST Programme of the EEC, Copenhagen Business School.

Bjørn-Andersen, N., Hedberg, B., Mercer, D., Mumford, E. and Sole, A. (1979), *The Impact of Systems Change in Organisations* (Amsterdam: Sijthoff & Noordhoff).

Blackler, F. H. M. and Brown, C. A. (1980), Job redesign and social change: case studies at Volvo. In Duncan, K. D., Gruneberg, M. M. and Wallis, D. (eds), *Changes in Working Life* (Chichester: John Wiley).

Buchanan, D. A. and Boddy, D. (1983), *Organisations in the Computer Age* (London: Gower).

Burchett, R. (1985), Data analysis and the LBMS structured development method (LSDM). *Information Technology Training*, **3**, 45-50.

Cakir, A., Hart, D. J. and Stewart, T. F. M. (1980), *Visual Display Terminals* (Chichester: John Wiley).

Central Computer and Telecommunications Agency (1980), *Stand Alone Word Processors; Report of Trials in UK Government Typing Pools 1979/80*, November (London: CCTA).

Checkland, P. (1981), *Systems Thinking, Systems Practice* (Chichester: John Wiley).

Cherns, A. B. (1976), The principles of socio-technical design, *Human Relations*, **29**, 783–792.

Congress of the United States (1985), *Automation of America's Offices 1985/2000* (Washington: Office of Technology Assessment).

Cutts, G. (1987), *SSADM*, (London: Paradigm).

Damodaran, L., Simpson, A. S. and Wilson, P. A. (eds) (1980), *Designing Systems for People* (Manchester: NCC).

Damodaran, L. (1984) Measures of user acceptability. In Pearce, B. G. (ed.), *Health Hazards Of VDTs?* (Chichester: John Wiley).

Damodaran, L. (1986), User support. In Bjørn-Andersen, N., Eason, K. D. and Robey, D. *Managing Computer Impact* (Norwood, NJ: Ablex).

Damodaran, L. (1986) Towards a human factors strategy for IT systems. *Proceedings of the SERC CREST course, Human factors for Information Usability*, Loughborough University of Technology, December 14–20.

Davies, D. G. (1989), Ergonomics applied to micro processors; the design of a novel micro processor based portable billing machine. In Harker, S. D. P. and Eason, K. D. (eds) *The Application of Information Technology* (London: Taylor & Francis).

Davis, L. E. and Taylor, J. C. (eds) (1972), *Design of Jobs* (London: Penguin).

Downing, H. (1980), Word processors and the oppression of women. In Forester, T. (ed.), *The Microelectronics Revolution* (Oxford: Basil Blackwell).

Dray, S. M. (1987), Getting the baby into the bathwater: putting organisational planning into the systems design process. In Bullinger, H.-J. and Shackel, B. (eds), *INTERACT '87; Human Computer Interaction* (Amsterdam: North–Holland).

DTI (1986), *Profiting from Office automation; Office Automation Pilots* (London: Department of Trade and Industry).

Eason, K. D. (1981), *Manager–computer interaction: A study of a task–tool relationship*. PhD thesis, Loughborough University of Technology.

Eason, K. D. (1982), The process of introducing information technology. *Behaviour and information Technology*, **1**, 197–213.

Eason, K. D. (1984a), The man-machine interface for the intermittent user. (Pergamon–Infotech State of the Art Review, The information initiative, Maidenhead).

Eason, K. D. (1984b), Towards the experimental study of usability. *Behaviour and Information Technology*, **3**, 133–144.

Eason, K. D. (1984c), Job design and VDU operation. In Pearce, B. G. (ed.), *Health hazards of VDTs?* (Chichester: John Wiley).

Eason, K. D. (1987), Methods of planning the electronic workplace. *Behaviour and Information Technology*, **6**, 229–238.

Eason, K. D. (1989), Patterns of usage of a flexible information system. In Harker, S. D. P. and Eason, K. D. (eds), *The Application of Information Technology* (London: Taylor & Francis).

Eason, K. D. and Harker, S. D. P. (1980), An open systems approach to task analysis. Internal Report, HUSAT Research Centre, Loughborough University of Technology.

Eason, K. D. and Harker, S. D. P. (1986), Effective human factors contributions to the design process. *Proceedings of the SERC CREST course Human Factors for Information Usability*, Loughborough University of Technology, December 14–20.

Eason, K. D. and Sell, R. G. (1980), Case studies in job design for information processing tasks. In Corlett, E. N. and Richardson, J (eds), *Stress, Work Design and Productivity* (Chichester: John Wiley).

Eason, K. D., Damodaran, L. and Stewart, T. F. M. (1974), A survey of man–computer interaction in commercial applications, LUTERG no. 144, HUSAT Research Centre, Loughborough University of Technology.

Eason, K. D., Harker, S. D. P., Raven, P. F., Brailsford, J. R. and Cross, A. D. (1987), A user centred approach to design of a knowledge based system. In Bullinger, H.-J. and Shackel, B. (eds), *INTERACT '87, Human–Computer Interaction* (Amsterdam: North-Holland).

Eason, K. D., Damodaran, L. and Stewart, T. F. M. (1989a), Evaluating the impact of a computer based system in a hospital. In Harker, S. D. P. and Eason, K. D. (eds), *The Application of Information Technology* (London: Taylor & Francis).

Eason, K. D., Gower, J. C. and Harker, S. D. P. (1989b),Task analysis in the specification of systems for electricity supply distribution. In Harker, S. D. P. and Eason, K. D. (eds), *The Application of Information Technology* (London: Taylor & Francis).

Eaton, J. and Smithers, J. (1982), *This is IT: A Managers' Guide to Information Technology* (Oxford: Philip Alan).

Emery, F. E. and Trist, E. L. (1969), Socio-technical Systems. In Emery, F. E. (ed.), *Systems Thinking* (London: Penguin).

Englebart, D. C. (1982), Integrated, evolutionary, office automation system. In Landau, R., Bair, J. H. and Siegman, J. H. (eds), *Emerging Office Systems* (Norwood, NJ: Ablex).

Fallik, F. (1987), *Managing Organizational Change* (London: Taylor & Francis).

Galer, I. A. R. (1987), *Applied Ergonomics Handbook* (London: Butterworths).

Galitz, W. O. (1981), *Handbook of Screen Format Design* (QED Information Services Inc.).

Gambino, T. J., Johnson, T. W. and Wilson, D. D. (1982) Microcomputer learning curve. *Computerworld*, 30 May, 35–42.

Gardiner, M. M. and Christie, B. (eds) (1987), *Applying Cognitive Psychology to User Interface Design* (Chichester: John Wiley).

Gardner, A. (1988), Human Factors in the Design of Computer-Based Systems, Final Draft MOD (PE) and DTI, London.

Gilb, T. (1988), *Principles of Software Engineering Management* (Wokingham: Addison–Wesley).

Gotlieb, C. C. and Borodin, A. (1973), *Social Issues in Computing* (New York: Academic Press).

Grandjean, E. (1987), *Ergonomics in Computerised Offices* (London: Taylor & Francis).

Gower, J. C. and Eason, K. D. (1989), The introduction of information technology in a city firm. In Harker, S. D. P. and Eason, K. D. (eds), *The Application of Information Technology,* (London: Taylor & Francis).

Hackman, J. R. and Oldham, G. R. (1975), Development of the job diagnostic survey. *Journal of Applied Psychology*, **60** (2), 159–170.

Hannigan, S. and Kerswell, B. (1986), Towards User Friendly Terminals, *Proceedings of the ISSLS '86 Conference*, Tokyo, Japan.

Harker, S. D. P. and Eason, K. D. (1984), Representing the user in the design process. *Design Studies*, 5.2, 79–85.

Harker, S. D. P. and Eason, K. D. (1985), Task analysis and the definition of user needs. *Proceedings of the IFAC Conference on the Analysis, Design and Evaluation of Man-Machine Systems*, Varese.

Harker, S. D. P. (1987a), The role of user prototyping in the systems design process. In Knave, B. and Wideback, P.–G. (eds), *Work With Display Units 86* (Amsterdam: North Holland).

Harker, S. D. P. (1987b), Rapid prototyping as a tool for user centred design. *Proceedings of the 2nd International Conference on Human–Computer Interaction*, Honolulu, August 1987.

Harker, S. D. P. and Eason K. D. (eds) (1989), *The Application of Information Technology: case studies in ergonomics*, Vol. 4, (London: Taylor & Francis).

Hedberg, B. (1975), Computer systems to support industrial democracy. In Mumford, E. and Sackman, H. (eds), *Human Choice and Computers* (Amsterdam: North–Holland).

Hedberg, B. (1980), Using computerised information systems to design better organisations and jobs. In Bjørn-Andersen, N. (ed.), *The Human Side of Information Processing* (Amsterdam: North-Holland).

Hedberg, B. and Mehlmann, M. (1984), Computer power to the people: computer resource centres or home terminals? Two scenarios. *Behaviour and Information Technology*, **3** (3), 235–248.

Hedberg, B. and Mumford, E. (1975), The design of computer systems: man's vision of man's own integral part of the systems design process. In Mumford, E. and Sackman, H. (eds), *Human Choice and Computers* (Amsterdam: North-Holland).

Hemming, S. A. H. (1986), *The Introduction of Computer Systems into Medical General Practice*. Master's Thesis, Loughborough University of Technology.

Hendersen, D. A. (1985), 'Escape Clauses', A solution for the problem of bounded technology in an unbounded world. In Brown, I. D., Goldsmith, R., Coombes, K. and Sinclair, M. A. (eds), *Ergonomics International 85* (London: Taylor & Francis).

Herzberg, F. (1968), One more time: how do you motivate employees? *Harvard Business Review*, **2**, (1), 53–62.

Hirschheim, R. A. (1985), *Office Automation: A Social and Organisational Perspective* (Chichester: John Wiley).

Hünting, W. (1984), Postural loads at VDT workstations. In Pearce, B. G. (ed.), *Health Hazards of VDTs?* (Chichester: John Wiley).

Hünting, W., Läubli, T. and Grandjean, E. (1980), Constrained postures of VDT operators. In Grandjean, E. and Vigliani, E. (eds), *Ergonomics Aspects of Visual Display Terminals* (London: Taylor & Francis).

Institute for Employment Research, University of Warwick (1984), Survey of job loss in engineering caused by information technology. Reported in *Computing*, October 4.

Irving, R. H., Higgins, C. A. and Safayeni, F. R. (1986), Computerised performance monitoring systems: use and abuse. *Communications of the ACM*, **29.8**, 794–801.

Jackson, M. A. (1975), *Principles of Program Design* (New York: Academic Press).

Janson, M. (1986), Applying a pilot system and prototyping approach to systems development and implementation. *Information and Management*, **10**, 209–216.

Japanese Ministry of Labour (1984), *Research on High Technology and Labour in Fiscal 1983* (Tokyo: Japan).

Jenkins, C. and Sherman, B. (1979), *The Collapse of Work* (London: Eyre Methuen).

Johnson, P. (1985), Towards a task model of messaging: an example of the application of TAKD to user interface design. In Johnson, T. and Cook, S. (eds), *People and Computers: Designing the Interface* (Cambridge: Cambridge University Press).

Judkins, P., West, D. and Drew, J. (1985), *Networking in Organisations* (London: Gower).

Keen, P. (1981), Information systems and organisational change. *Communications of the ACM*, **24.1**

Kinsman, F. (1987), *The TELECOMMUTERS* (Chichester: John Wiley).

Klein, L. (1976), *New Forms of Work Organisation* (Cambridge: Cambridge University Press).

Klein, L. and Eason, K. D. (1989), *Social Science in Practice*, (Cambridge: Cambridge University Press).

Kling, R. (1977), The organisational context of user–centred software designs. *MIS Quarterly*, December.

Lee, B. (ed.) (1982), *Introducing Systems Analysis and Design* (Manchester: National Computing Centre).

Maskery, H. (1986), *An Investigation into the Usage and Learning of Discretionary Computer Users*, PhD Thesis, Loughborough University of Technology.

McCosh, A. M. (1984), Factors common to the successful implementation of twelve decision support systems and how they differ from three failures. *Systems, Objective, Solutions*, **4**, 17–28.

Mitroff, I. I. (1980), Management myth information systems revisited: a strategic approach to asking nasty questions about systems design. In Bjørn-Andersen, N. (ed.), *The Human Side of Enterprise* (Amsterdam: North–Holland).

Moran, T. P. (1981), The Command Language Grammar: a representation for the user interface of interactive computer systems. *International Journal of Man–Machine Studies*, **15**, 3–50.

Mowshowitz, A. (1976), *The Conquest of Will: Information Processing in Human Affairs* (Reading: Addison–Wesley).

Mumford, E. (1983a), *Designing Human Systems* (Manchester: Manchester Business School Publications).

Mumford, E. (1983b), *Designing Secretaries* (Manchester: Manchester Business School Publications).

Mumford, E. and Henshall, D. (1979), *A Participative Approach to Computer System Design* (London: Associated Business Press).

Mumford, E. and Weir, M. (1979), *Computer Systems in Work Design: The ETHICS Method* (London: Associated Business Press).

Nora, S. and Minc, A. (1980) *The Computerisation of Society* (Cambridge: MIT Press).

Olphert, C. W., Eason, K. D. and Cockcroft, J. (1985), The Extent of Use of Office Automation, Phase 2, Report to the European Foundation for the Improvement of Living and Working Conditions, HUSAT Research Centre, Loughborough University of Technology.

Ouchi, W. (1981), *Theory Z* (New York: McGraw-Hill).

Parkin, A. (1980), *Systems Analysis* (London: Edward Arnold).

Paul, W. J., Robertson, K. B. and Herzberg, F. (1969), Job enrichment pays off. *Harvard Business Review*, **47**, 66–78.

Pava, C. (1983), *Managing New Office Technology: An Organisational Strategy* (New York: New York Free Press).

Pearce, B. G. (ed.) (1984), *Health Hazard of VDTs?* (Chichester: John Wiley).

Pearce, B. G. (1989), The workstation design of a modular counter for bank cashiers. In Harker S. D. P. and Eason K. D. (eds), *The Application of Information Technology* (London: Taylor & Francis).

Pomfrett, S. M. and Damodaran, L. (1989), An electronic messaging trial in a regional marketing organisation. In Harker, S. D. P. and Eason K. D. (eds), *The Application of Information Technology* (London: Taylor & Francis).

Pomfrett, S. M., Olphert, C. W. and Eason, K. D. (1985), Work organisation implications of word processing. In Shackel, B. (ed.), *Human Computer Interaction — INTERACT 84* (Amsterdam: North–Holland).

Pullinger, D. (1987), *The feasibility of electronic journals*. PhD thesis, Loughborough University of Technology.

Rice, A. K. (1958), *Productivity and Social Organisation: The Ahmedabad Experiment* (London: Tavistock).

Rothlisberger, F. J. and Dickson, W. J. (1939), *Management and the Worker* (Cambridge, Mass: Harvard University Press).

Shackel, B. (1984), The concept of usability. In Bennett, J., Case, D., Sandelin, J., and Smith, M, (eds) *Visual Display Terminals Usability Issues and Health Concerns*, (NJ: Prentice-Hall).

Shackel, B., Pullinger, D. J., Maude, T. and Dodd, P. (1983), The BLEND–LINC project on 'electronic journals' after two years. *Computer Journal* **26(3)**, 247–252.

Shackel, B., Eason, K. D. and Pomfrett, S. M. (1989), Organisational prototyping — a case study in matching the computer system to the organisation. In Harker, S. D. P. and Eason, K. D. (eds), *The Application of Information Technology* (London: Taylor & Francis).

Shneiderman, B. (1986), *Designing the User Interface* (Wokingham: Addison-Wesley).

Siemsens, (1978), Report on employment. Reported in *Computing* (Europe), 6 March 1980.

Simon, H. A. (1965), *The Shape of Automation for Men and Management* (New York: Harper and Row).

Smith, J. (1984), Beyond user friendly — towards the assimilation of multi-functional workstation capabilities. *Behaviour and Information Technology*, **3** (2), 205–220.

Smith, S. L. and Mosier, J. N. (1984), Design guidelines for user-system interface software. Mitre Corporation report MTD–9420 EST–TR–84–190, Mitre Corporation Burlington Road, Bedford. MA 01730.

Stewart, R. (1971), *How Computers Affect Management* (London: Macmillan).

Stewart, T. F. M. (1986), Task fit, ease-of-use and computer facilities. In Bjørn-Andersen, N. Eason, K. D. and Robey, D., *Managing Computer Impact* (Norwood, NJ: Ablex).

Sutcliffe, A and Old, A. C. (1987), Do users know they have user models? Some experiences in the practice of user modelling. In Bullinger, H.-J. and Shackel, B. (eds), *INTERACT '87, Human Computer Interaction*, pp. 35–41 (Amsterdam: North–Holland).

Tapscott, D. (1982), *Office Automation: A User Driven Method* (New York: Plenum).

Thompson, J. D. (1967), *Organisation in Action* (New York: McGraw–Hill).

Trist, E. L., Higgin, G. W., Murray, H. and Pollack, A. B. (1962), *Organisational Choice* (London: Tavistock).

Toffler, A. (1980), *The Third Wave* (London: Collins).

Tynan K. O. (1980), Improving the quality of working life in the 1980s. Work Research Unit Occasional Paper no. 16, London, ACAS.

Wainwright, J. and Francis, A. (1984), *Office automation, organisation and the nature of work* (Aldershot: Gower).

Walker, C. R. and Guest, R. H. (1952), *The Man on the Assembly Line* (Cambridge: Harvard University Press).

Wall, T. D. and Lischeron, J. A. (1977), *Worker Participation* (New York: McGraw–Hill).

Waterworth, J. (1984), Interaction with machines by voice: a telecommunications perspective, *Behaviour and Information Technology*, **3** (2) 163–178.

Weizenbaum, J. (1976), *Computer Power and Human Reason* (San Francisco: Freeman).

Whisler, T. L. (1970), *The Impact of Computers on Organisations* (New York: Praeger Publishers).

Wright, P. and Lickorish, A. (1983), Proof-reading texts on screen and paper. *Behaviour and Information Technology*, **2**, 227–235.

Wright, M. and Rhodes, D. (1985), *Manage IT: exploiting information systems for effective management* (London: Francis Pinter).

Wroe, B. (1986), *Contractors and computers: why systems succeed or fail*. PhD thesis, Loughborough University of Technology.

Index